ROUTLEDGE LIBRARY EDITIONS: JAPANESE LINGUISTICS

Volume 2

SUBJECTS IN JAPANESE AND ENGLISH

SUBJECTS IN JAPANESE AND ENGLISH

YOSHIHISA KITAGAWA

LONDON AND NEW YORK

First published in 1994 by Garland Publishing, Inc.

This edition first published in 2019
by Routledge
2 Park Square, Milton Park, Abingdon, Oxon OX14 4RN

and by Routledge
52 Vanderbilt Avenue, New York, NY 10017

Routledge is an imprint of the Taylor & Francis Group, an informa business

© 1994 Yoshihisa Kitagawa

All rights reserved. No part of this book may be reprinted or reproduced or utilised in any form or by any electronic, mechanical, or other means, now known or hereafter invented, including photocopying and recording, or in any information storage or retrieval system, without permission in writing from the publishers.

Trademark notice: Product or corporate names may be trademarks or registered trademarks, and are used only for identification and explanation without intent to infringe.

British Library Cataloguing in Publication Data
A catalogue record for this book is available from the British Library

ISBN: 978-1-138-36949-8 (Set)
ISBN: 978-0-429-40043-8 (Set) (ebk)
ISBN: 978-1-138-39367-7 (Volume 2) (hbk)
ISBN: 978-1-138-39412-4 (Volume 2) (pbk)
ISBN: 978-0-429-40138-1 (Volume 2) (ebk)

Publisher's Note
The publisher has gone to great lengths to ensure the quality of this reprint but points out that some imperfections in the original copies may be apparent.

Disclaimer
The publisher has made every effort to trace copyright holders and would welcome correspondence from those they have been unable to trace.

SUBJECTS IN JAPANESE AND ENGLISH

YOSHIHISA KITAGAWA

GARLAND PUBLISHING, INC.
NEW YORK & LONDON / 1994

Copyright © 1994 by Yoshihisa Kitagawa
All rights reserved

Library of Congress Cataloging-in-Publication Data

Kitagawa, Yoshihisa, 1953–
    Subjects in Japanese and English / Yoshihisa Kitagawa.
      p.   cm. — (Outstanding dissertations in linguistics)
    Originally presented as the author's thesis (doctoral-University of Massachusetts), 1986.
    ISBN 0–8153–1685–2
    1. Grammar, Comparative and general—Topic and comment.
2. Japanese language—Topic and comment. 3. English language—Topic and comment. 4. Government-binding theory (Linguistics)
I. Title. II. Series.
P298.K58 1994
495.6'5—dc20   93–38246
                                                                            CIP

Printed on acid-free, 250-year-life paper
Manufactured in the United States of America

To Isoko

TABLE OF CONTENTS

PREFACE	ix
ACKNOWLEDGMENTS	xiii
LIST OF TABLES	xvii
LIST OF ABBREVIATIONS	xix

I. INTRODUCTION 1

    1.1. Government and Binding Theory 1
    1.2. Outline 3
    1.3. Background Assumptions 9
    Footnotes to Chapter I 16

II. COMPLEX PREDICATES IN JAPANESE 17

    2.1. Introduction 17
    2.2. Lexical Derivation 33
    2.3. Affix Raising Hypothesis 53
    2.4. Further Motivations for the Affix
         Raising Hypothesis 116
    2.5. Arguments against Lexical Derivation 184
    Footnotes to Chapter II 204

III. DERIVING SUBJECTS 220

    3.1. Subjects in Japanese 220
    3.2. Subjects in English 231
    3.3. Summary 264
    Footnotes to Chapter III 266

IV. BINDING THEORY 273

    4.1. Introduction 273
    4.2. SUBJECTS 275
    4.3. Case Marking and Binding 289
    4.4. Further Implications and Problems:
         An Initial Sketch 350
    4.5. Concluding Remarks 365
    Footnotes to Chapter IV 366

APPENDIX: *zibun* 377

BIBLIOGRAPHY 383

ADDITIONAL FOOTNOTES 399

PREFACE

This work is a virtually unchanged reproduction of my doctoral dissertation submitted to the Department of Linguistics of the University of Massachusetts at Amherst in August 1986. Apart from the addition of new footnotes*, a few lines in the acknowledgments, and typo-graphical corrections, the present version is identical to the original dissertation.

In the spring of 1989, I started preparing a revised version of Chapter 2 of the original work for publication. While the project proceeded much more slowly than expected, it has undergone what I believe to be a remarkable qualitative and quantitative progress. In the meantime, the field of generative syntax faced a new challenge when Chomsky (1992) proposed the "minimalist design" of a linguistic theory, which advocates a shift of our attention from D-structure (and S-structure) to the representations and computations (= derivations) at the "Interface levels" (= LF- and PF-components). With the claim that "interface conditions" are the only truly relevant external conditions on representations and derivations, Chomsky abandoned the idea that the D-structure is the "pure thematic representation" and the portion of the Projection Principle that imposed uniformity of thematic marking on the representations at all syntactic levels. The plausibility of this new view of linguistic theory is yet to be fully examined. It has, however, certainly provided me with a fresh angle from which I can reinterpret and reevaluate what I attempted to make clear in the original work. Partly due to the availability of this new and exciting view of linguistic theory, and partly due to the fact that it has become increasingly clear that the final product of my "revision" project will end up being rather distant from what was originally planned, and finally because certain other portions of the original work would not have a chance to be brought to light, I have decided to have the original work published virtually as is, in hopes of having the "revised version" published as an independent piece of work.

Chapter 2 of the present work offers what I now call the 'Excorporation Approach' to complex predicates. It first offers three different phonological arguments for deriving morphologically complex predicates in Japanese, like 'Verb-*sase* (CAUSATIVE),' 'Verb-*rare* (PASSIVE),' and 'Verb-*ta* (DESIDERATIVE),' in the Lexicon. To the best of my knowledge, these arguments have not yet been seriously challenged to date, apart from concern for the plausibility of level-ordering assumptions in general. It is worthwhile emphasizing here that each of the three arguments is distinct, involving theoretical assumptions

---

*Additional Footnotes start on p. 399, and they are marked in the text as [AFN #].

varying from level-ordering to underspecification and the
Obligatory Contour Principle.

The chapter then offers two major arguments for motivating
the LF-application of 'Excorporation,' a type of Move α. First,
examination of scope- and locality-related phenomena such as
adverbial interpretation (2.3.5.3) and binding (4.3.10) will
lead us to reach a seemingly paradoxical conclusion that both
syntactically simplex and syntactically complex representations
must be made available at the interface level of the conceptual-
intentional nature. That is, morphologically complex predicates
in Japanese must undergo logical computation (= syntactic
derivation within the LF component). Combined with perhaps an
optimal hypothesis that no rule application and licensing of
linguistic expressions against principles need to be extrinsically ordered within a single component, the Excorporation
Approach is argued to offer an optimal solution to such a
paradox. Second, the chapter closely examines three cases of
"morphology-syntax mismatches," involving negative polarity,
honorification and reciprocalization, respectively. The
conclusion is drawn there that Excorporation, which can
correctly perform the required "non-string-vacuous" reordering
of morphemes at the logical interface, must be chosen over
approaches that adopt mechanisms like "reanalysis" or
"coanalysis," whose syntactic effects are necessarily string
vacuous.

Chapter 3 offers what now is often identified as the
Internal Subject Hypothesis (ISH). The particular version of
ISH proposed in this work is clearly distinguished from other
similar proposals in two respects. First, while what has been
labelled as ISH is usually regarded as a hypothesis concerning
phrase structures at the level of D-structure, it is claimed in
this work that ISH should be regarded as a hypothesis concerning
the relation between a predicate and its external argument at
the interface level, i.e., in the LF component. Second, it is
also argued for that English has a "purely" head-initial
interface representations in such a way that the instantiation
of a two-place relation involves VOS (or AOS) order (or more
precisely, a representation like [$_{VP}$ [$_{V'}$ V O] S] or
[$_{AP}$ [$_{A'}$ A O] S]).

Chapter 4 explores a theory of binding under ISH. The main
proposal there is that the binding category for anaphors and
pronouns is correctly defined only when we take into consideration the abstract Case assignment of these items couched in ISH.
We may perhaps characterize this proposal as an intermediate
step in the process of redefining Chomsky's (1986) "Least
Complete Functional Complex" in terms of the notion
"discharge/saturation" of all the selectional features of the
head predicate governing the anaphors and pronouns including

abstract Case as well as thematic roles. See Kitagawa (1991) for further discussion on this approach.

The strongest objection made since to the above proposals was that the two major theoretical claims offered — Excorporation and the Internal Subject Hypothesis — were so exotic that some of the major hypotheses which had been "standardly" adopted in the Principles and Parameters framework must be abondoned. Some of these hypotheses were: (i) that D-structure is a "pure" thematic representation, (ii) that the Projection Principle is inviolable, and (iii) that the theory of predication requires a subject (= an external argument) of a predicate to be syntactically realized "external" to a predicate phrase. The concluding remarks of the present work (4.5), in fact, end with a suggestion challenging the hypothesis in (i). The dilemma concerning the hypothesis (ii) was also discussed in 2.3.3., though I was not courageous enough to challenge the Projection Principle when I wrote it. (Later in Kitagawa (1990), I finally decided to bite the bullet and offered an argument against the Projection Principle in the process of motivating what I called "Anti-scrambling.")

Kitagawa (1989) offers, under ISH, a sketch of a view alternative to (iii). In that work, it is pointed out that 'predication' should not be viewed as a primitive notion but can and should be regarded as a derivative notion which arises as a special case of 'property assignment' in the semantic interpretation.

As stated above, I am currently preparing a book, which I expect to publish in the non-too-distant future. In that work, I cast the Excorporation Approach in the Minimalist Hypothesis, and attempt to extend it to broader empirical phenomena, thereby supporting the proposals in the original work as well.

I would like to thank here Jorge Hankamer, the editor of this series, for providing me with an opportunity to publish the present work.

Rochester, New York
July, 1993

References in Preface:

Chomsky, N. (1986) *Knowledge of Language*, Praeger.

Chomsky, N. (1992) "A Minimalist Program for Linguistic Theory," *MIT Occasional Papers in Linguistics* 1, 1-68.

Kitagawa, Y. (1989) "Deriving and Copying Predication," *Proceedings of the Nineteenth Annual Meeting of the North-Eastern Linguistic Society*, 279-300.

Kitagawa, Y. (1990) "Anti-scrambling," ms., University of Rochester.(The materials in this work had been presented previously in The Workshop on Japanese Syntax and Universal Grammar on Issues Pertaining to Movement (The Ohio State University: March 1989) and Tilburg Workshop on Scrambling (Tilburg University: October 1990).)

Kitagawa, Y. (1991) "Binding under the Internal Subject Hypothesis," in Nakajima, H. ed., *Trends in Linguistics State-of-the-Art Reports 16: Current English Linguistics in Japan*, Mouton de Gruyter.

ACKNOWLEDGMENTS

I have found myself one of the luckiest graduate students. Starting with the members of my thesis committee, let me express my gratitude here to the people who have turned my life into such an enjoyable one. (If I forget to mention your name, that is because you are such a natural part of my life.)

David Pesetsky, my thesis advisor and best friend, has provided me with what I have needed most as a graduate student. I would like to express my deepest gratitude for his kindhearted assistance and friendship. I have no hesitation to admit that no single page of this thesis escapes his influence. I simply wish I had the capability to make better use of it.

Emmon Bach has shown to me one very respectable way of living as a scholar. I am grateful to him for letting me know, in a very pleasant way, how much I do not know about language and linguistics.

It was a very fortunate accident that I had a chance to experience Edwin Williams' "Introduction to Transformational Syntax" for six hours a week in my first graduate year at UMass. Ever since, he has continually provoked my interest in linguistics.

One big advantage I have had at UMass is to have two talented and ambitious Japanese linguists on the same campus.

From the very beginning of my graduate life at UMass, Nobuko Hasegawa has always guided me in the right direction, academically and personally, with very useful suggestions.

I have also greatly benefited from the hours of discussion (and eating) with Hajime Hoji. Improvements to this thesis as well as my awareness as a linguist owe much to him.

Many other people in my department have helped me develop the ideas in this thesis.

Barbara Partee has provided me with many valuable comments on the main ideas of Chapter Two.

Lisa Selkirk and Scott Myers have kindly read the section on phonology and provided me with important comments as well as encouragement. I would also like to thank Junko Ito for her useful advice for the phonology section. I have had a chance to obtain pitch track diagrams of crucial examples, thanks to the assistance of John McCarthy and Scott Myers.

There are two fellow students to whom I would like to express special thanks --- Kiyoshi Kurata and Dave Lebeaux. As the reader will notice, some of the most important arguments in this thesis have been developed from their written works or the discussions I have had with them.

Thanks are also due to those who provided me with interesting discussions as well as native judgments, especially Steve Berman, T. Daniel Seely, Kenichi Mihara and Koichi Tateishi.

I am extremely grateful to Steve Berman for his excellent job of proofreading.

Let me also thank the following people outside UMass for useful comments and suggestions: Mamoru Saito, Susumu Kuno, Sige-Yuki Kuroda, Diana Archangeli, Eduardo Raposo and Mürvet Enç.

I would also like to express my gratitude to the following people and organization:

To the Rotary Foundation of Rotary International for providing me with an opportunity to launch my graduate studies in the United States.

To Lyn Frazier, Roger Higgins, Angelika Kratzer, Pieter Muysken, Alan Prince, Tom Roeper, and Tim Stowel for stimulating discussions and classes at UMass.

To Lynne Ballard and Kathy Adamczyk for making my life easier at UMass (and showing me how to spell "Mickey Mouse").

To Kazuko Inoue, Masatake Muraki and Kazuko Harada, my teachers in Japan, for the introduction to theoretical linguistics and warm encouragement thereafter.

To Heizo Nakajima and Chisato Kitagawa for their thoughtful advice when I needed it most.

To Masataka Tasaki for arousing my interest in language twenty years ago.

To "Pat" and "Trudy" Layton for their kind hospitality for my family.

To Norimasa and Kikuyo Yoshida for their generous assistance through my graduate years.

To our parents Isomatsu and Hanako Kitagawa, and Kenji and Toshiko Uetake for their love and encouragement.

To my late grandparents Kazumi and Yaeko Kinoshita for their devotion to me. How I wish my Ph. D. were in time.

Finally, I would like to thank my wife Isoko from the bottom of my heart for her love and patience in all these years. Together with our son Jun, she has always let me know for sure that there is at least one thing in my life that I have not (and will never) screw(ed) up.

LIST OF TABLES

1. Pitch track diagram of *umi-de oyog-u* 49
2. Pitch track diagram of *nom-ita-i* 50
3. Pitch track diagram of *o-nomi-ni-nar-u* 197
4. Pitch track diagram of *o-nom-ase-ni-nar-u* 198
5. Pitch track diagram of *imoya-ni nar-u* 199

LIST OF ABBREVIATIONS

ACC	accusative
COND	conditional
CONTR	contrastive
DAT	dative
DES	desiderative
DIST	distributive
GEN/gen	genitive
GER	gerundive
HON	honorific
NML	nominalizer
NOM/nom	nominative
PASS	passive
PRES	present
PROG	progressive
Q	question marker
TOP/top	topic
REC(IP)	reciprocal

CHAPTER I
INTRODUCTION

1.1. Government and Binding Theory

Throughout this thesis, our investigation will be conducted within the framework of the Extended Standard Theory (EST). More specifically, we will assume the basic features of the Government and Binding Theory sketched out by Chomsky (1981) and elaborated thereafter in various works.

In particular, we will assume the model of core grammar as schematized in (1) below:

(1)
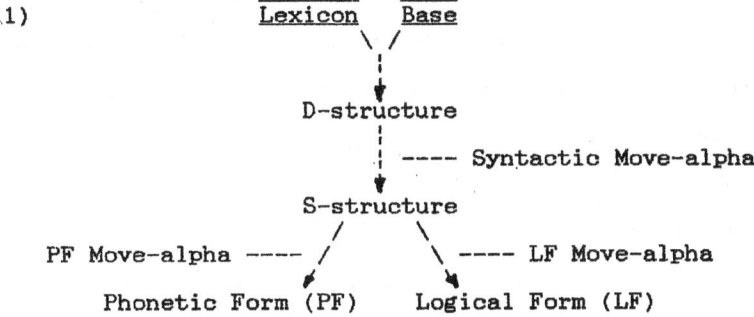

One characteristic of this model is that the mapping between different levels of representation is carried out by a single rule, Move-alpha, via various intermediate stages of derivation. For example, Move-alpha may map the

S-structure representation (2a) below onto the LF representation (2d) via pre-LF representations (2b) and (2c):[1]

(2)
a. S-str: [$_{S'}$ who$_1$ [$_S$ t$_1$ says what to someone everyday]]
b. pre-LF: [$_{S'}$ what$_2$ [$_{S'}$ who$_1$ [$_S$ t$_1$ says t$_2$ to someone everyday]]]
c. pre-LF: [$_{S'}$ what$_2$ [$_{S'}$ who$_1$ [$_S$ someone$_3$ [$_S$ t$_1$ says t$_2$ to t$_3$ everyday]]]
d. LF: [$_{S'}$ what$_2$ [$_{S'}$ who$_1$ [$_S$ everyday$_4$ [$_S$ someone$_3$ [$_S$ t$_1$ says t$_2$ to t$_3$ t$_4$]]]

The application of Move-alpha and the resulting representations are constrained by a limited number of universal principles which include: the X-Bar principles, the Theta (θ) Criterion, the Projection Principle, the Case Filter, the Empty Category Principle (ECP), the principles of Binding Theory and the Subjacency Condition. We will introduce the content of such principles when they become relevant in our discussions.

As has often been proposed in the literature, we will also assume (or in some cases propose) that one or more of such principles "hold at LF". One thing to be kept in mind here is that the expression "hold at LF" is used somewhat loosely to refer to "hold at pre-LFs and LF". In other words, both pre-LFs and LF are assumed to belong to a single LF component.

1.2. Outline

As its name suggests, the Government and Binding (GB) Theory has always placed the notion "government" at the center of its description and explanation of various grammatical phenomena.

"Government" here roughly refers to the relation holding between the head of a syntactic phrase and the non-head items located within that phrase. (We will provide a definition of this notion in 1.3.2. below.) For example, it has been a widely-accepted assumption in the GB Theory that a verb often both Case-marks and θ-marks its object NP under government, as illustrated in (3) below:

(3)
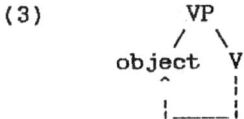

The main purpose of this thesis is to show that the structural relation "government" holds not only between the verbal head and its object but also between the verbal head and its subject at least at the level of Logical Form in both Japanese and English. In particular, we will propose and motivate LF representation in Japanese and English as illustrated in (4a) and (4b) below, in which the verbal head governs its subject:

(4) a. Japanese: b. English:²

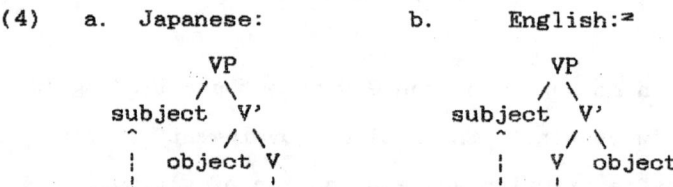

The chapters that follow are closely related to one another. Chapter Two offers an analysis of **complex predicate constructions** in Japanese. We will make two main proposals and provide supporting arguments for them. In 2.2., we will argue that complex predicates including their tense morphemes (e.g., V + *sase* (CAUSE) + *ru* (PRES)) are morphologically derived in the lexicon by means of affixation. We will conclude, in particular, that the complex predicate *tabe-sase-ru* (eat-CAUSE-PRES), for example, is inserted into a syntactic structure as a single and coherent lexical item of the form in (5) below:

(5)

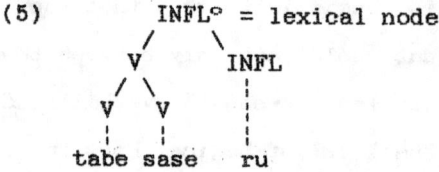

This extended version of a lexical approach to complex predicates (cf. Farmer's (1980) and Miyagawa's (1980)) will be supported in the light of various phonological phenomena such as accentuation, voicing spread and downdrifting.[3]

Another main proposal in Chapter Two will be presented in 2.3., where the complex predicates are analyzed as involving complementation at the level of Logical Form as a result of "Affix Raising" (cf. Pesetsky (1985)). In particular, we will propose that D- and S-structure representations like (6a) will be eventually mapped onto the LF representation (6b) due to the application of Move-alpha to the affixes *ru* (PRES) and *sase* (CAUSE):

(6) a. *D-/S-str*:
```
            IP
           /  \
         NP-ga  I"
              /  \
           NP-ni  I'
                /  \
              NP-o  I°      ===>
                   /  \
                  V    I
                 / \   |
                V   V  ru
                |   |
              tabe sase
```
b. *LF*:
```
            IP
           /  \
          VP    I
         / \    |
       NP-ga V' ru
            /  \
           VP   \
          / \    V
       NP-ni V'  |
            / \ sase
          NP-o  V
                |
              tabe
```

In the first half of 2.3.4., we will see that this analysis allows us to incorporate insights obtained by transformational approaches to these constructions (Kuroda (1965),

Kuno (1973), Shibatani (1973), etc.) while at the same time adhering to the spirit of the Lexicalist Hypothesis (Chomsky (1970)) and Government and Binding Theory. Then in 2.3.4.3. and 2.4., we will see that there are several reasons to consider that the complementation in the complex predicate construction takes place at the level of LF, and that it is derived there.

Extending the Affix Raising Hypothesis from complex predicates to simplex predicates, Chapter Three offers an account of phrase structure in Japanese and English. In particular, we will propose that the subject of a sentence in Japanese is normally base-generated under the sentence node headed by a (in a sense) "complex" predicate consisting of a verb and a tense affix, but ends up being located within the projection of the verb due to the raising of the tense affix at LF. This analysis is illustrated by the schematized derivation in (7) below:

(7) a. *D-/S-str*:   b.   *LF*:

```
              IP                                    IP
             /  \                                  /  \
         NP-ga   I'                              VP    I
                / \                             /  \   |
            NP-o   I°    ===>              NP-ga   V'  ru
                  / \                             / \
                 V   I                         NP-o  V
                 |   |                               |
               tabe  ru                            tabe
               eat  PRES
```

The subject in English, on the other hand, will be analyzed as being base-generated within the projection of a verb, but brought out of the verbal projection and placed under a sentence at S-structure, leaving a trace behind within the verbal projection (cf. Kuroda (1985), Sportiche (1986)). This analysis is illustrated in (8) below:

(8) a. *D-str*: b. *S-str/LF*:

```
        IP                        IP
       / \                       / \
          I'                   NP₁   I'
         / \                         / \
        I   VP    ===>          ¦   I   VP
       / \                      ¦      / \
     NP₁   V'                   ¦     t₁  V'
          / \                   ¦_____¦  / \
         V   NP₂                        V   NP₂
```

As a result, the θ-marking of a subject at LF, for example, is carried out directly in Japanese, whereas it is mediated by the trace of the "raised" subject in English. In either case, however, θ-marking of a subject at LF is carried out within the maximal projection of the θ-role assigner, i.e., within the VP.

Finally, in Chapter Four, we will develop a theory of binding in which the VP-internal subject at LF crucially behaves as a possible binder of anaphors and pronominals. We first adopt Chomsky's (1981) proposal that genitive Case in English, as opposed to nominative Case, is non-lexical in the sense that it is not assigned by a nominal head. We also adopt Saito's (1982,1983a,1985) proposal that the nominative *ga*-marking in Japanese is non-lexical as opposed to the accusative *o*-marking. Making an appeal to this dichotomy of Case marking and the notion of VP-internal subject, we will propose that Principles A and B of the Binding Theory require that, at LF, anaphors must be bound and pronominals must be free within the projection of their **lexical** Case assigner.

Among other things, the proposed Binding Theory yields the following desirable results. First, we can unify the Specified Subject Condition (Chomsky (1973)) and the Nominative Island Condition (Chomsky (1980)) without necessitating the notion "SUBJECT" (Chomsky (1981)). In 4.2. and 4.3.6., it will be shown that the notion "SUBJECT" is problematic both conceptually and empirically. Second, we can correctly predict that, descriptively, anaphors in Japanese are subject to the Specified Subject Condition but are immune to the Nominative Island Condition.

Thus, we may say that the main proposal of this thesis is that the postulation of VP-internal subjects at LF allows us to minimize the language-particular variations between Japanese and English.

1.3. Background Assumptions

At this point, let us briefly go over some of the novel terminology and assumptions adopted in this thesis.

1.3.1. X-Bar Notation

First, along the lines of Muysken (1982), we will adopt the X-bar notation in (9a) below to represent what is expressed in (9b) with a more familiar notation.

(9) a.   b.

We characterize the nodes X^{max}, X^{med} and X^{min} in (9a) as in (10) below in terms of "maximality" and "minimality" of nodes:

(10)   maximal   minimal

     X^{max} +   −
     X^{med} −   −
     X^{min} −   +

The convenience of this notation manifests itself immediately when we try to express what may be informally referred to as "non-phrasal" nodes (= $X^{[-max]}$) and "non-terminal" nodes (= $X^{[-min]}$). Although we may still

use the expression "XP" for convenience when what is meant
by that is obvious, a number of situations will arise in
which we appeal to the newly adopted notation to avoid
confusion as well as to capture certain generalizations.
For example, we will crucially distinguish the labelling
V^{max} in (11) below (for Japanese) from the traditional
notion of VP as in (12), in that V^{max} but not VP contains a
subject:

(11) V^{max}
            /   \
      subject V^{med}
              /   \
         object V^{min}

(12)   VP
            / \
        object V

Second, we follow Hale (1980), Farmer (1980) and
Stowell (1981), in assuming that the features of the head
item percolate up to the maximal node in the tree **both in
morphology and syntax** (cf. Williams (1981a), Lieber (1981)
for the head-feature percolation in morphology). We thus
obtain a morphological representation like (13) and a
syntactic representation like (14) below due to
head-feature percolation:

(13)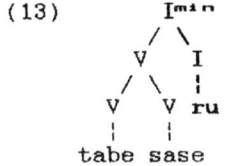

(14)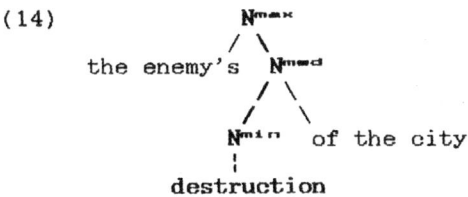

Third, we will adopt the following analysis of S' and S, following Stowell (1981) and Pesetsky (1982):

(15)
```
        C^max    (= S')
       /   \
     COMP   I^max   (= S)
           /  \
              I^med
             /  \
          INFL
```

We regard S' and S, in other words, as the maximal projection of COMP and INFL, respectively.

1.3.2. Government

Let us for the moment adopt (16) below as the definition of "government". (The definition here is essentially identical to that given in Chomsky (1986b), except for the treatment of "barriers" -- See below):

(16) *Government*:

  A governs *B* iff: (i) *A* does not dominate *B*, (ii) every *C* dominating *A* also dominates *B*, where *C* = maximal node, and (iii) no barrier intervenes between *C* and *B*.

Departing from the standard terminology, however, let us subclassify the notion "government" as in (17) below, depending on the status of *A*:

(17) a. *A max*-governs *B* if *A* is a maximal projection in (16).

  b. *A head*-governs *B* if *A* is a non-maximal projection (X^{min} or X^{med}) in (16).

"Max-government" plays a role, for example, in the binding of an NP by another NP. "Head-government", on the other hand, plays a role, for example, in the θ-marking and lexical Case marking of arguments by a verbal head.⁴

The clear departures the definition in (16) makes from that proposed by Aoun and Sportiche (1983) are: (i) that the governor is not limited to X^{min}, and (ii) that "head-government" is interpreted in such a way that any X^{min} is a possible governor, regardless of its lexical properties (e.g., whether or not INFL is [+AGR]). In Chapter Four, we will revise the PRO Theorem (Chomsky (1981)) based upon the Binding Theory newly proposed there. As a consequence, it will be unnecessary to stipulate that [+AGR] INFL, but not [-AGR] INFL, is a possible governor for a PRO subject.

As for the condition (16iii), we will leave it to future research how exactly "barriers" should be defined. Chomsky (1986b) attempts to provide uniform definitions for the barriers to max- and head-government. We will briefly discuss Chomsky's proposals in Chapter Four. Kitagawa (1986b) also proposes a definition for the barriers to head-government based upon the notion "head-feature percolation".

In the unmarked cases, the definition in (16) is sufficient. As we will see in Chapter Four, however, there are cases in which A must be considered to govern B even when the latter is located outside the first maximal projection X^{max} dominating A, as schematized in (18) below:

(18)
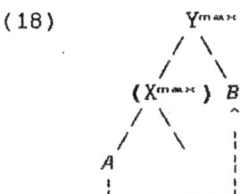

There are cases, in other words, in which some maximal projections are transparent with respect to "upward maximal-node counting". Taking this situation into consideration, let us redefine (16) above as in (19) below:

(19) *Government* (Revised):

A governs B iff: (i) A does not dominate B,
(ii) every C dominating A also dominates B,
where C = **non-transparent** maximal node, and
(iii) no barriers intervene between C and B.

In this thesis, we will refer to A, B and the first non-transparent maximal node dominating A (e.g., Y^{max} in (18)) as "governor", "governee" and "G(overment)-root", respectively.[5]

1.3.3. Isomorphy Constraint

As mentioned above, in the adopted model of core grammar (1), distinct levels of representation are related by the application of "Move-alpha", which states "Move anything anywhere". Since the application of Move-alpha is assumed to be optional, the derivation of an S-structure representation as in (20) below from a D-structure representation (21) must be made obligatory by some external force:

(20) D-structure: __ was kissed Mary

(21) S-structure: Mary₁ was kissed t_1

Chomsky (1981) has pointed out that this task can be achieved by the Case Filter (22) below:

(22) *The Case Filter* (Chomsky (1981)):

*NP, if NP has phonetic content and has no Case.

It has been assumed, in other words, that an NP in a non-Case position must move to a Case position in order to satisfy the Case Filter.

Further constraining the application of Move-alpha, Chomsky (1986a) strengthens this correlation to a biconditional and calls it the "Last Resort Principle".[6] The effect of the revision is that Move-alpha cannot move an NP to a Case position **unless** it is required by the Case Filter.

In this thesis, we will generalize the Last Resort Principle as in (23) below, and adopt it as one of our working hypotheses.[7]

(23) *Isomorphy Constraint*:

Representations at distinct syntactic levels are isomorphic unless principles of grammar require otherwise.

We will see various empirical supports for this principle in Chapters Two and Three below.

Footnotes to Chapter I

1. No claim is being made here as to the order of the various applications of Move-alpha at LF (e.g., *Wh*-movement before Quantifier Raising).

2. In Chapter Three below, we will propose an underlying constituent order for English different from that indicated here.

3. We will summarize Farmer's and Miyagawa's works in 2.1. below.

4. We will see the cases involving head-government by X^{max} in Chapters Two and Three below when we deal with modification and θ-marking.

5. From a graph-theoretic point of view, government may be considered to involve a coloring of those edges connected by three vertices *A*, *B* and *C* in a tree, as illustrated in (i) below:

(i)
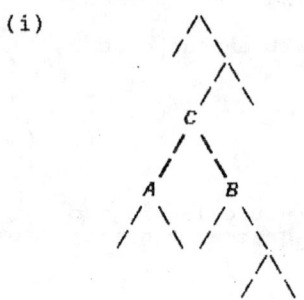

Note, then, that, with respect to this colored graph, *C* may be considered to be its "root". Based upon this observation, I have labeled *C* as "G(overnment)-root". The assumption implicit here is that the entire tree is a "rooted tree" (= an acyclic unipathic digraph) (cf. Nebesky (1979)).

6. Chomsky defines the Last Resort Principle in terms of the notion CHAIN (p. 137).

7. Isomorphy Constraint here is not to be confused with Sportiche's (1983) Isomorphy Principle on thematic structure.

CHAPTER II
COMPLEX PREDICATES IN JAPANESE

2.1. Introduction

In this chapter, we will examine some complex predicates in Japanese, of the type seen in (1):

(1)
a. V-*sase*-ru (V-CAUSE-PRES) 'make/let ... V'
b. V-*ta*-i (V-DESIDERATIVE-PRES) 'want to V'
c. V-*ta-gar*-u (V-DESIDERATIVE-display-PRES) 'appear to V'[1]
d. V-*rare*-ru (V-PASSIVE-PRES) 'be V-en'

Among these, we will pay special attention to the causative of the form V-*sase* ((1a)), one of the most extensively studied topics in Japanese syntax. As we shall see in 2.1.1. below, one of the most interesting issues under this topic has been **how** and **where** in the grammar we can reconcile two contradictory properties of the causative construction: that V-*sase* is a coherent word, and that *sase* involves complementation.

I will begin with an overview of two approaches to this problem offered in the literature: the "Verb Raising" Approach and the "Lexical" Approach. We then present our own analysis, which will allow us to incorporate the

observations and insights attained in both the Verb
Raising and the Lexical Approaches without conflicts.

2.1.1. Verb Raising Approach

The line of research we will refer to as the Verb
Raising Approach to Japanese causatives seems to have been
initiated by Kuroda (1965a), and later adopted, articulated
and modified by Kuno (1973), Shibatani (1973, 1976), Inoue
(1976), Kuroda (1978), among others.

All these works agree on the analysis of causatives
summarized in (2) below:[2]

(2) (i) A causative morpheme *sase* takes a syntactic complement.

    (ii) This complementation takes place at the level of deep structure.

    (iii) The complement is clausal (i.e., either S or S').

    (iv) A complex verb V-*sase* is derived at surface structure by means of a transformational rule called Verb Raising.

On the other hand, there hardly exists a consensus on
the exact differences between the two types of causatives
exemplified in (3) below --- the *ni*-causative and the
o-causative:[3]

(3) a. kooti ga sensyu *ni* hasir-ase-ru
       coach NOM player DAT run-CAUSE-PRES

   'The coach makes/lets the player run.'

   b. kooti ga sensyu *o* hasir-ase-ru
      coach NOM player ACC run-CAUSE-PRES

   'The coach makes/lets the player run.'

For example, there has been a long and heated controversy over:

(4) (i)   How the different Case marking (*ni* vs. *o*) is realized.

    (ii) Whether they have different underlying structures, and if they do, how exactly they differ.

    (iii) Whether they can be clearly distinguished semantically, and if they can be, how exactly they differ.

Although (4i-iii) are interesting and important problems and we will return to some of these problems when they become relevant, let us for the moment concentrate on the various proposals summarized in (2).[4]

If we suppress Case marking, the derivation of the *o*-causative sentence (3b) in the Verb Raising Approach, for example that proposed by Kuno (1973), will proceed as in (5) below:

(5)
a. Deep Structure: kooti sensyu [₈ sensyu hasir-u] sase-ru
b. Equi-NP Deletion: kooti sensyu [₈ ∅ hasir-u] sase-ru
c. Aux Deletion: kooti sensyu [₈   hasir-∅] sase-ru
d. Verb Raising: kooti sensyu [₈ ∅   ] *hasir*-sase-ru
e. Tree Pruning: kooti sensyu hasir-sase-ru

In this analysis, the Verb Raising (5d) is triggered by the lack of a complement Aux induced by the Aux Deletion (5c).

The Verb Raising Approach is rooted in the Standard Theory (Chomsky (1965)). Notably, this theory advocates a model of grammar in which the **deep** structure is assumed to be the sole input to the **semantic interpretation**, and the **surface** structure to be the sole input to the **phonological rules**, as schematized in (6) below:

(6)
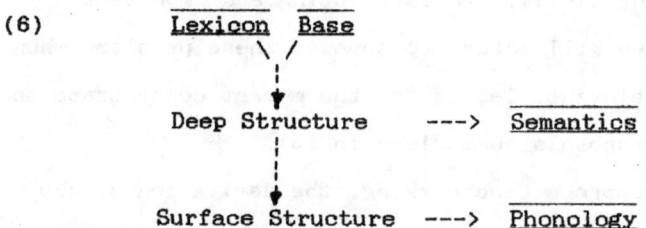

In the above mentioned works, especially Kuroda (1965a) and Shibatani (1978), many interesting semantic facts were discovered that suggest that the causative constructions involve complementation at the syntactic level where semantic interpretation is relevant.

In (7) below, some of these arguments are summarized: (We will spell out the details of these arguments below when they become relevant to our discussion.)

(7) (i) The **subject**-oriented reflexive pronoun *zibun* (self), may refer to either a causer (= matrix subject) or a causee (= complement subject). (Kuroda (1965a))

(ii) The pro-VP *soo-s* (do so) may refer to either a "matrix" VP headed by *sase* or a "complement" VP. (Shibatani (1973))

(iii) Some adverbs may ambiguously modify either the "matrix" verb *sase* or a "complement" verb. (Shibatani (Ibid.))

Thus, the deep structure complementation (2i-ii) was a rather natural consequence of the analysis of causatives conducted within the framework of the Standard Theory.

On the other hand, native speakers of Japanese have a clear intuition that a complex predicate of the form V-*sase* constitutes a single surface word. In this connection, it has been pointed out by McCawley (1968) and Hayata (1971) that complex predicates exhibit the same accent pattern as simplex predicates. (See 2.2.3. for a summary of McCawley's analysis.) Since all phonological rules were assumed to apply to the surface structure, it was again a natural move to come up with an analysis, in which a transformational rule like Verb Raising agglutinates two independent deep structure verbs (V and *sase*) into a single verb V-*sase* at the surface structure.

In short, arguments for the Verb Raising Approach, especially (2ii) and (2iv), are quite insightful and straightforward within the theoretical framework of the Standard Theory.

Although we have presented the Verb Raising Approach above from a historical perspective, there does not exist any reason why this analysis must be confined to the framework of the Standard Theory. It may, in principle, be adapted to any theoretical framework, for example, into the theory that incorporates Logical Form as a level of representation. In 2.4. below, we will take up this possibility and discuss it.

2.1.2. Lexical Approach

The idea that Japanese causatives involve syntactic complementation has been challenged by Farmer (1980) and Miyagawa (1980), who independently proposed that "V-*sase*", as well as other complex predicates, are derived in the lexicon by means of a morphological rule of affixation. Let us refer to this line of investigation as the "Lexical" Approach.[6]

2.1.2.1. Theoretical Background

The Lexical Approach to the complex predicates in Japanese is an extension of the Lexicalist Hypothesis (Chomsky (1970)), which confines all the derivational morphology to the lexicon. Another important theoretical backdrop to the Lexical Approach is the rapid development and organization of the theory of the lexicon that followed up Chomsky's work mentioned above. Mostly based upon data from English, such works as Halle (1973), Siegel (1974), Jackendoff (1975) and Aronoff (1976), to name only a few, convincingly argue that the lexicon is not merely a list of the idiosyncratic properties of lexical items but is, in many ways, a highly structured autonomous component of grammar. This view has derived support and been extended by the analyses presented by Pesetsky (1979), Lieber (1981), Williams (1981a), Kiparsky (1982), Selkirk (1982), among others.

The Lexical Approach, thus, considers the morphemes like *sase* (CAUSE), *rare* (PASSIVE) and *ta* (DESIDERATIVE) to be derivational suffixes, and lets the productive rules of derivational morphology attach them to a verbal root or stem. Accordingly, the derived complex predicates, for example, the causative expression *tabe-sase*, (eat-CAUSE) will be inserted into a syntactic structure as a single coherent lexical item, as in (8) below:

(8)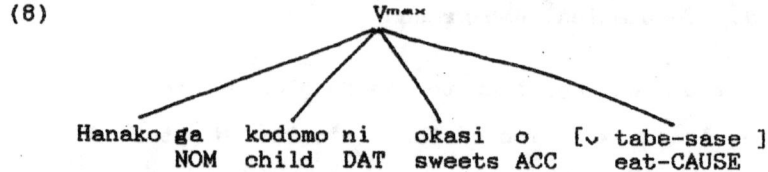

'Hanako's making/letting the child eat sweets'

Both Farmer and Miyagawa adopt a **non-configurational** (or **flat**) analysis of Japanese phrase structure as in (8).[7] Hale (1980) has pointed out that this analysis allows the base-generation of a free word order as in (9) below without recourse to the syntactic rule of scrambling, assuming that there now exists no necessity for the object NP to maintain any special relation with the verb.

(9)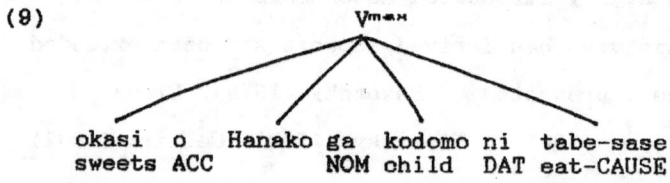

On the other hand, it is important to realize that the lexical derivation of complex predicates and the non-configurational analysis of the phrase structure are two independent matters. It is perfectly plausible, therefore, to adopt the former but not the latter, as illustrated in (10) below:

(10)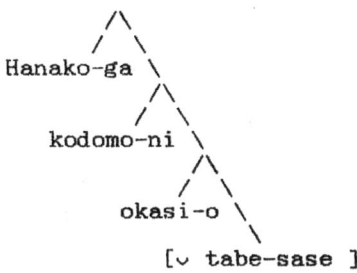

We will, in fact, adopt an analysis similar to (10) rather than (8) in 2.3. below, with the assumption that the free word order is explained in terms of a movement rule in syntax (Harada (1977), Saito (1985), etc.). There is a growing body of literature, for example, Whitman (1982), Saito (1985) and Hoji (1985), among others, which provides many different arguments for a configurational phrase structure in Japanese.

Neither Farmer nor Miyagawa, on the other hand, treats tense morphemes on a par with other "derivational" suffixes like *sase*. Miyagawa, for example, explicitly claims that tense morphemes are, by virtue of being [+Aux], inserted into syntactic structures as lexical items independent of predicates (p. 89). Farmer, on the other hand, assumes tense as one of the lexical features which does not have its own categorial status (p. 73). Therefore, a sentence equals a V^{max} in her analysis. In short, tense morphemes are not attached to predicates by way of affixation in either analysis.

In 2.2. below, we will provide evidence for the lexical derivation of complex predicates. The version of the Lexical Approach we will argue for is, in a sense, even more radical than Miyagawa's or Farmer's, in that it introduces not only derivational morphemes like *sase* (CAUSE) and *rare* (PASSIVE) but also inflectional morphemes like *ru* (PRES) and *ta* (PAST) by means of affixation in the lexicon.

In the remainder of this section, we will briefly describe the major differences betwen Miyagawa's and Farmer's works.

2.1.2.2 Miyagawa (1980)

Aside from the lexical derivation of complex predicates mentioned above, the most distinctive feature of Miyagawa's proposal concerning the complex predicates is that it denies the presence of complementation in any grammatical level, be it syntactic or lexical.

In order to maintain this claim, Miyagawa attempts to undermine some of the arguments for the complementation analysis introduced in (7) above. We will examine some of Miyagawa's counterarguments in 2.4. below, and conclude that they are either invalid or valid but problematic for his own positions. In fact, the biggest problem with the position Miyagawa takes concerning the complementation issue is that he does not offer any alternative account for the observed facts in (7).

Contrary to these problematic claims concerning complementation, Miyagawa offers very interesting and convincing evidence for the lexical derivation of complex predicates. He observes that "verb-*sase*" formed with, for example, an intransitive verb may undergo semantic drift only if it lacks an independent transitive counterpart. (Miyagawa assumes that causativization is basically a transitivizing process.) For example, intransitive verbs *nak* (cry) and *niow* (smell), which lack transitive counterparts, may acquire non-compositional meanings via causativization:

(11) a. nak-ase   'trouble'
        cry-CAUSE
     b. niow-ase   'hint'
        smell-CAUSE

An intransitive verb like *sin* (die), which has a transitive counterpart *koros* (kill), on the other hand, may never undergo such semantic drift.

In order to account for this generalization, Miyagawa makes an appeal to the notion "blocking" (Aronoff (1976)) in the following way. All verbal stems in Japanese are arranged in the lexicon in terms of a Paradigmatic Structure (PDS) of the form in (12) below. Each PDS has

three related meaning slots labelled "intransitive",
"transitive" and "ditransitive":

(12)

intransitive	transitive	ditransitive
sin (die)	koros (kill)	

While an underived predicate fills each meaning slot
solely based upon their meanings as in (12), a derived
predicate (e.g., V-*sase*) is "blocked" from entering the PDS
if there already exists an underived stem in the
corresponding meaning slot (e.g., transitive slot), as
illustrated in (13) below:[e]

(13)

intransitive	transitive	ditransitive
sin (die)	koros (kill) *sin-ase (die-CAUSE)	

If there is no such "preoccupying" stem in the PDS, on the
other hand, a derived predicate will fill the meaning slot
as a stem, as illustrated in (14) below:

(14)

intransitive	transitive	ditransitive
nak (cry)	nak-ase (cry-CAUSE)	

Miyagawa's claim is that only those derived predicates
that enter the PDS, hence are registered as stems, may
undergo semantic drift and be listed in the permanent

With the extension of the theory of the lexicon proposed by Aronoff (1976), this argument provides an indirect but good piece of motivation for the lexical derivation of complex predicates.

2.1.2.3. Farmer (1980)

Farmer (1980) does not argue explicitly for the lexical derivation of complex predicates, but claims:

(15) (i) The causative morpheme *sase* is "bound", in that it must be attached to a verb.

    (ii) If we treat *sase* as an affix, we can capture the bound property of *sase* in terms of the notion "morphological subcategorization" of an affix (Lieber (1981)).

    (iii) If *sase* is an affix, it cannot be syntactically introduced.

Although these assumptions are not implausible, they by no means constitute evidence for the lexical derivation of V-*sase*, since even the Verb Raising Approach can incorporate the "morphological subcategorization" mentioned in (16ii) as a surface structure constraint without much trouble.

Unlike Miyagawa, on the other hand, Farmer recognizes the validity of at least (7i) (the argument concerning *zibun*) and offers an alternative account to the syntactic complementation assumed in the Verb Raising Approach. Her logic goes as follows:

(16) (i) Complex predicates are lexically-derived.
 (ii) A lexically-inserted complex predicate remains a coherent word throughout the syntactic derivation.
 (iii) Therefore, syntactic complementation is not available to account for the facts in (7).

Her solution to the problem raised in (16iii) is to explain (7) in terms of what she calls "Propositional Argument Structure (PAS)". PAS is a **lexical** representation in which the θ-roles of a predicate are associated with linearly ordered argument positions, as illustrated in (17) below:

(17) (**Agent** **Theme** tabe)
                    eat

Crucially, it is assumed that PAS may involve complementation as in (18) below:

(18) (**Agent** (**Agent** **Theme** tabe) sase)
                         eat   CAUSE

Farmer claims that it is this **lexical** complementation structure that allows us to capture the facts in (7i). In particular, she proposes that a rule of the form in (19) **cyclically** applies and identifies both the matrix and the complement subjects that may behave as an antecedent of *zibun*:[7]

(19) Assign the diacritic 'S(=Subject:Y.K.)' to the
primary argument position in a propositional argument
structure, as in:

(<u>Agent</u> (<u>Agent</u> <u>Theme</u> tabe) sase)
  S   S   eat   CAUSE

Since Farmer maintains a "non-configurational" syntactic structure headed by a lexically derived complex predicate in addition to such a "configurational" lexical structure, it amounts to the claim that causative sentences in Japanese have **dual** structural representations as in (20) below throughout the syntactic derivation (cf. also Chomsky (1981) and Hale (1983)):

(20) *Syntactic Representation:*

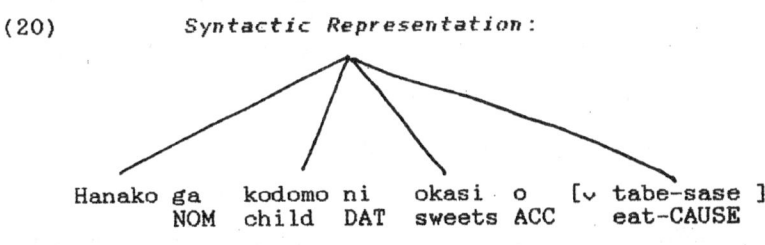

Hanako ga   kodomo ni   okasi o   [v tabe-sase]
NOM   child DAT   sweets ACC   eat-CAUSE

'Hanako's making/letting the child eat sweets'

(21) *Lexical Representation:*

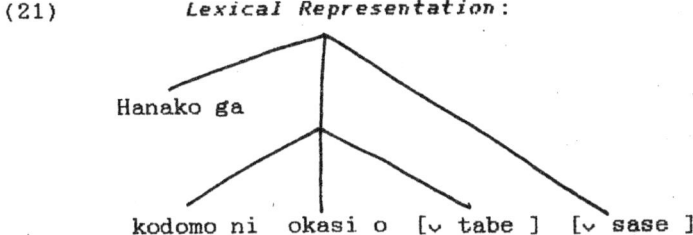

Note that Farmer is, in a sense, bringing syntax into lexical representations by permitting complementation of PASs (cf. also Bresnan (1978) and various subsequent works in Lexical Functional Grammar). The dual structural representations can be viewed as an interesting alternative to the analysis of Japanese causatives involving syntactic complementation, but one desires independent motivation for the need of a lexical process like "lexical complementation". It should be clear here that the need for a lexical representation of an argument structure (PAS) and the need for compounding of PAS's when complementation is involved are two independent matters. While it has been convincingly shown that a lexical argument structure is a part of the lexical representation of predicates (Gruber (1965), Jackendoff (1972), Bresnan (1978), Williams (1980), etc.), introducing complementation into such lexical representations, as Farmer does, is an issue which requires independent empirical justification, and that has not yet been provided.[10]

In 2.3. and 2.4. below, we will note: (i) that the lexical derivation of complex predicates does not necessarily preclude us from adopting syntactic complementation to account for the facts in (7) above, and (ii) that there are various semantic facts peculiar to complex predicates that cannot be successfully accounted for in the PAS approach without also requiring complementation in syntax. We will argue, in other words, that the dual structural representation, particularly the complementation in the lexical representation, is superfluous even in the lexical analysis of causatives.

Saito (1985) argues that the dual structural representations are not essential to the account of free word order phenomena in Japanese. Our proposals below, if plausible, will make it unnecessary to adopt the retreat he made, whereby dual structural representations are necessary only for the causative (and similar) constructions.

The rest of this chapter proceeds as follows. In 2.2., we will present phonological motivations for the lexical derivation of complex predicates. We then make our own proposals in 2.3., extending the Affix Raising analysis proposed by Pesetsky (1985) and further developed by Lebeaux (1984) and Kitagawa (1986a). Various motivations for the proposals will be provided in 2.4., and the counterarguments to the lexical derivation analysis will be examined in 2.5.

2.2. Lexical Derivation

In this section, we will argue that complex predicates in Japanese are derived in the lexicon.

Although our main purpose is to show that suffixes like *sase* (CAUSE), *rare* (PASSIVE) and *ta* (DESIDERATIVE) are attached to a verbal stem in the lexicon, the discussion will lead us to conclude that both these derivational morphemes and tense morphemes like *ru* (PRES) and *ta* (PAST) are attached to a stem in the lexicon.

We will first provide a brief overview of a model of grammar that incorporates the distinction between phonology **before** syntax (lexical phonology) and phonology **after** syntax (post-lexical phonology).

Later in the section, we will observe that quite regular dependencies exist between certain phonological rules and both derivational and inflectional suffixes in Japanese when they are involved in the derivation of simplex predicates and/or complex predicates. It will be argued, then, that those dependencies can be straightforwardly captured in the theory of lexical phonology if we assume that all verbal and adjectival predicates in Japanese, including the complex predicates, are derived in the lexicon together with their tense morphemes.

2.2.1. Lexical and Post-lexical Phonology

It has long been noted that there exist dependencies between certain phonological and morphological processes (Sapir (1921), Bloomfield (1933), etc.). A much discussed problem has been how such dependencies -- known as "morphophonemics" -- can be systematically captured.

Important progress on this issue was made by Siegel (1974), who showed that those affixation processes in English which trigger the cyclic stress assignment (Class I affixation) and those which do not (Class II affixation) are ordered in blocks --- or in more recent terms, are "level-ordered" in the lexicon. (cf. also Allen (1978)) For example, Class I suffixes like -ity, (adjective-forming) -al, (noun-forming) -y and -ation influence the placement of primary stress, as illustrated by the examples in (1) below:[11]

(1) a. accident ===> accident-al ===> accidental-ity
    b. photograph ===> photograph-y
    c. limit ===> limit-ation

Class II suffixes like -less, -ness and -ed, on the other hand, play no role in the assignment of stress:[12]

(2) a. use ===> use-less ===> useless-ness
    b. decide ===> decid-ed ===> decided-ness

Siegel has proposed that if we level-order some of the phonological rules as well as morphological processes, we can straightforwardly capture the fact that certain classes of morphemes trigger particular sets of phonological rules. For example, the facts in (1) and (2) above can be accounted for by the following level-ordering:[13]

(3)   morphlogical   phonological
            process   process
Level I: -ity, -al, -y, -ation   ===>   Cyclic Stress
                                             Assignment
Level II: -less, -ness, -ed

The proposed ordering of the two classes of affixation processes (Class I < Class II) can be confirmed by the existence of a word like *accident-al-ness* (Class I < Class II) and the absence of a word like **decid-ed-ity* (Class II < Class I).[14]

In short, "lexical" phonology was introduced in addition to "post-lexical" (or post-syntax) phonology.

The theory of lexical phonology has been elaborated in such works as Pesetsky (1979), Kiparsky (1982), Mohanan (1982), Pulleyblank (1983), Halle and Mohanan (1985) to name only a few. This work has been guided by the observation that lexical and post-lexical phonology exhibit clusters of distinctive properties with respect to the mode of rule application. Let us summarize here the portion of these distinctions relevant to us:[15]

(4) (i)   Lexical phonology is word-bound, whereas post-lexical phonology may take a phrase as a domain.

    (ii) Lexical phonology precedes post-lexical phonolgy.

(iii) Lexical phonology may exhibit sensitivity to morphological information, whereas post-lexical phonology may not.

The difference of domains ((4i)) and the relative order ((4ii)) follow from a model of core grammar we have introduced in Chapter One, if we assume that post-lexical phonology takes place at the level of PF (See (1) in Chapter One). In this model, lexical phonology precedes syntax. Hence, it must be word-bound as well as ordered before post-lexical phonology.

There are at least two types of morphological sensitivity that lexical phonology exhibits ((4iii)). One is sensitivity to a class of morphemes as observed in (1) and (2) above with respect to English stress assignment. The other is sensitivity to particular morphemes, which results in the presence of exceptions to the rules. The first type of sensitivity can be considered to be a result of level-ordering. It has been argued, on the other hand, that the second type of morphological-sensitivity is related to the possibility for lexical phonology to have access to word-internal structure, including idiosyncratic information of particular morphemes (cf. Pesetsky (1979), Mohanan (1982)).

There seems to be no consensus as to where in each lexical level the internal brackets of words become inaccessible to further morphological and phonological processes. It seems to be a quite stable assumption, however, that such internal brackets become inaccessible (or erased) at least at the end of the last lexical level. From this, it follows that post-lexical phonology cannot have access to word-internal structures, hence exhibits no morphological sensitiveity of either type mentioned above.

2.2.2. Accentuation

The first argument for the lexical derivation of complex predicates comes from the investigation of accents in verbs and adjectives.

It is well-known that the accent patterns of verbs and adjectives systematically differ depending on the tense morphemes attached to them (Chew (1961), McCawley (1968), etc.). As illustrated in (5) below, verbs and adjectives have an accent on the stem-final mora[16] when they are accompanied by a present tense morpheme. When accompanied by a past tense morpheme, on the other hand, they exhibit a stem-penultimate accent, as in (6):
(M' = accented mora)

(5) a. tabe'-ru   (eat-PRES)
    b. siro'-i   (white-PRES)

(6) a. ta'be-ta   (eat-PAST)
    b. si'ro-katta (white-PAST)

In order to capture the contrast between (5) and (6), Chew (Ibid.) and McCawley (Ibid.) stipulate that the present tense morphemes *ru* and *i* do, but the past tense morphemes *ta* and *katta* do not, trigger Accent Attraction Rule, which has the effect of shifting the underlyingly specified accent one mora toward right.

Haraguchi (1977), on the other hand, proposes the accent assignment rules in (7) below, assuming that verbs and adjectives need not be specified with the location of their underlying accent:[17]

(7) (i) V ===> V' / ___ stem] i Adj]
                        [+Acct]

 (ii) V ===> V' / ___ C₀ V stem] + Q Adj]
                              [+Acct]

;where Q = the maximal sequence of segments,
 V = vowel,
 [+Acct] = Accented.

The application of these rules is restricted to underlyingly accented adjectives as the condition [+Acct] indicates. Here the variable Q is meant to include not only the past tense ending but also some other conjugational endings like *te/kute* (GERUNDIVE) and *kereba* (CONDITIONAL). Let us concentrate here, however, on the past tense morpheme for ease of exposition.

The verbal version of (7i-ii) will presumably look something like (8i-ii) below: (cf. Clark (1983))

(8) (i) V ===> V' / ___ ₛₜₑₘ] ru ᵥₑᵣᵦ]
                        [+Acct]

(ii) V ===> V' / ___ C₀ (V) ₛₜₑₘ] + Q ᵥₑᵣᵦ][19]
                              [+Acct]

The basic intuition behind Haraguchi's rules seems to be that an accent falls on the penultimate mora of both adjectives and verbs in all their conjugated forms, if the present tense endings (*ru/i*) but not past tense endings (*ta/katta*) belong to the derived words. Both in McCawley's and Haraguchi's analyses, in other words, the rules manipulating accents see the present tense endings but they do not see the past tense endings. What we observe here, then, is an interdependency of phonology and morphology quite comparable to that involving cyclic stress assignment in English --- a case that led Siegel to postulate a level-ordering of derivational affixes in English.

It has been pointed out earlier (independently) by Clark (1983) and Kurata (1984) that the "present-past asymmetry" in accentuation observed above can be straightforwardly captured by assuming that the accent assignment (or accent attraction) is a lexical process, and that the present and past tense morphemes are introduced in different lexical levels. Clark further points out that this level-ordering allows us to simplify the accent assignment rules in (7) and (8) by eliminating (7ii) and

(8ii). The simplified rule will presumably look like (9) below:

(9) *Penultimate Accent Placement Rule*:

$$V ===> V' / \underline{\quad} C_0 V_{verb/adj}]$$
$$[+Acct]$$

(10) below is a simplified version of the level-ordering in question:

(10)   morphological   phonological
           process   process
Level *i*:   -*ru/i* (PRES)   ===>   Penult Accent Assignment (9)
Level *j*:   -*ta/katta* (PAST)

If this level-ordering approach to accentuation is on the right track, we are led to conclude that both present and past tense morphemes are attached to a relevant stem in the lexicon.

One may still insist that Penultimate Accent Assignment (9) applies post-lexically, taking a derived word as its domain. This approach would force one, however, to assume either: (i) that present tense morphemes are attached to the stem in the lexicon, but past tense morphemes are introduced in syntax, or (ii) that both types of tense morphemes are introduced in syntax, but only present tense morphemes are attached to the stem by some syntactic operation. This is a possible but highly dubious move to take, however, when we consider the similar syntactic functions of present and past tense morphemes.

One might also attempt to account for the present-past asymmetry in accentuation by positing an "extratonal" status for past tense morphemes (cf. Archangeli and Pulleyblank (1984)).[17] As illustrated in (11) and (12) below, this assumption permits us to consider that accent is placed on the penultimate mora in both present and past forms in post-lexical phonology:

(11) a. tabe'-ru   (eat-PRES)
     b. ta'be-(ta)   (eat-PAST)

(12) a. siro'-i   (white-PRES)
     b. si'ro-(katta) (white-PAST)

The contrast in (13) below indeed motivates the extratonality of the adjectival tense morpheme *katta* (PAST):[20] (__ = Low Tone, ‾‾ = High Tone)

(13) a. nemu-i   (sleepy-PRES)
     b. nemu-katta   (sleepy-PAST)

At first sight, (13a) and (13b) appear to provide us with the contradictory conclusion that the adjectival stem *nemu* (sleepy) is both unaccented and accented. The seeming accentedness of the mora *mu* in (13b), however, can be accounted for if the immediately following low tone arises from the extratonality of *katta*.

The lack of such a contrast in (14) below, on the other hand, suggests that the verbal tense morpheme *ta* cannot be considered to be extratonal:

(14)   a.   ȳame-ru   (stop-PRES)

        b.   ȳame-ta   (stop-PAST)

The contrast between (13b) and (14b), in other words, forces us to reject the extratonality approach to the present-past asymmetry of accentuation observed in (11) and (12) above.

We thus adopt the level-ordering approach, and assume that tense morphemes are attached to verbal and adjectival stems in the lexicon.[21]

With this conclusion in mind, let us now turn to the following paradigm (cf. McCawley (1968)):

(15)   a.   tabe-sase'-ru   (eat-CAUSE-PRES)

        b.   tabe-sa'se-ta   (eat-CAUSE-PAST)

(16)   a.   tabe-sase-rare'-ru   (eat-CAUSE-PASS-PRES)

        b.   tabe-sase-ra're-ta   (eat-CAUSE-PASS-PAST)

Crucially, *sase* (CAUSE) and *rare* (PASSIVE) in (15a) and (16a) not only appear inside the tense morpheme *ru* but also carry an accent on their final mora due to the application

of the lexical rule of penultimate accent placement, which
counts *ru* as the final mora of the derived word. The only
logical conclusion we can draw, then, seems to be that *sase*
and *rare* have already been attached to the verbal stem when
the tense morpheme *ru* is introduced in the lexicon.

Second, the complex predicates in (15) and (16)
exhibit a present-past asymmetry in accent placement
already familiar to us from simplex predicates. This
asymmetry can be also straightforwardly accounted for if
sase and *rare* are also assumed to be introduced in the
lexicon as Level *i* suffixes (Kurata (1984)):[22]

(17)   morphological   phonological
         process   process

Level *i*: -*sase* (CAUSE)
            -*rare* (PASSIVE)   ===> Penultimate Accent
            -*ru/i* (PRES)   Assignment (9)

Level *j*: -*ta/katta* (PAST)

We thus conclude that complex predicates together
with tense morphemes are derived in the lexicon.[23]

2.2.3. Voicing Spread

In this subsection, we will present another
phonological argument for the lexical derivation of a
tensed verb of the form V-*ta* (PAST). It will again lead us
to the lexical derivation of complex predicates.

Observe, first, the phonological change in (18) below triggered by the suffixation of Level *j* morphemes *ta* and *te*:

(18) a. tob + ta ===> ton-da
          jump PAST
      b. tob + te ===> ton-de
               GER

In addition to the Consonant Assimilation discussed in footnote 12, there are two other phonological processes involved in the derivation of these examples --- Voicing Spread and Coda Nasalization, as illustrated in (19) below (Ito and Mester (1986)):[24]

(19) -*ta*:   tob-ta
      Voi Spr: tob-da
      C Assim: tod-da
      Coda Nas: ton-da

Let us here concentrate on Voicing Spread, and present the following observation made by Ito and Mester (Ibid.). In contrast to verbs ending in a voiced obstruent as in (18) above, not only verbs ending in a voiceless consonant but also verbs ending in a sonorant fail to trigger Voicing Spread, as illustrated in (20) below:[25]

(20) a. but-ta ===> but-ta
hit-PAST

b. tabe-ta ===> tabe-ta
eat

c. tor-ta ===> tot-ta
take

d. kaw-ta ===> kat-ta
buy

Adopting the theory of underspecification (Kiparsky (1982)), Ito and Mester account for this contrast, especially the contrast bentween (18) and (20b-d), with the hypothesis that redundant features ([+voi] for sonorants and [-voi] for obstruents) are not present underlyingly or during the cyclic phonology but are filled in by post-cyclic default rules. It has been claimed, in other words, that Voicing Spread as in (21) below formalized as an autosegmental rule of lexical phonology, does not have a chance to apply even in (20b-d), since the stem-final sonorants in these exmaples are not yet associated with [+voi], which is provided for the first time by a default rule in the post-lexical phonology:

(21) *Voicing Spread*:

There is good reason, in other words, to assume that Voicing Spread applies lexically. Then, since the past tense morpheme ta may undergo Voicing Spread, as seen in (18) above, we may again conclude that it is attached to the verbal stem in the lexicon.[26]

2.2.4. Downdrift

One final argument for the lexical derivation of complex predicates concerns the desiderative suffix -ta (want). Observe first the contrast in (22) below, which indicates that ta (want) is accented:

(22) a. a̅ke-ru
       open-PRES

 b. a̅ke-ta̅-i
       want-PRES

Suppose, then, that ta (want) is suffixed to an accented verbal root like tabe (eat) and nom (drink). Here, following Pulleyblank (1983), we represent underlying accents "non-linearly" as high tones, as illustrated in (23) below:[27]

(23) a. tabe-ta-i   (eat-want-PRES)
        | |
        H   H

 b. nom-ita-i   (drink-want-PRES)[28]
        | |
        H   H

The resulting representation, then, will violate the
Obligatory Contour Principle (Leben (1973)), which
prohibits a sequence of identical elements in the melodic
tier.

In order to solve this problem, let us assume that
there exists a cyclic rule of tone deletion as in (24),
which applies at least in Level i (cf. Archangeli and
Pulleyblank (1984)):

(24) *Tone Deletion*:

   H H ... ===>   Ø H ...

This rule will provide derivations as in (25) below:

(25) a. tabe-ta   ===>   tabe-ta
             | | | |
             H H   Ø H
      b. tabe-ta-gar ===> tabe-ta-gar
             | | |
             H H   Ø H

That this approach is on the right track can be
confirmed when we examine the accent patterns of V-*ta*
(want) in the light of so-called downdrift phenomena.
Kawakami (1973) observes that when a phrasal expression
containing two accented items is read in a fast,
uninterrupted manner, the second of the two accents will
undergo the downdrift, as illustrated in (26) below
(cf. McCawley (1968) and Haraguchi (1977)):

(26) u'mi-de + oyo'g-u ===> u̅m̅i̅-̅d̅e̅ ̅o̅y̅o̅g̅-u
    sea LOC   swam-PRES   ---

This intuition can be confirmed by the pitch track diagram in Table 1 below: (The speech was digitized at 10 kHz, and the pitch was computed within an AMDF pitch tracker at 200 Hz.)

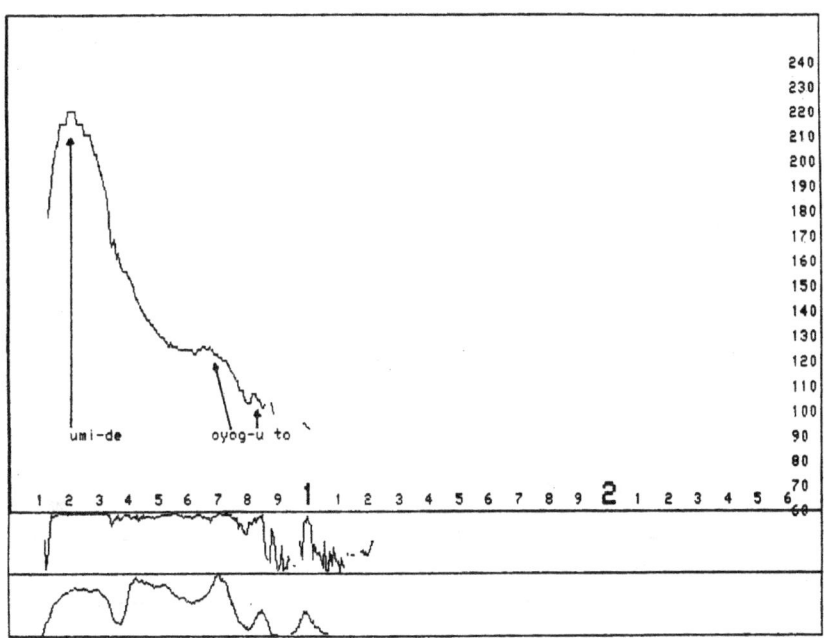

Table 1. Pitch track diagram of u'mi-de oyo'g-u

Crucially, however, the complex predicates in (23) above, which involve an accented verbal root and *ta* (want), do

not undergo downdrift but exhibit a lexical penultimate-
accent pattern, as in (27) below:

(27) a. ta̅be̅-ta̅-i̅
      b. no̅m̅-i-ta̅-i̅

This intuition is confirmed by the pitch track diagram
in Table 2 below:

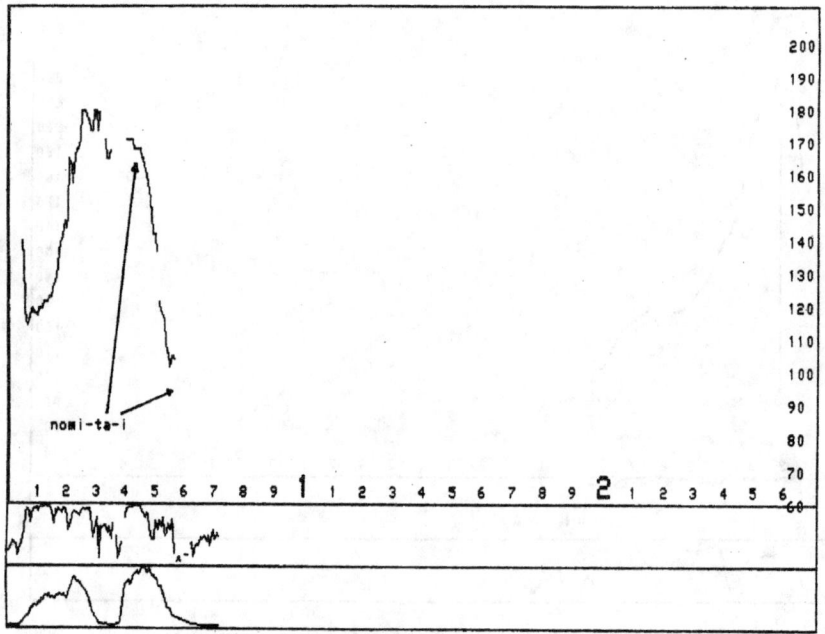

Table 2. Pitch track diagram of no'm-ita'-i

This means that the complex predicate *nom-ita-i*
(drink-want-PRES), for example, is **not** represented as in
(28) below when downdrift takes place:

(28) nom-ita-i
       | |
       H   H

Whether downdrift is a phonological process (Haraguchi (1977)) or is a result of a phonetic implementation rule (Pierrehumbert (1980)), it must be considered to take place **post-lexically**, since its domain is unquestionably phrasal (cf. (26)). The contrast between (26) and (27) above, then, argues for the lexical derivation of V-ta (want). Under an approach which derives V-ta in syntax, the two accents, i.e., two high tones, in the examples like (23) are put together for the first time **post-lexically**. They are, therefore, incorrectly predicted to undergo downdrift, leaving the contrast between (26) and (27) unexplained.

On the other hand, in the lexical-derivation approach incorporating a lexical tonal deletion rule, this contrast will be expected, since the complex predicates in (23a-b) lose one of the high tones during the lexical derivation, hence will be unable to undergo downdrift post-lexically.

2.2.5. Summary

In this section, we have concluded that all tensed prediates including complex predicates are derived in the lexicon.

Follwoing Kurata (1984) and Clark (1983), we first argued that the present-past asymmetry in the accentuation of tensed verbs and adjectives is best accounted for by ordering the present tense morphemes *ru/i* and the past tense morphemes *ta/katta* in different lexical levels.

Drawing on Ito and Mester's (1986) work, we have seen that the lexical introduction of the past tense morpheme *ta* is also motivated in the light of voicing spread.

Since *sase* (CAUSE) and *rare* (PASSIVE) not only appear inside the tense morphemes but also are affected by Penultimate Accent Assignment triggered by the lexical process of *ru/i*-suffixation, we have concluded that they are also lexically introduced.

Finally, we have seen that lexical introduction of the desiderative morpheme *ta* (want) is motivated in the light of downdrift. While phrasal expressions containing two accented items may undergo downdrift, a complex predicate consisting of an accented verbal stem and the accented suffix *ta* (want) (e.g., *tabe-ta-i*) never undergoes this **post-lexical** process. We have pointed out that this contrast can be explained if V-*ta* (want) is assumed to be derived in the lexicon, where one of the high tones is deleted by a cyclic rule of tone deletion.

The following is a summary of the proposed level-ordering:

(28)   morphological   phonological
                    process   process

    Level i: -sase (CAUSE)   Penultimate Accent
               -rare (PASIVE)   Assignment (9)
               -ta (want)   ==>   Tone Deletion (24)
               -ru (PRES)
               -i (PRES)

    Level j: -ta (PAST)   Voicing Spread (21)
               -te (GER)   ===>   Coda Nasalization
               -katta (PAST)

If our conclusion in this section has any validity, it will force us to reject virtually all versions of the Verb Raising Approach, in which complex predicates are derived in syntax.

2.3. Affix Raising Hypothesis

2.3.1. Initial Sketch

We have concluded in 2.2. that complex predicates are derived in the lexicon. Within the model of grammar we have adopted ((1) below), this means that we cannot adopt the Verb Raising Approach to account for the two contradictory sets of properties of the causative construction. In particular, D-structure complementation is not an available option for us to account for the facts in (2) below. These facts require structural complexity in the complex predicate construction.

(1)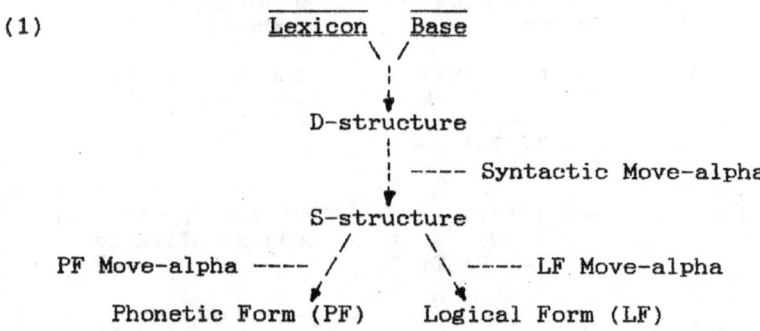

(2) (i) The **subject**-oriented reflexive pronoun *zibun* (self) may refer to either a causer (= matrix subject) or a causee (= complement subject). (Kuroda (1965a))

(ii) The pro-VP *soo-s* (do so) may refer to either a "matrix" VP headed by *sase* or a "complement" VP. (Shibatani (1973))

(iii) Some adverbs may ambiguously modify either the "matrix" verb *sase* or a "complement" verb. (Shibatani (Ibid.))

Miyagawa (1980) and Farmer (1980) take it for granted that the syntactically simplex D-structure representation containing a complex predicate must remain simplex throughout the derivation. As a consequence, they do not capture the facts in (2) in terms of syntactic complementation. In this thesis, however, we will deny this assumption. We will propose that a simplex syntactic representation of a complex predicate construction at S-structure may be mapped onto a complex structure at Logical Form. In particular, our analysis makes an appeal to the syntactic rule of Move-alpha at LF. Move-alpha raises both inflectional and derivational affixes out of complex predicates to yield a syntactically complex structure.

Let us begin to illustrate our "Affix Raising" Hypothesis by presenting typical (schematized) S-structure representations of the complex predicate constructions as in (3) below:[30]

(3) a. S-structure:

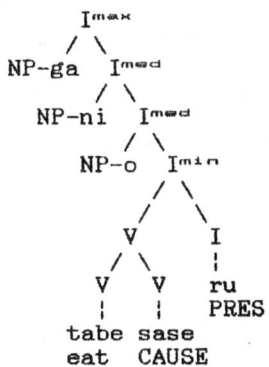

b. S-structure:

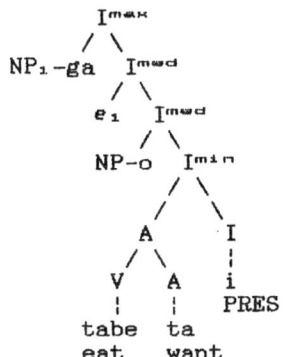

In 2.2. above, we have seen that a complex predicate accompanied by a tense morpheme is derived in the lexicon. When we consider the general head-final character of the morphology in Japanese,[31] it becomes a quite natural assumption that the entire complex predicate (headed by INFL) is inserted as a lexical item of the category INFL (I^{min}), as in (3a) and (3b). Given the basic claim of the X-bar Theory that the category of a non-terminal constituent in syntax corresponds to that of its head lexical item (cf. Chomsky (1970), Emonds (1976), Jackendoff (1978), Hale (1980), Farmer (1980), Stowell (1981), etc.), the syntactic labelling in (3a-b) also is quite straightforward.[32,33]

To these S-structure representations, Move-alpha applies and brings the affixes one by one out of the complex predicates, as illustrated in (4) and (5) below:[34]

(4) a. *S-structure:*   b. *Pre-LF:*

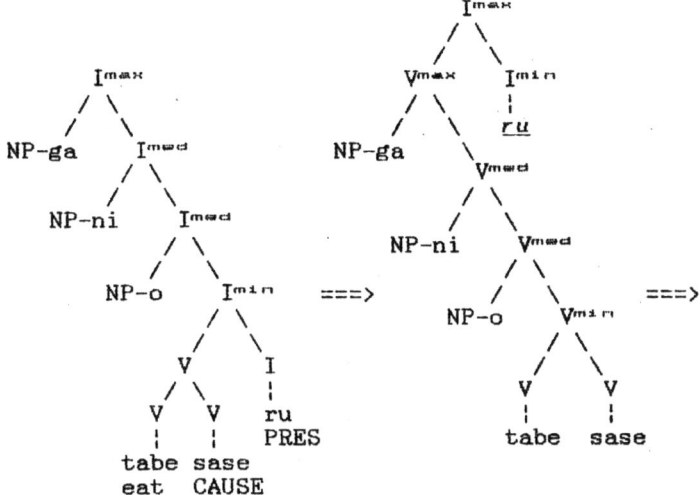

c. *LF:*

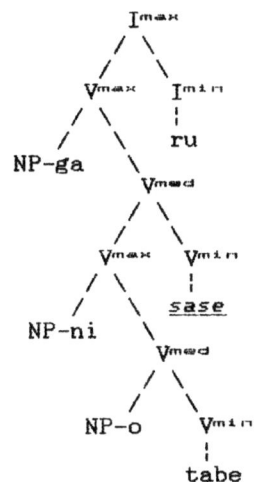

(5) a. *S-structure:* b. *Pre-LF:*

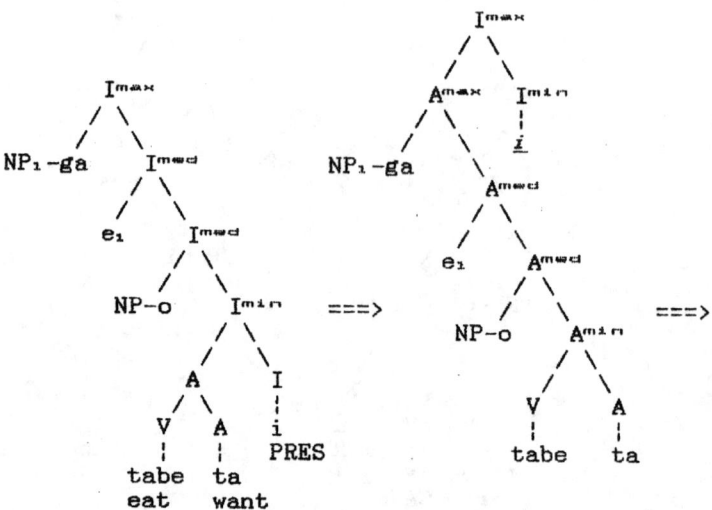

===>

c. *LF:*

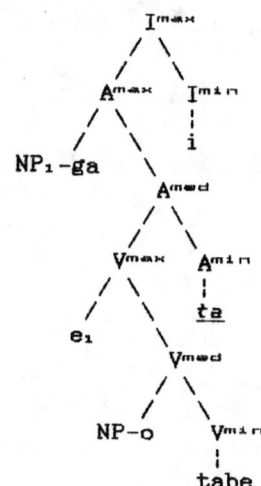

An important feature of this analysis is that the resulting LF representatins in (4) and (5) do contain the complement (V^{max}) to sase (CAUSE) and ta (want). The emergence of such complements will play a crucial role in our account of (2 i-iii) and other facts presented below. On the other hand, since the affix raising in this analysis maps S-structure onto LF, it should have no effect on the phonological and phonetic properties of complex predicates determined at PF. The coherence of a complex predicate as a word, in other words, is inherited from D-structure to PF in this analysis. This result is quite compatible with the intuition reported in 2.1.1. above that a complex predicate constitutes a single surface word, although, at this moment, we have not presented any direct evidence to support this intuition. Note also that the complex predicate's inheritance of "coherent word status" from D-structure through S-structure to PF results from the Isomorphy Constraint ((23) in 1.3.3.), since there does not seem to exist any principle of grammar that requires otherwise.

2.3.2. Bracketing Paradoxes

A further important point to be noted is that the application of Move-alpha to affixes is by no means peculiar to the analysis of complex predicates but should

be considered as a general option available in the
grammar. Its motivation comes from morphological problems
known as "bracketing paradoxes" (cf. Siegel (1974),
Williams (1981a)).

The Affix Raising Approach to bracketing paradoxes
stems from Pesetsky (1985), who dealt with various problems
in English and Russian. For example, English is known to
exhibit bracketing paradoxes like those in (6) below:
(cf. Siegel (Ibid.))

(6) a. un [$_N$ analyze-able-ity]
    b. [un [$_A$ analyze-able]] ity

Here, a well-established level-ordering in English requires
the word-internal structure in (6a), -*ity* and *un*- being
Level 1 (+) and Level 2 (#) affixes, respectively (See
2.2.1. above). When it comes to the categorial selectional
properties of affixes, on the other hand, (6b) rather than
(6a) is motivated, since the prefix *un*- selects an
adjective rather than a noun. The Affix Raising Analysis
proposed by Pesetsky is illustrated in (7) below:

(7) a.   S-structure: b.   LF:

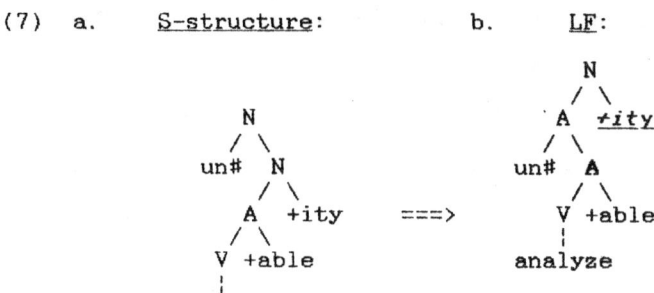

Pesetsky's claims here are: (i) that categorial selection of lexical items including affixes (e.g., un-: +[__ A]) is checked only at LF, and (ii) that the potential violation of c-selection as in (7a) triggers the application of Move-alpha.

The theory of subcategorization mentioned in (i) has been proposed by Pesetsky (1982). First, this theory divides classical subcategorization frames into two independent lexical properties --- theta-marking properties and categorial selectional (c-selectional) properties. The theory argues, moreover, that only the theta-marking properties of lexical items are subject to the Projection Principle, hence only those properties are obligatorily realized throughout a syntactic derivation (i.e., at all D-structure, S-structure and LF). C-selectional properties of lexical items, on the other hand, are checked only at the level of LF. This allows the categorial specification of syntactic constituents to be altered in the course of a derivation. Pesetsky provides various quantifier phrases in Russian --- certain numeral phrases, distributive *po*-phrases, "genitive of negation", etc. --- as examples requiring such an alteration of categorial specification, and motivates this analysis by explaining some puzzling subject-object asymmetries involving these quantifier phrases. Pesetsky (1985) further extends this analysis to morphology, and proposes the analysis introduced in (7) above, in which affix raising by Move-alpha is triggered by the c-selectional property checking.

Japanese as well shows bracketing paradoxes for which the affix raising approach provides a simple solution. In Kitagawa (1986a), for example, I have discussed the following cases:

(8) a. [$_N$ ko-gosi] o kagame
        little-waist ACC bend

   b. *ko* [$_{VP}$ gosi o kagame]

     '*lightly* bend oneself'

(9) a. [$_N$ oo-guti] o ake
        big-mouth ACC open

   b. *oo* [$_{VP}$ guti o ake]

     'open one's mouth *wide*'

Here, the word-bound process of *rendaku* voicing[30] (*k̲osi* (waist) ==> *g̲osi*, *k̲uti* (mouth) ==> *g̲uti*) motivates the bracketing in (8a) and (9a) but the interpretation of the prefixes *ko-* (little) and *oo-* (big) as verbal modifiers suggests the bracketing in (8b) and (9b). With the application of affix raising at LF as in (10) below, we can explain why such adverbial interpretation of the affixes becomes possible:[36]

(10)   a.   S-structure: b.   LF:[37]

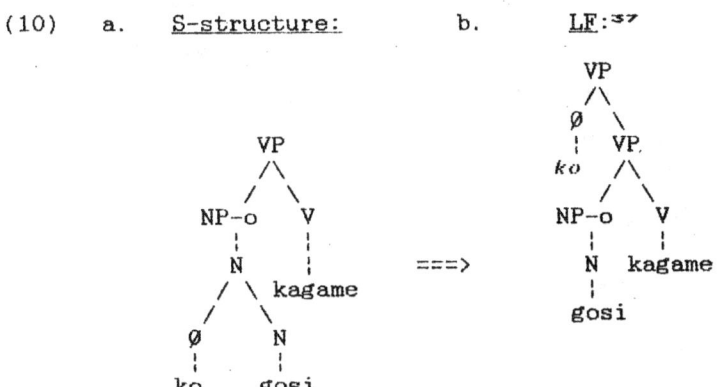

Furthermore, as illustrated in (11) below, the nominal expressions in these examples may never provide an acceptable interpretation by themselves:

(11) a. *kanozyo-no *ko   waki*
                her   *little armpit*

    'her little armpit'

    b. *boku-no *oo   guti*
            my   *big mouth*

    'my big mouth'

Based upon this observation, it has also been suggested that the application of Move-alpha in these examples is triggered by the Principle of Full Interpretation (Chomsky (1986b)), which requires every entity at LF to be interpreted.

Lebeaux (1984b) extends this approach to English nominalization in an interesting way. He argues that the distinction between result and action readings of deverbal nominals reflects a difference in attachment sites for the nominalizing affix at LF, as illustrated in (12)-(14) below:[38]

(12)   the destruction   [result nominal]

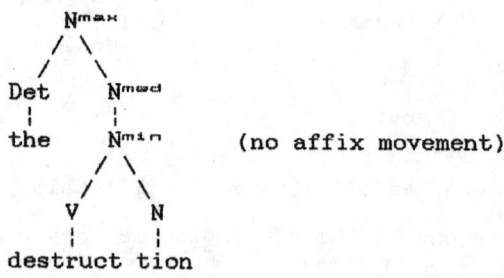

(13) the destruction of the city [action nominal]

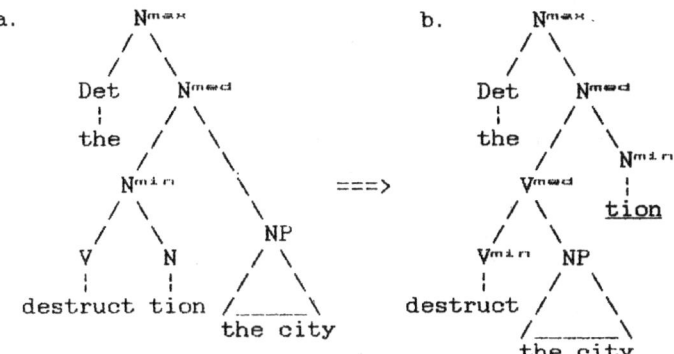

(14) the enemy's destruction of the city [action nominal]

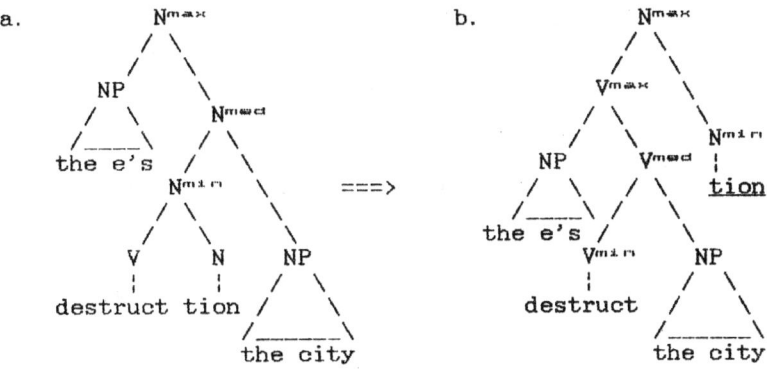

In short, a grammatical device we have adopted for the analysis of complex predicates in Japanese, namely, the application of Move-alpha to an affix is independently well-motivated. In this thesis, we will follow Pesetsky (1982,1985), and assume: (i) that both syntactic and morphological c-selection are checked at LF but nowhere else, and (ii) that c-selectional properties checked at LF trigger the affix raising by Move-alpha.

2.3.3. C-selection and θ-marking

In order to complete our analysis presented in 2.3.1. above, we will make the following proposals concerning the complex predicate forming suffixes *sase* (CAUSE), *rare* (PASSIVE), *ta* (want), *gar* (display) and the tense morphemes in Japanese.

First, these morphemes in Japanese have **morphological** c-selectional properties as in (15) below:

(15) *Morphological C-Selection*:

      a.   sase (CAUSE):   +[V __]
      b.   rare (PASSIVE):   +[V __]
      c.   ta (want):   +[V __]
      d.   gar (display):   +[A __]
      e.   ru/ta (PRES/PAST): +[V __]
      f.   i/katta (PRES/PAST): +[A __]

We propose these as the formal representation of the "boundness" of these morphemes. For example, (15a) states that *sase* (CAUSE) must be attached to a verbal stem. Since we have adopted the position that all c-selectional properties are checked at LF, it follows that a complex predicate containing one or more of the suffixes in (15) must be analyzed as a single lexical item in at least one of the representations at LF. Later in this section and in Chapter Four below, we will see that the facts concerning adverbial scopes and binding in complex predicates are exactly as predicted in this analysis. We thus have a representation like (16) below (=(4a) above) as both an S-structure and a pre-LF representation:

(16) $S-structure/Pre-LF_1$:

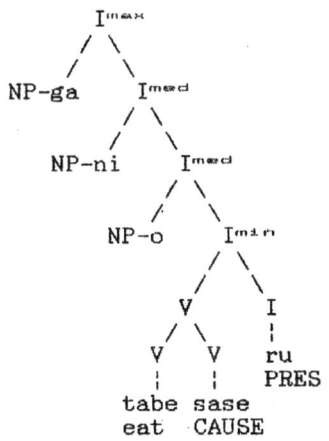

Second, the tense morphemes have **syntactic** c-selectional properties as summarized in (17) below:

(17) $Syntactic\ C-Selection$:

    a.   ru/ta: +[V^{max} ___]

    b.   i/katta: +[A^{max} ___]

Our claim here, in other words, is that the tense morpheme *ru*, for example, syntactically selects a maximal projection of a verb just as a transitive verb selects a maximal projection of a noun (i.e., an object NP). Again, c-selectional properties checked at LF trigger the application of Move-alpha in the example (16). We now motivate the derivation of (18) below from (16) above by means of affix raising:

(18) b. $Pre-LF_2$:

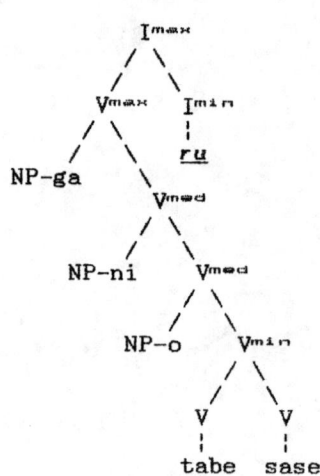

Finally, the various derivational suffixes have the θ-marking properties as summarized below:

(19) θ-marking Properties:

   a. sase (CAUSE):   [AG [ET __]]
   b. rare (PASSIVE):   [EX [ET __]][37]
   c. ta (want):   [EX [ET __]]
   d. gar (display):   [AG/EX [ET __]]

   (AG = AGENT, EX = EXPERIENCER, ET = EVENT-TYPE[40])

Extending Pesetsky's claims, we will assume that the
θ-Criterion as in (20) below also triggers affix raising:

(20) θ-Criterion (Chomsky (1982)):

   (i)   Each term of LF (= each argument) is assigned a
         θ-role uniquely.

   (ii) Each θ-role determined by lexical properties of
         a head is uniquely assigned to an argument at LF.

Thus, the LF representation in (21a) below is derived from
(18) in order to satisfy the θ-Criterion:

(21) a.   *LF*:   b.   *LF*:

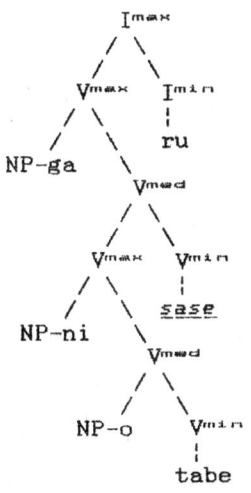
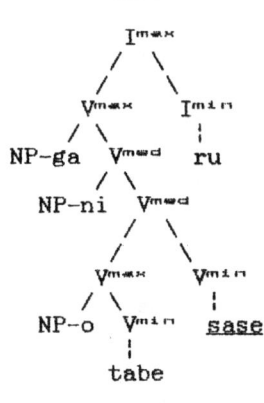

Now in (21a), the θ-marking properties of *sase* ((19a)) and *tabe* ([AG [TH __]]) are both satisfied, in contrast to (21b). Our claim here is, in other words, that once the θ-marking properties of each predicate (including derivational suffixes like *sase* (CAUSE)) are stipulated, the θ-Criterion will force the affixes to take correct landing site when they are raised at LF. Note also that the Isomorphy Constraint guarantees that affix raising is terminated at this point, every principle of grammar being satisfied.

One important question that naturally arises here is whether the analysis in (21) with the proposed θ-marking property in (19a) is compatible with the Projection Principle (Chomsky (1981)), which can be summarized as in (22) below:

(22) *Projection Principle*:

> Representations at each syntactic level (i.e., LF, and D- and S-structure) are projected from the lexicon, in that they observe the θ-marking properties of **lexical items**.

At first sight, the answer to this question appears to be "no". In the (D- and) S-structure representation in (16), for exmaple, there exists no syntactic constituent that can receive the event-type θ-role assigned by *sase* (CAUSE). Note, however, that the Projection Principle is meant to preserve the θ-marking of each **lexical item** inserted into a syntactic representation as an independent word rather than each morpheme making up such a word. In this respect, we may consider that the derivation of (21) from (16) does not violate the Projection Principle. The crucial assumptions here are that neither *tabe* (eat) nor *sase* (CAUSE) is an independent lexical item introduced into syntax, and that the complex lexical item *tabe-sase* (eat-CAUSE) does not have its own θ-marking properties[41], hence is immune to the Projection Principle.

Another possibility pointed out to me by David Pesetsky (personal communication) is to consider that the Projection Principle is in fact satisfied even in the (D- and) S-structure representation in (16), assuming that the event-type θ-role of *sase* is assigned to the I^{max} immediately dominating "NP *ni*". Notice that this node turns into V^{max} at LF, as illustrated in (21) above. Whichever account we may adopt, it seems to be the case that the derivation in question does not have to be considered to violate the Projection Principle.

2.3.4. Mechanisms of Affix Raising

Let us now describe in greater detail how Move-alpha and other conventions map one representation onto another in the Affix Raising Approach. Take, for example, the mapping from (23a) (=(5a)) to (23b) and (23c) below:

(23) a. *S-str/Pre-LF₁*: b. *Pre-LF₂*:

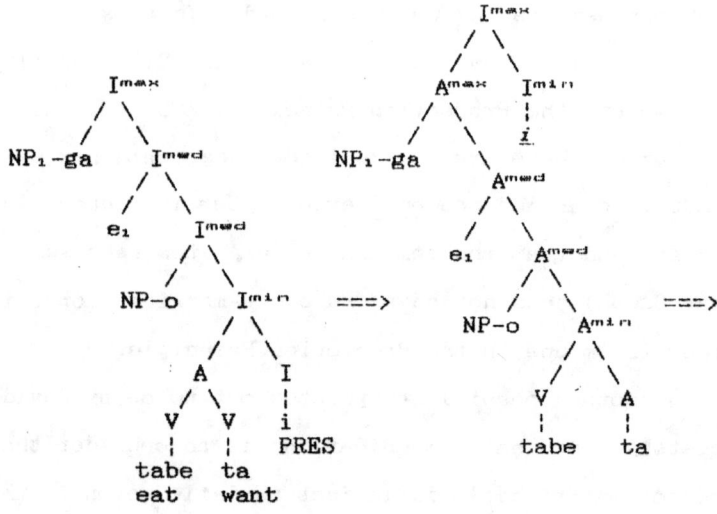

c. *LF*:

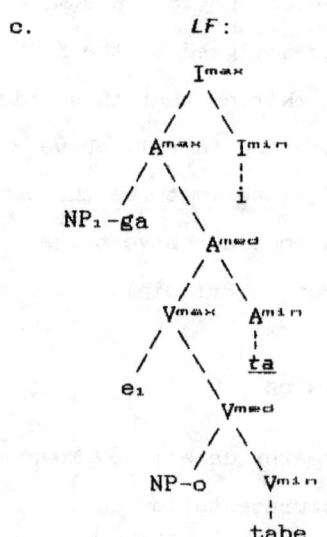

First, when the adjectival tense morpheme *i* (PRES) moves out of the I^{max} in (23a), an intermediate structure as in

(24) below derives by way of the head feature percolation (Williams (1981), Lieber (1981)):

(24)
```
         A^max
        / \A_med
      /  / \
    NP  /  A_med
     NP /   \
      /    A^min
     NP     |
            A^min
           /  \
          V    A
          |    |
         tabe  ta
```

We are assuming, in other words, that the head-feature percolation applies at each syntactic representation.

Also, we are assuming here, following Pesetsky (1982), rather than Pesetsky (1985), that movement leaves a trace behind only when its presence is required by principles of grammar. In our analyses, in other words, affix movement does not leave a trace because no principles of grammar seem to require its presence.

The representation in (24), then, will be mapped to (23b) with two more structural operations. One is the adjunction of the adjectival tense morpheme *i* (PRES) to the derived A^{max} node in (24). Note that this landing site for *i* automatically follows once we stipulate the c-selectional property of this morpheme ([A^{max} ___]).[42]

Note that we are assuming one crucial difference between morphology and syntax: only in morphology does the application of Move-alpha as an adjunction process give rise to percolation of the head features from the moved item, as illustrated in (25) below:

(25)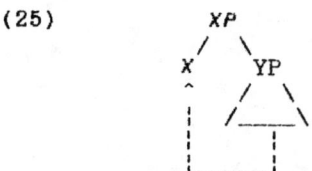

The other mechanism involved is a convention as in (26) below, which has an effect of eliminating one of the A^{min} nodes in (24): (cf. Lasnik-Kupin (1977))

(26)   x   x
       | |
       y   ===>   y
       |
       y

The mapping of (23b) onto (23c) proceeds quite similarly via an intermediate structure as in (27) below:

(27)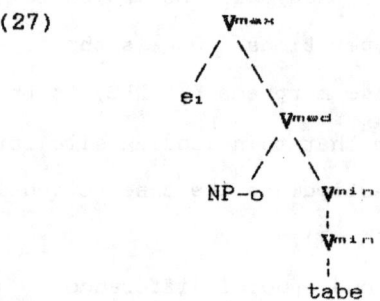

2.3.5. Complementation in the Affix Raising Approach

In this subsection, we will describe how the following arguments for the syntactic complementation in the causative construction fit into the Affix Raising Approach.

(28) (i) The subject-oriented reflexive pronoun *zibun* (self) may refer to either a causer (= matrix subject) or a causee (= complement subject). (Kuroda (1965a))

(ii) The pro-VP *soo-s* (do so) may refer to either a "matrix" VP headed by *sase* or a "complement" VP. (Shibatani (1973))

(iii) Some adverbs may ambiguously modify either a "matrix" verb *sase* or a "complement" verb. (Shibatani (Ibid.))

2.3.5.1. zibun

Let us start with the argument based upon the binding of the reflexive pronoun *zibun* (self) (Kuroda (1965)). Unlike the reflexive anaphors in English, *zibun* may be bound across clause boundaries but must in general take a subject as its antecedent.[43] If a causative sentence truly involves complementaion, the argument goes, we expect it to be possible for an embedded *zibun* to be bound ambiguously either by the matrix subject or the complement subject --- or more crucially, a surface non-subject can be an antecedent of *zibun* in some cases. This prediction is borne out, as the contrast between the simplex sentence (29a) and the causative sentence (29b) below illustrates:

(29) a. Taroo$_1$ ga Hanako$_2$ o zibun$_{1/*2}$ no heya ni
              NOM   ACC self   GEN room to

    ire-ta
    let=in-PAST

    'Taro let Hanako into his room.'

b. Taroo$_1$ ga Hanako$_2$ o zibun$_{1/2}$ no heya ni
              NOM   ACC self   GEN room to

    hair-*ase*-ta
    enter-CAUSE-PAST

    'Taro made/let Hanako enter his/her room.'

Thus, binding of *zibun* provides an argument for the complex status of a causative sentence or at least for analyzing an NP denoting the causee as a subject at some level of representation.

In the Affix Raising Approach, we will account for this fact with the LF complementation of V^{max} as in (30) below:

(30)   LF:

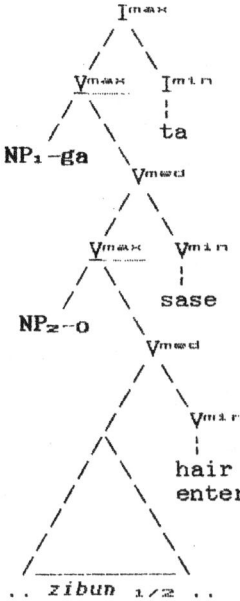

This account crucially differs from the account offered in the Verb Raising Approach in at least two different aspects.

First, complementation exists at LF rather than at D-structure. In 2.3.5.3. and 2.4.2. below, we will see independent motivation for this analysis.

Second, the complement is a projection of V rather than INFL or COMP (i.e., the complement is not S or S'). Accordingly, what functions as the antecedent of *zibun*, i.e., subject, is identified as the outermost argument of

the verbs *sase* (NP₁ ga) and *hair* (NP₂ o), along the lines
of Stowell (1981, 1983).

One clear advantage of an analysis like this has been
pointed out by Hasegawa (1980). In the Verb Raising
Approach, the lack of tense in the complement of complex
predicates is accounted for by the postulation of Aux
Deletion (cf. (5) in 2.1.). This rule, however, must be
conditioned to obligatorily apply to the sentential
complements in the complex predicate construction, but
never to other instances of sentential complements. If we
assume, on the other hand, that the complements in the
complex predicate construction are non-sentential in the
first place, this problem will automatically disappear.[44]

2.3.5.2. soo s

The V^{max} complementation analysis can also be
directly applied to (28ii) -- Shibatani's argument
involving *soo s* (do so).

What exactly the pro-form *soo s* (do so) refers to has
been a matter of controversy. Nakau (1973) claims that *soo
s* is a pro-VP. Hinds (1973), Inoue (1976) (among others),
on the other hand, question the validity of this claim.
Hasegawa (1980), in turn, supports Nakau's claim,
questioning the validity of Hinds' and Inoue's
counterarguments. In this thesis, we will not commit

ourselves to this issue. The sole purpose of this section is to point out that if soo s turns out to be a pro-VP, we still have a means to capture the facts observed by Shibatani ((28ii)) in our Affix Raising Approach.

Observe the following examples (cf. Nakau (1973)):

(31) a. Taroo ga [vp sara o   arat] ta   no   wa
         NOM   dish ACC wash   PAST NOMNL TOP

   matigai-nai ga, Ziroo ga soo si-ta   keiseki wa
   sure   NOM   NOM so do-PAST trace   TOP

   nai
   does=not=exist

   'Taro has for sure done the dishes, but there is
   no trace that Jiro has done so.'

b. ?*Taroo ga [vp sara o   arat] ta   no   wa
             NOM   dish ACC wash   PAST NOMNL TOP

   matigai-nai ga, Ziroo ga koppu o   soo si-ta
   sure   NOM   NOM glass ACC so do-PAST

   keiseki wa nai
   trace   TOP does=not=exist

   'Taro has for sure done the dishes, but there is
   no trace that Jiro has done so to glasses.'

(32) a. Taroo ga [vp sensei ni   soodan-si] ta   no
         NOM   teacher DAT consult=with PAST NOMNL

   wa tasika da roo   ga, Ziroo ga soo si-ta
   TOP sure   is perhaps NOM   NOM so do-PAST

   to   wa omo-e-na-i
   COMP TOP think-cannot

   'It is perhaps true that Taro has consulted with
   the teacher, but I cannot imagine that Jiro has
   done so.'

b. ?*Taroo ga [ᵥₚ sensei ni soodan-si] ta no
         NOM   teacher DAT consult=with PAST NOMNL

wa tasika da roo   ga, Ziroo ga
TOP sure   is perhaps NOM   NOM

oya   ni soo si-ta   to   wa omo-e-na-i
parent DAT so do-PAST COMP TOP think-cannot

'It is perhaps true that Taro has consulted with
the teacher, but I cannot imagine that Jiro has
done so with his parents.'

(33) a. Taroo ga [ᵥₚ koibito to nige] ta   koto wa
          NOM   lover   with flee PAST fact TOP

suguni sirewatat-ta ga, Ziroo ga soo si-ta
soon   spread   but NOM   so do-PAST

koto wa dare-ni-mo-sirare-nakatta
fact TOP no=one=came=to=know

'Everyone has learned soon that Taro ran away
with his lover. No one noticed, however, that
Jiro did so.'

b. ?*Taroo ga [ᵥₚ koibito to nige] ta   koto wa
         NOM   lover   with flee PAST fact TOP

suguni sirewatat-ta ga, Ziroo ga hitori de
soon   spread   but NOM   alone with

soo si-ta   koto wa dare-ni-mo-sirare-nakatta
so do-PAST fact TOP no=one=came=to=know

'Everyone has learned soon that Taro ran away
with his lover. No one noticed, however, that
Jiro did so alone.'

The awkwardness of the *b*-examples here is predicted if a pro-verb form *soo s* (do so) takes what is normally labeled as VP as its antecedent. This proposal derives the anomaly of the resulting readings **koppu o sara o araw* (glass ACC dish ACC clean) in (31b), **oya ni sensei ni soodan-s*

(parent DAT teacher DAT consult=with) in (29b), and
*hitoride koibito to nige (alone lover with flee) in (33b).

Shibatani's (1973,1976) argument here is similar to the argument from zibun: if causatives involve complementation, not only the matrix but also the embedded VP should be a potential antecedent of soo s. This prediction is borne out:

(34) Sin-tyan ga [$_{VP1}$ otooto   ni [$_{VP2}$ obentoo o   ake]
                 NOM   y.brother DAT   lunch   ACC open

      sase] ru   to   mukai-no seki ni suwatteita ko
      CAUSE PRES when opposite seat in sitting   child

      mo   soo si$_{1/2}$-ta
      also so   do-PAST

      'When Shin-chan made/let his younger brother open the
      lunch box, the boy sitting in the opposite seat did
      so, too.'

Again, the LF complementation of V^{max} provides us with a similar account of the interpretation of soo s. We have two instances of V^{max} at LF as in (35) below, which corresponds to the two VPs in (34):

(35)   LF:

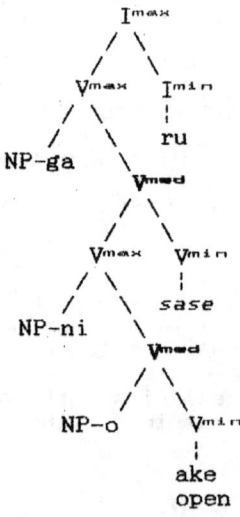

Since the *soo s* test works in a parallel fashion in both the complex predicate construction and the simplex sentence construction, our analysis above implies that, at LF, the traditional notion VP is replaced by V^{med} even in simplex sentences as illustrated in (36) below --- a position further argued for in Chapters Three and Four:

(36)
```
            Vmax
           /    \
       NP-ga    Vmed
               /    \
            NP-o    Vmin
                     |
                    ake
```

2.3.4.3. Adverbial Scope

Let us now deal with the argument in (28iii), which concerns the scope of adverbial modifiers. Shibatani (1973, 1976) observes that, in the causative sentence in (37a) below, the adverb *damatte* (silently) may modify either the derivational affix *sase* (cause) or the verbal stem *hair* (enter), while such ambiguity does not arise in a simplex sentence like (37b), which involves a lexical (non-affixal) causative *ire* (let=in):

(37) a. Taroo ga Hanako o   heya ni   *damatte* hair-
              NOM   ACC room into silectly   enter-

   ase-ta
   CAUSE-PAST

   'Taro made Hanako enter the room silently'

   b. Taroo ga Hanako o   heya ni   *damatte* *ire*-ta
             NOM   ACC room into silently let=in-PAST

   'Taro let Hanako into the room silently.'

The ambiguity of adverbial scope in (37a), according to Shibatani, can be attributed to the presence of complementation in this sentence.

In fact, complementation in causative constructions is even more clearly attested by the lack of anomaly created by two contradictory adverbials, *doyasitukete* (by=bawling=out) and *damatte* (silently) in (38a) below. Compare (38a) with a simplex (38b):

(38) a. *doyasitukete* Taroo ga [kodomotati o heya ni
       by=bawling=out   NOM children ACC room into

   damatte hair]-*ase*-ta
   silently enter]-CAUSE-PAST

   'By bawling them out, Taro made the children enter
   the room silently.'

b. **doyasitukete* Taroo ga kodomotati o heya ni
      by=bawling=out   NOM children ACC room into

   damatte ire-ta
   silently let=in-PAST

   '*By bawling them out, Taro let the children into
   the room silently.'

In (38a), if an embedded domain for adverbial interpretation (as indicated by the bracketing) were not present where the scope of adverbials is determined, the sentence would be ruled out just as (38b) is. Thus, we must assume the presence of complementation at some level of representation --- at D-structure in the framework of the Standard Theory, and at LF in our model of grammar, which incorporates this level as the immediate linguistic input to semantic interpretation.

The following examples, involving the passive suffix *rare* and the desiderative suffix *ta*, exhibit basically the same facts:

(39) *Indirect Passive*: (cf. Makino (1972))

a. Hanako wa Taroo ni wazato asi o
       TOP   by intentianally foot ACC

   hum-are-ta
   step=on-PASSIVE-PAST

   'Hanako had her foot stepped on intentionally by Taro.'

b. *siranai-aida-ni* Hanako wa Taroo ni wazato
   while-unnoticed   TOP   by intentionally

   asi o hum-are-ta
   foot ACC step=on-PASSIVE-PAST

   'Hanako unwittingly had her foot intentionally stepped on by Taro.'

(40) *Direct Passive*:

a. Hanako wa Taroo ni wazato butukar-are-ta
       TOP   by intentionally bump-PASSIVE-PAST

   'Hanako was intenionally bumped into by Taro.'

b. *siranai-aida-ni* Hanako wa Taroo ni wazato
   while=unnoticed   TOP   by intentionally

   butukar-are-ta
   bumped-PASSIVE-PAST

   'Hanako was intentionally bumped into by Taroo unwittingly.'

(41) *Desiderative*:

a. watasi wa *kokoro-no-soko-kara ayamar-ita*-i
   I   TOP heartily   apologize-want-PRES

   'I want to apologize from the bottom of my heart.'

b. *kokoro-no-soko-kara* watasi wa *itiou uwabe-dake-demo*
   heartily   I   TOP anyway surface=only=even

   ayamar-ita-i
   apologize-want-PRES

   'I truly want to apologize at least on the surface.'

All the a-examples here exhibit a matrix-complement ambiguity involving adverbs comparable to (37a); the b-examples permit the co-occurrence of two contradictory adverbials.[45]

As Miyagawa (1980) points out, however, assuming the mere presence of complementation in causative constructions does not provide a full account of ambiguous adverbial scope. As illustrated by the diagram in (42) below, for example, this analysis shows how the embedded scope of adverbials is possible in (37a) but it does not explain how the matrix scope is also possible there.

(42)

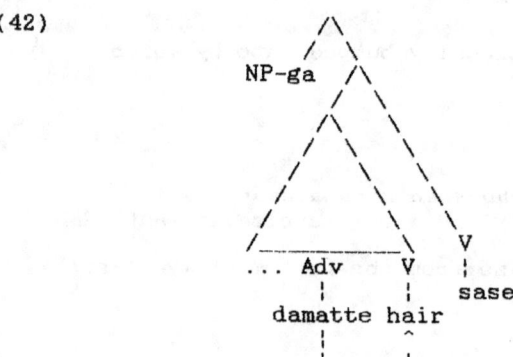

As a result, the Verb Raising Approach would require that not only the D-structure as in (42) but also the S-structure as in (43) below be the input to semantic interpretation.

(43)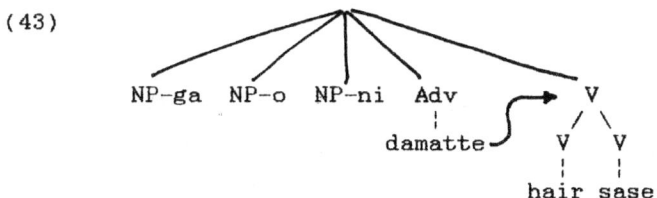

Thus, it seems to be the case that the Verb Raising Approach cannot be maintained at least in its original version to account for the facts in (37).

On the contrary, Miyagawa claims, if one assumes a simplex structure as in (43) throughout the derivation, one can account for the ambiguity of adverbial scope in (37a) without having to modify the model of grammar.

Reporting a lack of embedded adverbial scope in causative sentences like (44a-b) below, Miyagawa further questions the validity of Shibatani's claim that causatives involve complementation: (Compare (44a-b) with (37a) above, paying attention to the different positions of adverbials.)

(44) a. Taroo ga *damatte* Hanako o heya ni hair-ase-ta
     b. *damatte* Taroo ga Hanako o heya ni hair-ase-ta

We certainly agree with Miyagawa that the full account of adverbial scope in causative constructions requires further investigation. We do not accept his conclusion, however, that the simplex structure analysis of causatives provides a better account for the problem in question, for the following reasons.

First, contrary to what Miyagawa claims, the simplex structure analysis does not provide any satisfactory account of the ambiguity of adverbial scope in a sentence like (37a) above. This is so because the verbal stem *hair* (enter) and the causative affix *sase* in the simplex syntactic structure (43) makes up a complex predicate headed by *sase*, and there is no reason to expect that the morphological non-head subconstituent of a complex predicate (*hair* in (43)) provides a domain for adverbial interpretation. In other words, it is highly unlikely, in the light of a theory of morphology, that a VP adverb modifies the morphological non-head subconstituent of a complex verb. The simplex structure analysis, in other words, seems to fail to account for the presence of embedded adverbial scope in (37a).

Even more seriously, the simplex structure analysis also fails to provide an account for the contrast in (38) above with respect to the contradictory adverbial interpretation, since both (38a) and (38b) are analyzed to be simplex.

One might try to save the simplex structure analysis of (37a) and (38a) by supplementing it with a convention to allow the non-head subconstituent of a complex verb to provide a domain for adverbial interpretation. Although such revision may solve the problems mentioned above, it would also predict, incorrectly, that adverbial interpretation can be ambiguous even in a sentence like (44b) above. In short, the simplex structure analysis does not provide a satisfactory account of adverbial interpretation in causative constructions.

Before we turn to our own analysis, let us first clarify the facts to be considered. We agree with Miyagawa that the adverbial *damatte* (silently) in (44b) above is unambiguously interpreted to take matrix scope. Contrary to the judgment reported by Miyagawa, on the other hand, I find (44a) and similar examples in (45) below perfectly ambiguous with respect to adverbial interpretation, although the matrix scope tends to be a preferred reading in some of them.

(45) a. watasi wa *tue o tukatte* Hanako ni
        I   TOP cane ACC using   DAT

    tat-ase-ta
    stand=up-CAUSE-PAST

    'I made Hanako stand up with a cane.'

b. sensei   wa   *oogoe o hariagete*   minna   ni
    teacher TOP big=voice ACC raising everyone DAT

    utaw-ase-ta
    sing-CAUSE-PAST

    'The teacher made everyone sing with a big
     voice.'

The availability of an embedded adverbial scope in the
sentences with this particular position of adverbials can
be demonstrated, first, by the acceptability of the
examples in (46) below:

(46) a. kanseikan   wa *dootai o tukatte*
         air=traffic=controller   TOP body ACC using

         pairotto ni tyakurikus-ase-ta
         pilot   DAT land-CAUSE-PAST

         'The air traffic controller made the pilot
          crashland.'

     b. omoi-mo-kake-na-i atatakai motenasi   ga
         unexpected   warm   hospitality NOM

         kokoro-no-soko-kara karera o   yorokob-ase-ta
         heartily   they   ACC pleased-CAUSE-PAST

         'An unexpected warm hospitality made them pleased
          from the bottom of their hearts.'

Note that (46a-b) are both well-formed despite the fact
that the adverbials there are compatible only with the stem
of the complex verb rather than the causative affix (i.e.,
**dootai o tukatte sase* 'cause with a body', **kokoro no soko
kara sase* 'cause from the bottom of the heart'). The same
point can be made by the lack of anomaly in (47a):

(47) a. *doyasitukete* Taroo ga *damatte* kodomotati o
by=bawling=out   NOM silently children ACC

heya ni   hair-*ase*-ta
room into enter-CAUSE-PAST

'By bawling out, Taro made the children enter the room silently.'

b. **doyasitukete* Taroo ga *damatte* kodomotati o
by=bawling=out   NOM silently children ACC

heya ni   *ire*-ta
room into let=in-PAST

'By bawling out, Taro let the children into the room silently.'

If an embedded adverbial scope were not possible, the two contradictory adverbials in (47a) should give rise to an anomaly just as they do in (47b).

We can now summarize the facts to be explained concerning the adverbial interpretation in causative constructions as in (48) below, with the relevant examples repeated in (49):[46]

(48)   ambiguity

   (49a):   +
   (49b):   +
   (49c):   −

(49) a. Taroo ga Hanako o   heya ni   *damatte*
              NOM   ACC room into silectly

   hair-*ase*-ta
   enter-CAUSE-PAST

   'Taro made Hanako enter the room silently'

   b. Taroo ga *damatte* Hanako o heya ni hair-ase-ta

   c. *damatte* Taroo ga Hanako o heya ni hair-ase-ta

Incidentally, quite comparable paradigms can be obtained in the passive and desiderative constructions, as illustrated in (50)-(52) below:

(50) *Indirect Passive*:

a. Hanako wa Taroo ni asi o   *wazato*
         TOP   by foot ACC intentionally

   hum-are-ta
   step=on-PASSIVE-PAST

   'Hanako had her foot stepped on intentionally by Taro.'

b. Hanako wa Taroo ni *wazato*   asi o
         TOP   by intentionally foot ACC

   hum-are-ta
   step=on-PASSIVE-PAST

   'Hanako had her foot stepped on intentionally by Taro.'

c. Hanako wa *wazato*   Taroo ni asi o
         TOP intentionally   by foot ACC

   hum-are-ta
   step=on-PASSIVE-PAST

   'Hanako had her foot stepped on intentionally by Taro.'

d. wazato　　　　　Hanako wa　Taroo ni　asi o
   intentionally　　　　TOP　　　by foot ACC

   hum-are-ta
   step=on-PASSIVE-PAST

   'Intentionally, Hanako had her foot stepped on by Taro.'

(51) *Direct Passive*:

a. Hanako wa　Taroo ni　wazato　　　　　butukar-are-ta
   　　TOP　　by　intentionally bump-PASSIVE-PAST

   'Hanako was intentionally bumped into by Taro.'

b. Hanako wa　wazato　　　　Taroo ni　butukar-are-ta
   　　TOP　intentionally　　by bump-PASSIVE-PAST

   'Hanako was intentionally bumped into by Taro.'

c. wazato　　　　　Hanako wa　Taroo ni　butukar-are-ta
   intentionally　　　　TOP　　by bump-PASSIVE-PAST

   'Intentionally, Hanako was bumped into by Taro.'

(52) *Desiderative*:

a. watasi wa　imooto ni　　kokoro-kara　ayamar-ita-i
   I　　　TOP　y. sister DAT　heartily　　apologize-want-PRES

   'I want to apologize to my sister from the bottom of my heart.'

b. watasi wa　kokoro-kara　imooto　　ni　ayamar-ita-i
   I　　　TOP　heartily　　y. sister DAT apologize-want-PRES

   'I want to apologize to my sister from the bottom of my heart.'

c. kokoro-kara　watasi wa　imooto　　ni　ayamar-ita-i
   heartily　　　I　　　TOP y. sister DAT apologize-want-PRES

   'From the bottom of my heart, I want to apologize to my sister.'

All but the last examples in (50)-(52) exhibit matrix-complement ambiguity in the adverbial, while the last examples have only the matrix interpretation. In other words, an adverbial may be ambiguously interpreted in the complex predicate construction in general, except when it appears to the left of all the arguments in the sentence.

Consider now the derivation of the sentence (49a) above in the Affix Raising Approach:

(53) a. *S-str/Pre-LF₁*:   b. *Pre-LF₂*:

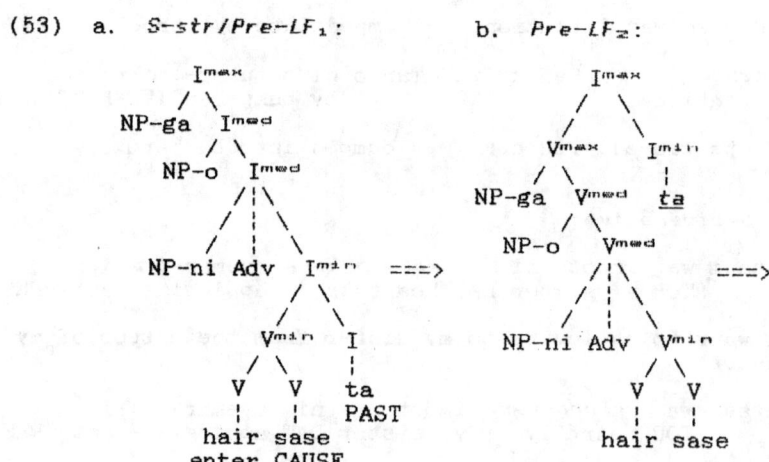

c.   LF:

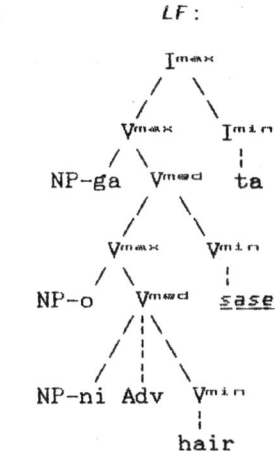

Suppose, as has usually been assumed, that Move-alpha applies only to one item at a time. Given the c-selectional property of *ta* (PAST) and the θ-marking property of *sase* (CAUSE) as in (54) below, there arise at least two representations at LF that are distinct from the S-structure representation, as exemplified in (53b-c):

(54) a. ta (want):   +[V^{max} __]   (= (17a))
     b. sase (CAUSE): [AG [ET __]]   (= (19a))

Let us assume here: (i) that there exists a licensing condition at LF, as in (55) below, for modifiers in general, and (ii) that this licensing is formally represented as co-indexation of the modifier and the modifiee as in (56) and (57):

(55) *Modifier Licensing Condition*:

Each modifier (= non-argument and non-head) must be licensed at LF by being head-governed by a modifiee.

(56) a.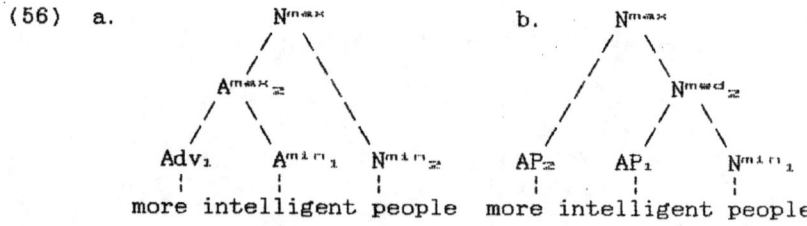

(57)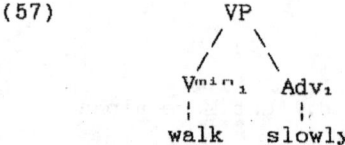

Note that in (56b), for example, the modifier phrases *intelligent* and *more* are licensed by the modifiees *people* (N^{min}) and *intelligent people* (N^{med}), respectively. This is one of the cases in which head-government defined in terms of the notion "non-maximal projection" ([-max]) is relevant.

The licensing condition (55) probably is only one specific instantiation of the Principle of Full Interpretation (FI).[47] Let us further assume that this licensing may take place anywhere in the mapping to LF -- in particular, before or after Move-alpha raises *sase* in (53). All the facts summarized in (48) can now be accounted for quite straightforwardly.

Let us begin with the ambiguity in (49a) (repeated below):

(49) a. Taroo ga Hanako o   heya ni   damatte
             NOM   ACC room into silectly

   hair-*ase*-ta
   enter-CAUSE-PAST

   'Taro made Hanako enter the room silently'

   b.   Taroo ga *damatte* Hanako o heya ni hair-ase-ta

   c.   *damatte* Taroo ga Hanako o heya ni hair-ase-ta

The Affix Raising Analysis provides two distinct LF representations in either of which the adverbial may be licensed by a modifiee, as illustrated by the coindexation in (58) and (59) below:

(58)
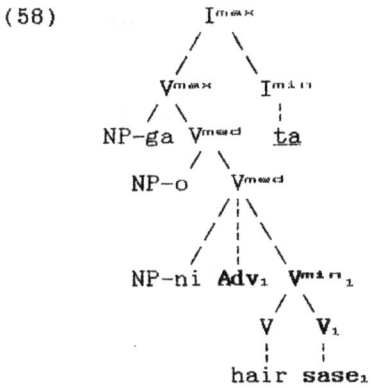

(59)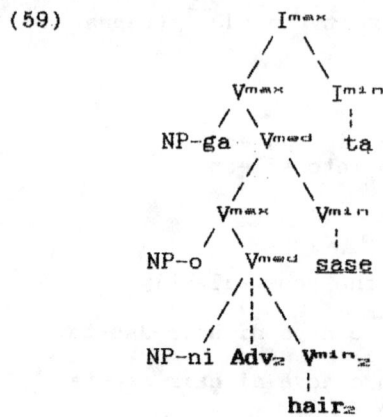

In (58), the adverb is licensed by the causative suffix *sase*.[48] In (59), on the other hand, the adverb is licensed by the verbal stem *hair* (enter). (We may call the maximal projection of the licenser in each representation (i.e., V^{max}) the "scope" of the licensed adverbial.) Thus, the ambiguity of adverbial scope in (49a) can be ascribed to the availability of two possible derivations as in (60) and (61) below:

(60) *Matrix Scope:*

a. *S-str/Pre-LF$_1$:* 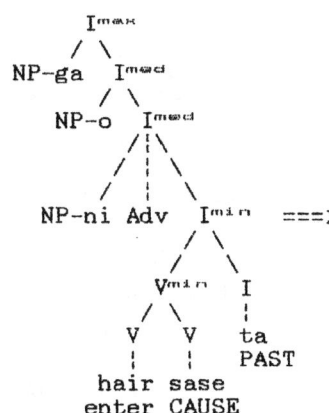 ===>

b. *Pre-LF$_2$:* 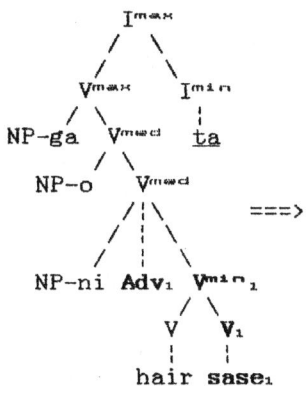 ===>

c. *LF:*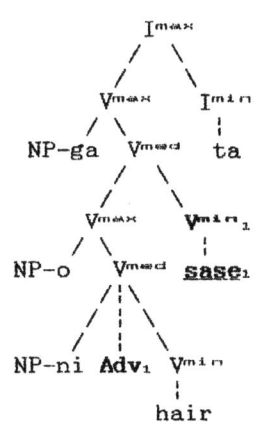

(61) *Lower Scope:*

a. *S-str/Pre-LF₁:* 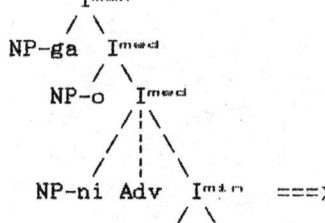   b. *Pre-LF₂:*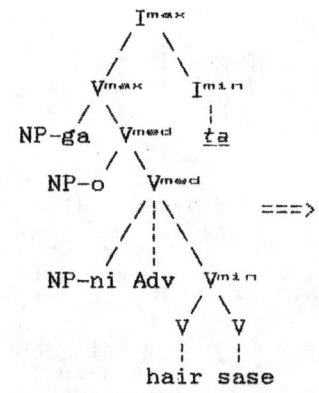

c. *LF:*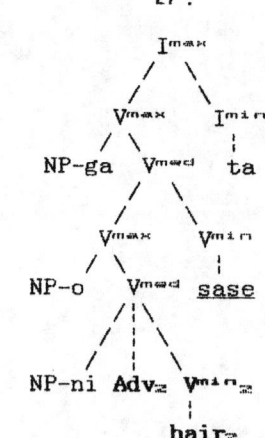

Note that the licensing of the modifier by the verbal root *hair* does not take place in (60c) because the adverbial has already been coindexed with a different legitimate licensor (*sase*) in the earlier stage of the derivation.

The ambiguity in (49b) above arises in quite a similar way, as the derivations in (62) and (63) below illustrate. The adverb can be licensed either by *sase* as in (62b) or by *hair* as in (63c):[49]

(62) *Matrix Scope*:

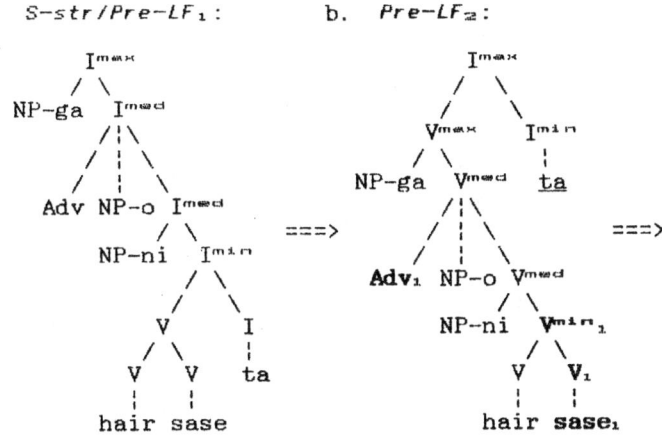

c.   *LF*:

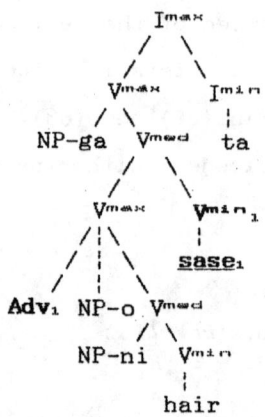

(63) *Lower Scope*:

a. *S-str/Pre-LF₁*:   b. *Pre-LF₂*:

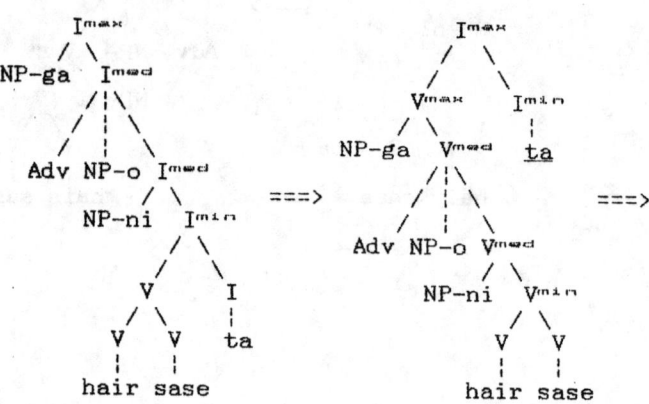

c.   LF:

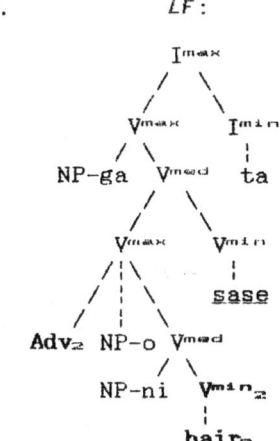

Thus, the ambiguity of adverbial interpretation in (49a) and (49b) can be straightforwardly accounted for in the Affix Raising Approach when we incorporate the Modifier Licensing Condition (55) holding at LF.

How can the lack of ambiguity in (49c) explained, then? The affix raising in (49c) also provides two distinct LF representations, as illustrated in (64) below:

(64) a.   *S-str/Pre-LF₁*:   b.   *Pre-LF₂*:

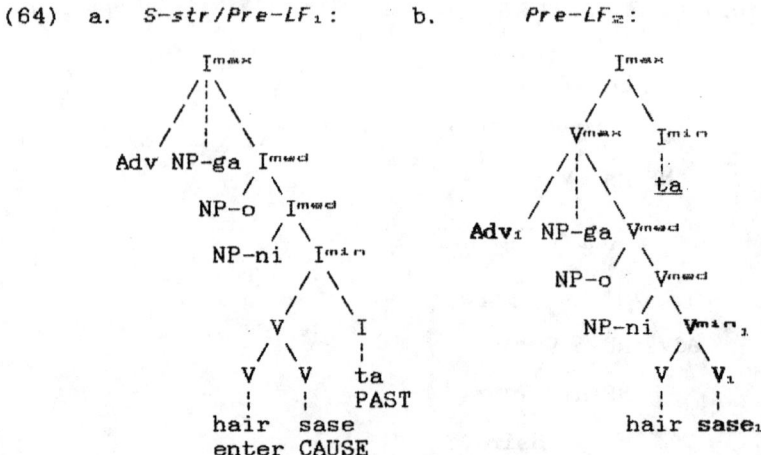

c.   *LF*:

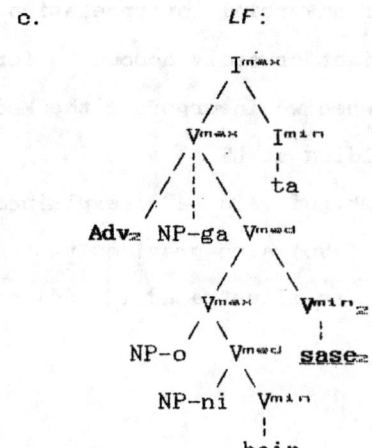

Unlike in the other two cases, however, the adverbial crucially does **not** have a chance to be licensed by the verbal root *hair* (enter) in this sentence. This is precisely because it appears to the left of the matrix subject (NP-ga) in a right-branching construction, i.e., at the same or higher (bar) level as/than NP-ga appears. Recall that sase (cause) must govern NP-ga to assign its external thematic role AG ((54b)). From this, it follows that the adverb is located outside the V^{max} complement of sase even after sase moves out of the complex predicate, as in (64c). Thus, the lack of embedded adverbial scope in (48c) also follows naturally from the Affix Raising Analysis supplemented by the Modifier Licensing Condition in (55) above.

Notice that this analysis crucially requires the presence of both a simplex and a complex syntactic representation **at different stages of the mapping to LF**. The facts concerning adverbial interpretation are, in other words, exactly as we predict on the follwoing assumptions: (i) the lexical unity of complex predicates must be retained at least in one representation at LF due to the morphological c-selectional properties of various suffixes ((15)), (ii) affix raising creates complementation at LF when principles of grammar require it.

Our observation in (48) above concerning adverbial interpretation in the causative construction will provide us with another basis to reject some other alternative analyses of the complex predicate construction in Japanese.

First, we now have another reason to reject not only the original version of the Verb Raising Approach but also some of its variants. If one assumes, for example, that verb raising applies at PF and that the syntactic representation of the complex predicate remains to involve complementation throughout the rest of derivation, the ambiguity in (49a) will be left unexplained, since it will provide no explanation of how the matrix scope of adverbs is made possible there. For exactly the same reason, the verb raising in syntax without clause union and the PAS Complementation Approach (cf. 2.2.) are also rejected.

We now also have a reason to reject a non-configurational analysis of Japanese phrase structure as in (66) below, and also to reject any version of the "extra NP" analysis of causatives as in (67): (We are disregarding tense here for simplicity.)

(66)
a. *damatte* Taroo ga Hanako o heya ni hair-ase-ta
   silently   NOM   ACC room into enter-CAUSE-PAST

   'Silently, Taro made/let Hanako into the room.'

b.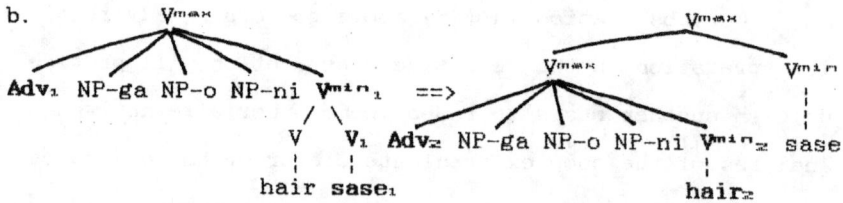

(67)
a. Taroo ga *damatte* Hanako₁ ni/o e₁ heya ni
      NOM silectly   DAT/ACC   room into
   hair-ase-ta
   enter-CAUSE-PAST

   'Taro made Hanako enter the room silently'

b.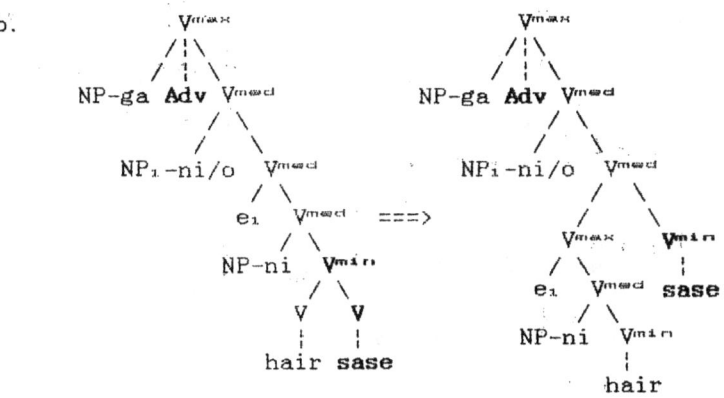

In the non-configurational analysis in (66b), it would be incorrectly predicted that even a sentence like (66a) (= (49c)) exhibits ambiguous interpretation of the adverb, since the adverb has a chance to be licensed either by *sase* (CAUSE) or *hair* (enter) in the derivation. In the extra NP analysis in (67b), on the other hand, it would be incorrectly predicted that a sentence like (67a) (= (49b) with an additional Case particle *o* (ACC)) exhibits only the matrix scope of the adverb, since the presence of the extra matrix NP (NP-*ni/o*) in the matrix precludes the adverb from being head-governed by the verbal head *hair* at any stage of the derivation.

2.3.6. Order of Affix Raising

In all the derivations involving affix raising above, we have crucially assumed that Move-alpha raises an affix out of the complex predicate one by one **starting with the outermost affix**. The importance of this assumption can be verified when we consider a hypothetical derivation as in (69) below for a sentence (68) (= (49c)), which exhibits only matrix scope of the adverbial:

(68)
damatte Taroo ga Hanako o   heya ni   hair-ase-ta
silently   NOM   ACC room into enter-CAUSE-PAST

'Silently, Taro made/let Hanako enter the room.'

(69) a. $S\text{-}str/Pre\text{-}LF_1$:   b. $Pre\text{-}LF_2$:

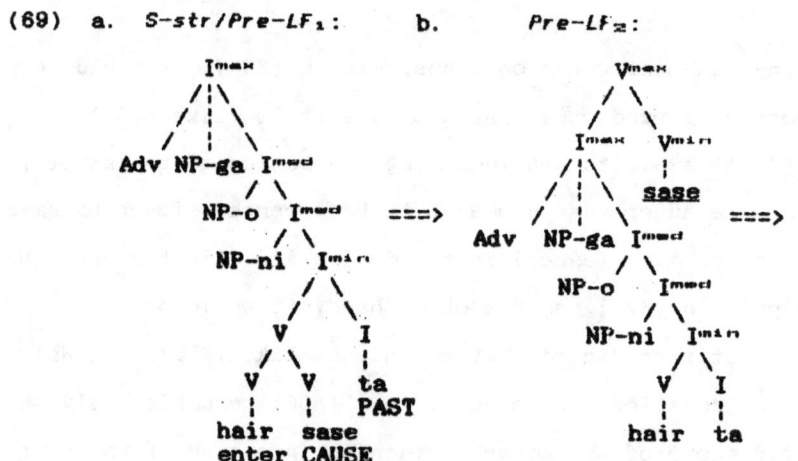

c.   LF:

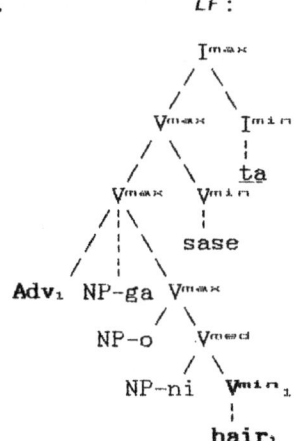

In (69), Move-alpha raises the inner suffix *sase* (CAUSE) before it raises the outermost suffix *ta* (PAST). As a result, it yields an LF representation (69c), in which the adverbial is incorrectly licensed by the verbal root *hair* (enter). The correct ordering of affix raising, therefore, must be guaranteed somehow. An important question to be asked, then, is whether such an order must be extrinsically specified or follows from more general properties of the grammar.

In the case of (68), we can make an appeal to the θ-Criterion to rule out the LF representation (69c), since NP-*ga* as an argument remains θ-less, and the agent θ-role of *sase* (cf. (73a) below) is not assigned to any argument in this representation.

There is one case, however, in which even the
θ-Criterion cannot rule out the incorrect order of affix
raising. Consider, for example, a sentence like (70)
below:

(70) Taroo ga tomodati ni uisukii o   nom-*ase-rare*-ta
     NOM   friend   by whiskey ACC drink-CAUS-PASS-PAST
    'Taro was made to drink whiskey by his friend.'

If Move-alpha "peels" the affixes off the complex predicate
one by one from the outside in, we will obtain an LF
representation as in (71c), which corresponds to the
correct interpretation of (70): (Let us again disregard
tense for simplicity.)

(71) a.   *S-str/Pre-LF$_1$*:   b.   *Pre-LF$_2$*:

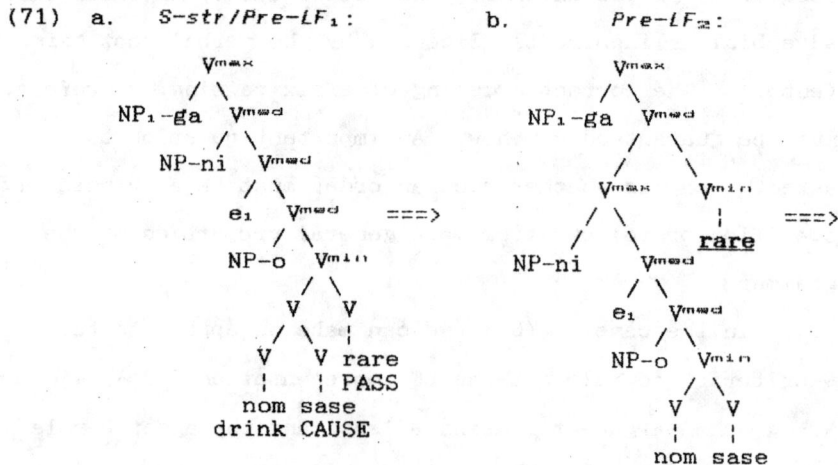

c.   *LF*:

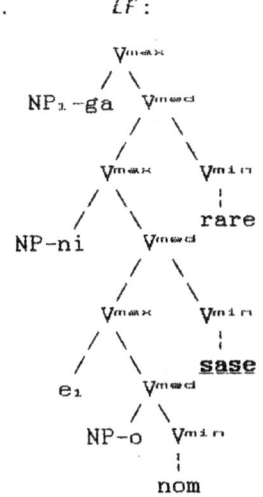

If, on the other hand, Move-alpha raises *sase* (CAUSE) and *rare* (PASSIVE) out of the complex predicate in this order, we will obtain the LF representation (72c) below:

(72)   a.   *S-str/Pre-LF$_1$*:   b.   *Pre-LF$_2$*:

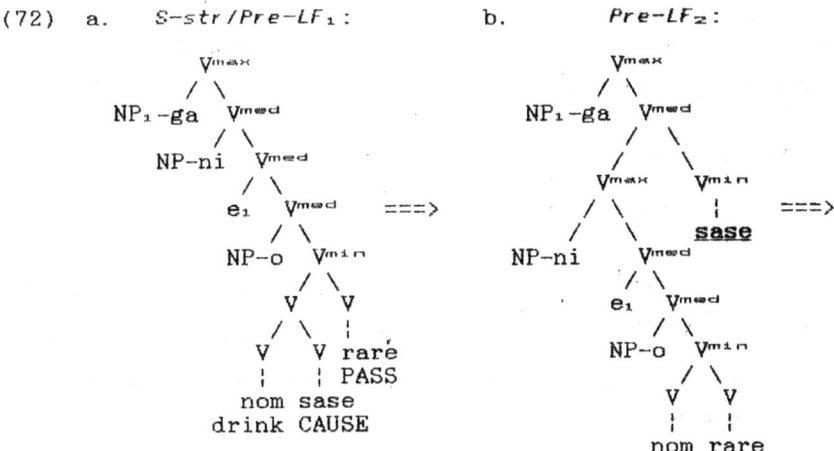

c.   LF:

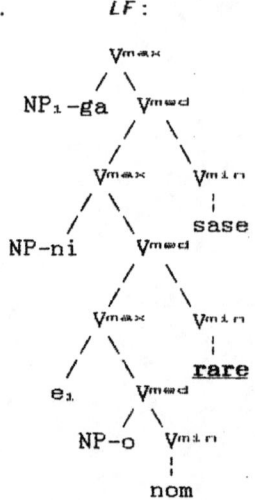

This representation corresponds to the incorrect
interpretation "Taro₁ made a friend suffer from his₁
drinking whiskey". This LF-representation, however,
satisfies the θ-Criterion with respect to the arguments
involved there and the θ-marking properties of *sase* and
rare as in (73) below:

(73) a. sase: [AG [ET __]
      b. rare: [EX [ET __]

It therefore seems to be the case that the order of
LF complementation in the complex predicate construction
must reflect the order of the morphemes involved in the
formation of the complex predicate involved, as can be seen
from the comparison of (71) and (72) above.

This generalization is reminiscent in its effects of what
Baker (1985) labels the "Mirror Principle", stated in (74)
below: (See also Muysken (1979).)

(74) *The Mirror Principle*:
      Morphological derivations must directly reflect
      syntactic derivations (and vice versa).

Actually, if we compare the order of affixation (= morphological process) and the order of affix raising (= syntactic process), the relation between morphological and syntactic derivations stated in (74) is an inversed one. In the complex predicate structure in Japanese, the order of morphological derivations (e.g., *nom* ==> *nom* + *sase* ==> *nomase* + *rare*) is **inversely** reflected in the application of Move-alpha at LF (e.g., ... *nom-sase-rare* ==> ... *nom-sase*] *rare* ==> ... *nom*] *sase*] *rare*]). We, thus, obtain (75) below as a descriptive generalization:

(75) *The Mirror Image Derivations*:
      Syntactic derivations **inversely** reflect morphological
      derivations (and vice versa).

Let us emphasize here that (75) is a restatement of the generalization captured by (74) from the new point of view provided by the Affix Raising Hypothesis.

 Again, the relevant question to be asked is whether (75) must be stipulated as a principle of grammar or whether (75) follows from other aspects of the grammar. Our proposal is that (75) follows from a quite simple assumption that the only morphological information accessible to syntax is that which is reflected on (or percolated up to) the lexical node, in the unmarked case, from its head morpheme.[50] In the case of the complex predicate *nom-(s)ase-rare* (drink-CAUSE-PASSIVE) in (76) below, for example, the θ-Criterion can see the θ-marking property of *rare* (PASSIVE), but not that of *sase* (CAUSE) or *nom* (drink). This difference arises because, in general, only the head features are percolated up to the lexical node V^{min} (Williams (1981), Lieber (1981)). The predicates *nom* (drink) and *sase* (CAUSE) in (76), however, are non-heads:

(76)
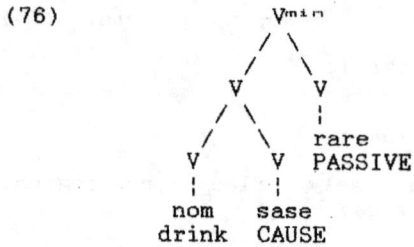

After *rare* (PASSIVE) is raised out of the complex predicate, however, *sase* (CAUSE) becomes the head of the complex predicate, as in (77) below, and syntax can now "see" the θ-marking property of *sase reflected on the lexical node* V^{min}:

(77)
```
        V(main)
        /  \
       /    \
      V      V
      |      |
     nom    sase
```

As a result, affix raising of *sase* is triggered to satisfy the θ-Criterion. This way, the Mirror Image Derivations can be correctly captured --- the last morpheme attached is the first morpheme accesible to syntax, its properties reflected on the lexical node due to the head feature percolation. This perhaps explains why affix raising applies to a head item in a string vacuous fashion in most cases.

In 2.4.2. below, we will see some exceptions to the Mirror Image Principle. As will be pointed out there, however, there exists good reason for the grammar to permit a marked option of non-string-vacuous affix raising in such exceptional cases.

2.3.7. Summary

To summarize this section, we have proposed that affix raising is triggered by the checking of c-selection and the θ-Criterion. Affix Raising causes the lexically-derived complex predicates to involve complementation at LF. In effect, we have come up with a purely syntactic analysis that permits us to reconcile two

contradictory observations concerning complex predicates
--- that they are lexically-derived and that they involve
complementation. We have also claimed that the unity of
complex predicates must be inherited from the lexicon to
LF, since the morphological c-selection of the suffixes is
checked at LF. It has been shown that this assumption,
combined with the Affix Raising Approach and the Modifier
Licensing Condition, will provide us with a strightforward
account of otherwise mysterious facts concerning adverbial
scopes in the complex predicate construction. Finally, it
has been pointed out that the relevant order of affix
raising follows from the assumption that a syntactic
rule has only a limited access to morphological
information, namely, it may only look at those properties
of morphemes percolated up to the lexical node.

2.4. Further Motivations for the Affix Raising Approach

We now turn to motivating the following claims made
by the Affix Raising Approach: (i) complementation in the
complex predicate construction is found in a **syntactic**
rather than a lexical representation, (ii) complementation
in the complex predicate construction is found at the level

of **Logical Form** rather than D-structure, and (iii) complementation in the complex predicate construction is **derived** by the application of affix raising at LF.

Given that the complex predicates are derived in the lexicon, the first two claims will be supported by the observation that complementation in the complex predicate construction can serve as a scope domain for various items with quantificational force. The third claim will be also supported when we observe that negative, honorific and reciprocal affixes are sometimes interpreted in a fashion that can be explained via non-string-vacuous movement of an affix at LF, as schematized in (1) below:

(1)

```
                C^max                              C^max
               /  \                               /   \
          ... C^min      ===>              ...  /     B
              / \                              C^min
             /\  \                             / \
          [ A  B  C ]                       [ A   C ]
```

(C = negative, honorific or reciprocal suffix)

Before we turn to these arguments, however, we will first make clear how and where in the grammar we assume the scope of quantifiers to be determined.

2.4.1. Scope Determination at LF

May (1977) proposes that the S-structure representations of quantified sentences are mapped onto LF-representations by the application of Quantifier Raising (QR), an instance of Move-alpha, as illustrated in (2) below:

(2) a. S-str: [$_S$ he saw everyone]
    b. LF: [$_S$ *everyone*$_1$ [$_S$ he saw t_1]]

QR Chomsky-adjoins a quantified phrase to one of the S-structure constituents dominating that quantifier phrase, leaving a coindexed trace behind. (In May (1977), the adjunction site was limited to S but in Fiengo and Higginbotham (1980) and May (1985), it has been extended to include at least VP and NP as well.) The function of QR, in a sense, may be considered to be deriving a syntactic representation that can be the input to the semantic interpretation of quantified expressions.

Pointing out the structural overlap between an LF-representation like (2b) above and an S-structure *wh*-construction as in (3) below, May (1977, 1985) provides some arguements for this "LF-movement" approach to quantification, as summarized below:

(3) S-str/LF: [$_S$ *who*$_1$ [$_S$ he saw t_1]]

First, this analysis allows us to offer a simple and uniform definition of "scope" for both *wh*-expressions and quantifiers in terms of the syntactic notion of "c-command" --- any LF constituent c-commanded by ß (ß = quantifier or *wh*-phrase) is ß's potential scope. The notion "c-command" is defined as in (4):[51]

(4) *C-Command*: (cf. Reinhart (1976))
   A c-commands B iff the first branching node dominating A dominates B, and A does not dominate B.

Second, if "downgrading" movement, which yields a trace non-c-commanded by its antecedent, is assumed to be proscribed (Fiengo (1977), May (1981)), the ill-formedness of the *wh*-construction in (5) below and the lack of the scope of *someone* lower than *believes* in (6a) can be uniformly accounted for. Compare (5) and (6b):

(5) S-str/LF: *[s t_1 wondered [s· who_1 [s Bill was lying]]]

(6)
a. S-str: [s someone believes [s Bill is lying]]
b. LF: *[s t_1 believes [s $someone_1$ [s Bill is lying]]]

Third, both *wh*- and quantified sentences exhibit the "weak crossover" effect. This uniformity can now be captured if we assume that weak crossover is caused when the variable left by *wh*-movement and QR is construed at LF

as the antecedent of a pronoun that it does not c-command,
as illustrated in (7b) and (8b) below:[32]

(7) a. S-str: *who$_1$ did his$_1$ mother see t_1

b. LF: *[$_S$· who$_1$ [$_S$ did his$_1$ mother [$_{VP}$ see t_1]]]

(8) a. S-str: *his$_1$ mother saw everyone$_1$

b. LF: *[$_S$ everyone$_1$ [$_S$ his$_1$ mother [$_{VP}$ saw t_1]]]

Interestingly, wh- and quantified sentences uniformly exhibit weak crossover also in Japanese, a language that lacks S-structure wh-movement (Saito and Hoji (1983), Hoji (1985)). If all quantified phrases including wh-phrases are subject to LF-movement in this language (cf. Huang (1982)), the phenomena can be completely assimilated to the English case, as illustrated in (9) and (10) below: (pro in the examples represents a "zero" pronoun (Kuroda (1965a)).)

(9) a. S-str: *[$_S$· [$_{NP}$ e$_2$ hitome   pro$_1$ mi-ta hito$_2$] ga
                              one=glance   saw   person NOM

   [$_{VP}$ dare$_1$ o   sukininat-ta] no]
        who   ACC came=to=like   Q

   '*Who$_1$ did the person that took a glance at him$_1$ come to like?'

b. LF: *[$_S$· dare$_1$ o [$_{NP}$ e$_2$ hitome pro$_1$ mi-ta hito$_2$] ga

   [$_{VP}$ t_1 sukininat-ta] no]

(Hoji (1985, 51))

(10) a. S-str: *[s· [NP e₂ hitome   pro₁ mi-ta hito₂] ga
                    one=glance   saw person   NOM

              [VP daremo₁ o   sukininat-ta]]
                  everyone ACC came=to=like

              '*The person that took a glance at him₁ came
              to like everyone₁.'

     b. LF: *[s· daremo₁ o [NP e₂ hitome pro₁ mi-ta

              hito₂] ga [VP t₁ sukininat-ta]]

Having recognized the empirical content of the QR Approach to quantification, we adopt it as one of our working hypotheses. We will assume, in other words, that, at the level of **Logical Form**, a quantified phrase is adjoined to a constituent dominating it, leaving a coindexed trace behind, as illustrated in (11) below:

(11) a.   b.

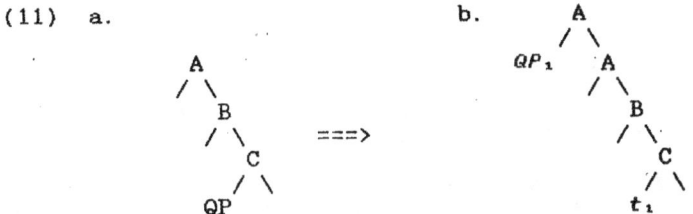

Moreover, the constituent to which the QP is adjoined (e.g., the lower A in (11b)) becomes the scope of that QP at LF.

2.4.2. Relative Scope

In this subsection, we will observe that some quantified expressions take scope narrower than the complex predicate forming suffixes like *ta* (want) and *sase* (CAUSE). This observation will lead us to conclude that the complex predicates do take syntactic complements at the level of LF.

In fact, it is not too difficult to come up with examples like (12a) and (12b) below, in which a universal quantifier seems to take scope narrower than *ta* (want) and *sase* (CAUSE), respectively:

(12)
a. watasi wa disateisyon ga owat-tara *mainiti* hiru
   I   top dissertation nom end-COND every=day noon
   made netei-*ta*-i
   until sleeping-want-PRES

   'I now have a desire to sleep until noon every day
    when my dissertation is finished.' (**WANT > ∀**)

b. watasi ga rusu-no-aida wa uti-no yome   ni
   I   nom absent=while top my   daughter=in=law DAT
   mainiti ko-*sase*-masu   kara ansin-site-kudasai
   every=day come-CAUSE-PRES since feel=easy=please

   'Don't worry. I will make my daughter-in-law come
    everyday while I am away.' (**CAUSE > ∀**)

In (12a), for example, the universal quantifier *mainiti* (every day) seems to take scope below *ta* (want), modifying the complement verb *netei* (sleeping). What takes place every day, in other words, is not that "the speaker feels desire" but that "(s)he sleeps until noon". Similarly in (12b), what takes place every day is "for the daughter-in-law to come" rather than "for the speaker to make her do that remotely from a distant place".

2.4.2.1. Scope Ambiguity (I)

The presence of a scope domain below the suffixes like *ta* (want) and *sase* (CAUSE) is even more clearly attested when we examine how more than one quantified expression interacts with the complex predicates containing these suffixes in regard to their scope properties.

Let us begin with an English sentence, as in (13) below:

(13) Bill *intends* to visit [a *museum*][*every day*].

Arguing against the postulation of the feature [+/-specific], and attributing the original observation and analysis to Bach (1968) and McCawley (1970), Karttunen (1976, p.379) reports the scope ambiguity in this sentence as in (14) below:[53]

(14) a. Bill intends that there be some museum that he visits every day. (INTEND > E > V)
   b. Bill intends to do a museum visit every day. (INTEND > V > E)

The contrast between (14a) and (14b) is quite relevant to our discussion, since the presence of scope ambiguity between the existential quantifier and the universal quantifier here indicates the presence of a scope domain narrower than the predicate *intend*. The ambiguity between (14a) and (14b), in other words, arises due to the presence of the complement of *intend*.

Consider now Japanese sentences as in (15) and (16) below, which contain complex predicates *ik-(i)ta-i* (go-want-PRES) and *okur-ita-i* (present-want-PRES), respectively.

(15)
a. watasi wa kono natu [*mainiti*]
   I   TOP this summer every=day

   [*dokokano*   hakubutukan e] ik-*ita*-i
     somewhere   museum   to go-want-PRES

   'I want to go to some museum every day.'

b. wasi wa nanazyussai no tanzyoobi ni [*nanika*
    I   TOP 70=years=old GEN birthday   on   something

    kinen-ni-naru mono   o][magotati   no *daremo* ni]
    commemorative thing ACC grandchildren GEN everyone to

    okur-*ita*-i
    present-want-PRES

    'I want to present something commemorative to every
    one of my grandchildren on my seventieth birthday.'

These sentences exhibit at least the ambiguity as indicated in (16) and (17) below, which is completely comparable to (14a-b) above:[54]

(16) a. I desire that there be some museum that I visit every day. (**WANT > E > ∀**)

   b. I want to do a museum visit every day. (**WANT > ∀ > E**)

(17) a. I desire that there be some common commemorative item, which all my grandchildren will receive. (**WANT > E > ∀**)

   b. I desire that each of my grandchildren will receive some commemorative item. (**WANT > ∀ > E**)

Crucially, then, the ambiguities observed in (14) and (15) require that *ta* (want) have a complement constituent in these examples, which can be the domain of a scope narrower than *ta* (want) at the level the scopes of quantifiers are determined -- i.e., at the level of Logical Form.

A complex predicate containing *sase* (cause) as in (20) and (21) below also exhibits a similar scope ambiguity, as described in (22) and (23):

(20) watasi wa konya settokusi te kare o [mainiti]
     I   TOP tonight persuade and he ACC every day

    [dokokano hakubutukan e] ika-ase-masu
      somewhere museum   to   go-CAUSE-POLITE=PRES

    'By persuading him tonight, I will make him visit
     some museum every day.'

(21) Tanaka wa sono enkai   no sekizyoo-de   [genkin
            TOP that banquet GEN on=the=occasion cash

    mosikuwa syoohinken o][syusseki-si-te-iru
    or   gift=card ACC attending

    yuukensya-tati no daremo   ni] gooin-ni
    voters   GEN everyone DAT forcibly

    uketor-ase-ru   tumori-de-iru
    receive-CAUSE-PRES   have=intention

    'Tanaka is planning to make every attending voter
     receive cash or gift cards at the banquet.'

(22) a. I will bring about a situation s.t. there be
        some museum that he visits every day.
        (CAUSE > E > V)

     b. I will make him do a museum visit every day.
        (CAUSE > V > E)

(23) a. Tanaka is planning to give rise to a situation
        s.t. every attending voter will uniformly receive
        either cash or gift cards.   (CAUSE > OR > V)

     b. Tanaka is planning to give rise to a situation
        s.t. each attending voter will receive either
        cash or gift cards.   (CAUSE > V > OR)

Thus, with our assumption that the scope of quantifiers is determined at LF, we may conclude that the derivational affixes like *ta* (want) and *sase* (cause) involve syntactic complementation at the level of LF.

This conclusion will lead us to reject the PAS
Approach to complex predicates proposed by Farmer (1980).
Our observations above concerning the scope of quantifiers
might also be captured in this approach in terms of
complementation of PAS, letting the embedded PAS function
as a scope domain narrower than the suffix. On the other
hand, given the parallelism between quantifiers like *every*,
some and *wh*-expressions with respect to weak crossover
phenomena (cf. 2.4.1. above), a syntactic analysis of
quantified sentences seems to be called for even in the PAS
Approach. Therefore, if we can capture the interaction of
quantifiers and complex predicates in terms of syntactic
complementation, as we have just suggested above, the use
of syntactic complementation rather than complementation of
PAS becomes a null hypothesis.[55]

2.4.2.2. Scope Ambiguity (II)

Carlson (1985) provides an interesting study of the
expressions *same* and *different* in English.[56] He observes
that one of the uses of these expressions involves implicit
comparison between two or more elements within a sentence.
Such an S-internal comparison by *same* or *different*,
furthermore, requires the presence of a plural or
distributive NP as a "licenser" within a certain local

domain.[57] These observations can be illustrated by the examples in (24) and (25) below:

(24) a. *Bob and Alice* attend *different* classes.

 (e.g., Bob attends Biology 101 and Alice attends Philosophy 799.)

 b. The *same* salesman sold me *these two magazine subscriptions*.

 (e.g., Salesman Jones sold me this subscription to Consumer Report and Jones, too, sold me this subscription to Cosmopolitan.)

 c. *Two men* who belonged to the *same* political party met me at the train station.

 (e.g., Two Democrats met me at the train station.)

 (Carlson (1985, 2))

(25) a. *The two gorillas* saw [a woman who fed them/*different* men][58]

 b. *The men* wanted to see [Jill's pictures of them/*different* dogs]

 (Carlson (Ibid., 4))

The contrast between (24a-c) and (25a-b) illustrates the locality condition on the licensing of *same* and *different* by a plural/distributive NP, which is reminiscent of the Subjacency Condition on movement (Chomsky (1973)).

Quite parallel paradigms can be obtained in Japanese as well, with the expressions *tiga(w)u* (different) and *onazi* (same).[57] Observe the contrast between (26a-b) and

(27a-b) as well as the contrast between (28a-b) and (29) below:

(26)
a. *hutari no tuukoonin* ga [*tigau* doroboo] o
    two   GEN passerby NOM different thief ACC

    mokugekisi-ta
    witnessed

    'Two passersby witnessed different thieves.'

b. aru tuukoonin ga [*tigau*   ie   ni   sinobikomoo-to-
    a   passerby NOM different house into going=to=sneak=

    siteiru *hutari no doroboo*] o   mokugekisi-ta
    in   two   GEN thief   ACC witnessed

    'Some passerby witnessed two thieves that were sneaking into different houses.'

(27)
a. **hutari no tuukoonin* ga [*tigau*   ie   ni
    two   GEN passerby NOM different house into

    sinobikom-oo-to-siteiru aru doroboo] o mokugekisi-ta
    going=to=sneak=in   a   thief   ACC witnessed

    '*Two passersby witnessed some thief who was sneaking into different houses.'

b. ?**hutari no tuukoonin* ga [aru doroboo ga *tigau*
    two   GEN thief   NOM a   thief   NOM different

    ie   ni   sinobikom-oo-to-siteiru tokoro] o
    house into going=to=sneak=in   occasion ACC

    mokugekisi-ta
    witnessed

    'Two passersby witnessed some thief's sneaking into different houses.'

(28)
a. *watasi-tati* wa [*onazi* kusuri-uri   kara]
   we   TOP same medicine=peddler from

   kanpoo-yaku   o   kat-ta
   Chinese-medicine   ACC bought

   'We bought Chinese medicine from the same medicine peddler.'

b. watasi wa [*onazi* mura   kara kita *hutari no*
   I   TOP same   village from came two   GEN

   kusuri-uri   kara] kanpoo-yaku   o   kat-ta
   medicine=peddler   from   Chinese=medicene ACC bought

   'I bought Chinese medicine from two medicine=peddlers who came from the same town.'

(29) *watasi-tati wa [*onazi* mura   kara kita aru
     we   TOP same   village from came a

   kusuri-uri   kara] kanpoo-yaku   o   kat-ta
   medicine=peddler from   Chinese=medicine ACC bought

   '*We bought Chinese medicine from some medicine peddler who came from the same town.'

We will not pursue here what exactly constitutes the local domain in which the S-internal comparison is licensed. Instead, we will turn to another interesting observation made by Carlson, which is directly relevant to our discussion on complex predicates. Observe now the example in (30) below:

(30) John and Bill *want* to live in *different* cities.

With the S-internal comparison, *different cities* in (30) exhibits two distinct readings. On one reading, *John* and

Bill each has a particular city in mind (e.g., New York and Boston, respectively), and each person wants to live in that city. On the other reading, however, neither *John* nor *Bill* has any particular city in mind, but each person wants to live in a city the other person does not live in. Following Carlson, let us adopt an analysis in which the two readings are assigned two distinct LF representations, as illustrated in (31) below, and call them a wide scope reading and a narrow scope reading, respectively:

(31) a. *Wide Scope* (==> two particular cities):
[*different cities*$_1$ [John and Bill$_2$ want [PRO$_2$ to live in t_1]]]

b. *Narrow Scope* (==> any two non-identical cities):
[John and Bill$_2$ want [*different cities*$_1$ [PRO$_2$ to live in t_1]]]

In each of these representations, LF-movement adjoins the NP containing *different* to a constituent containing the licensing NP --- *John and Bill* in (31a) and PRO controlled by *John and Bill* in (31b). The difference in the two readings, in other words, is captured in terms of the scope of *different* relative to the predicate *want* --- the wide scope reading involves the scope of *different* being wider than the predicate *want* as in (31a), whereas the narrow scope reading involves the scope of *different* being narrower than *want* as in (31b).

A point of particular interest to us here is the availability of the narrow scope reading in (30), since it will suggest to us: (i) that there exists an LF constituent below *want*, which can function as the scope domain of *different*, and (ii) that this scope domain contains a plural NP functioning as the licenser of *different* (PRO controlled by *John and Bill* in (31b)).

Recall now our conclusion in 2.4.2.1. above that the desiderative suffix *ta* in Japanese takes a complement at LF, which functions as the scope domain of quantifiers. If this conclusion is correct, we may expect that a similar scope ambiguity, especially the presence of the narrow scope reading, may be observed when Japanese counterparts of *same* and *different* are used in this complex predicate construction. This prediction is borne out, as illustrated by the examples in (32) and (33) below:

(32)   ore to aniki   ga *tigau*   syokuba   de
       I   and e. brother NOM different workplace at

       hatarak-*ita*-i   (koto)
       work-want-PRES (fact)

       'My elder brother and I want to work at different places.'

(33) kanozyo to boku ga *onazi daigaku* ni
      she   and I   NOM same college into

      hair-*ita*-i   (koto)
      enter-want-PRES (fact)

      'She and I want to get into the same college.'

The availability of the narrow scope reading in these examples can be confirmed when we observe that an expression like *dokodemo iikara* (wherever it may be) can be added immediately before *tigau* (different) and *onazi* (same).

Note that, in the analysis adopted here, the narrow scope reading of (32), for example, is assigned an LF representation like (34) below:

(34) LF: ore to aniki$_2$ ga [$_{Vmax}$ *tigau syokuba*$_1$ *de* [$_{Vmax}$ e$_2$ t$_1$ hatarak]] *ta*

Crucially, *tigau syokuba de* (at different workplaces) takes a scope narrower than *ta* (want). We thus have another motivation to postulate a complement to *ta* (want) at LF.

Notice also that the availability of a narrow scope reading combined with the licensing condition on *tigau* (different) and *onazi* (same) also motivates the postulation of an empty licenser NP (e$_2$ in (34)) below the predicate *ta* (want), i.e., within the comlement of *ta* at LF. This motivates the control structure of *ta* (want) construction as proposed in 2.3.1. above.

2.4.3. Morphology-Syntax Mismatches

In this subsection, we will examine how negative, honorific and reciprocal affixes in Japanese interact with complex predicates. In the course of the investigation, some observations will be made which will lead us to conclude that a complex predicate structure of the form in (35) below must sometimes be analyzed to have a syntactic representation in (36) at some level of representation:

(35)
```
           C^max
          /  \
     ...   C^min
            /  \
           /\   \
         [ A  B  C ]
```

(C = negative, honorific or reciprocal suffix)

(36)
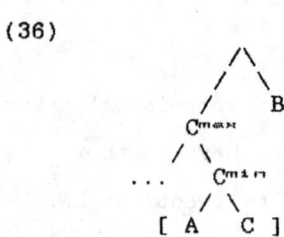
```
              /\
             /  \
            /    B
          C^max
          /  \
     ...   C^min
            /  \
          [ A   C ]
```

It will be argued below that a simple account of such a morphology-syntax mismatch and its related matters will call for, hence will argue for, the application of non-string-vacuous affix raising at LF.

2.4.3.1. Negative Polarity

2.4.3.1.1. Background

Sika ((anything) but) is one of the negative polarity items in Japanese (cf. McGloin (1972)). Compare *sika* in (37a-b) with another negative polarity expression (numeral 'one' + counter +) *mo* (even) in (38a-b):[40]

(37) a. *[kare ga biiru-*sika* nom-u]   (koto)
         he NOM beer-*but*   drink-PRES (fact)

    b. [kare ga biiru-*sika* nom-ana-i]   (koto)
         he NOM beer-*but*   drink-NEG-PRES (fact)

       'He drinks only beer.'

(38)
a. *[kare ga osake-o *itteki-mo*   nom-u]   (koto)
      he NOM liquor-ACC one=drop-even drink-PRES (fact)

b. [kare ga osake-o *itteki-mo*   nom-ana-i]   (koto)
      he NOM liquor-ACC one=drop-even drink-NEG-PRES (fact)

   'He does not drink even a drop of liquor.'

Combined with the negative morpheme *(a)na*, *sika* ((anything) but) in (37b), for example, yields an interpretation representable as in (39) below (cf. McGloin (1976), Muraki (1978)):

(39) **ONLY**x, x=beer, [DRINK (he, x)]

While an account of the full paradigm involving *sika* requires complication, I will tentatively assume that the

basic licensing condition for *sika* is its co-occurrence
with a negative expression within a single clause (Oyakawa
(1975), McGloin (Ibid.), Muraki (Ibid.), Kuno (1986),
etc.). The basic correctness of this condition can be most
clearly shown by the ill-formedness of a sentence like (40)
below in addition to the ill-formedness of (37a) above:

(40) *watasi wa [kare ga biiru-*sika* nom-u] to
     I   TOP he NOM beer-but drink-PRES COMP

     sir-*ana*-katta
     know-NEG-PAST

    '*I didn't know that he drinks anything but beer.'

In the Affix Raising Approach, which provides an LF
derivation in (41) below for (37b), we can capture this
co-occurrence restriction in terms of the notion
(head)-government, as in (42):

(41)

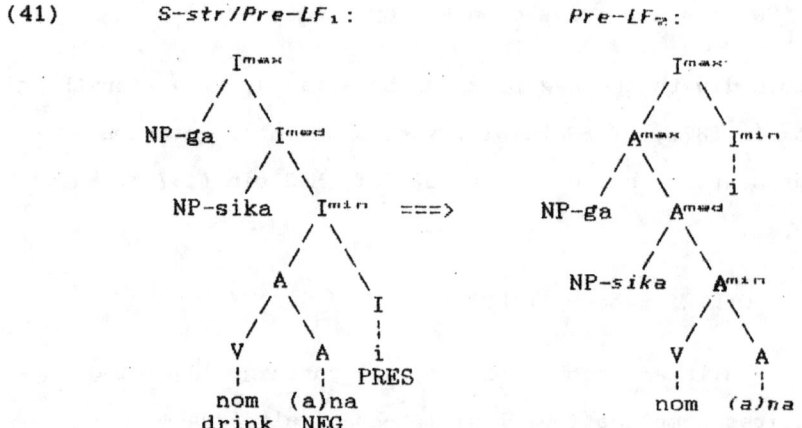

(42) *Negative Polarity Licensing Condition*:

A phrase containing a negative polarity item (e.g., *sika*, ... *mo*) must be head-governed at LF by a predicate headed by a negative morpheme.[61]

Let us again adopt coindexation as a formal notation to represent the relation between the licenser and the licensee. The derivation in (41), then, will be completed as in (43) below. The raising of *na* (NEG) is triggered by the potential violation of both the θ-Criterion and the syntactic c-selection of *na* (+[V^{max} __]):

(43) a. *Pre-LFs*:   b.   *LF*:

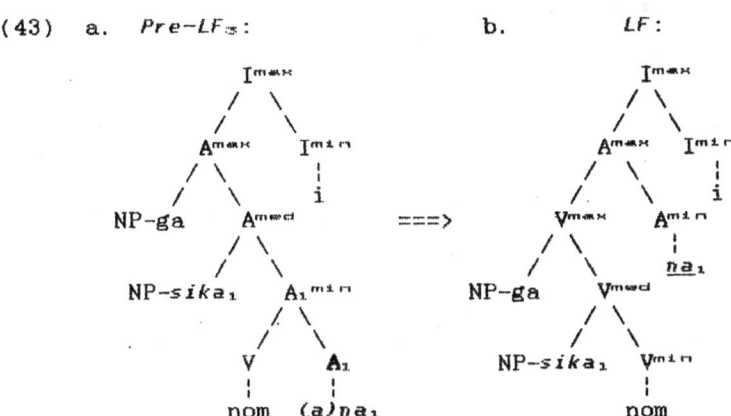

The LF-representation (43b) provides a basis for the correct scope relation represented in (39) --- i.e., *sika na* interpreted as "ONLY" has the V^{max} headed by *nom* (drink) as its scope, in which the base position of the *sika* phrase is converted into a variable bound by "ONLY". Such a semantic conversion is possibly mediated by a further LF movement of NP-*sika* --- perhaps an adjunction of the *sika*-phrase to *na* itself or its projection, leaving a trace behind. I will leave the details of such a conversion open.

2.4.3.1.2. *sika na* in the Complex Predicate Construction

With this much background in mind, let us now turn to the following sentences:

(44)   ano   ban   watasi wa   Taroo ni   biiru-*sika*
       that night I   TOP   DAT   beer-but

       nom-ase-*na*-katta
       drink-CAUSE-NEG-PAST

       'That night, I made/let Taroo drink only beer.'

(45)   Rupan wa   tesita   ni   hooseki-sika
       Lupin TOP   follower DAT jewelry-but

       nusum-ase-*na*-katta
       steal-CAUSE-NEG-PAST

       'Lupin made/let his followers steal only the jewelry.'

These sentences may be interpreted ambiguously with respect to the scope of *sika na* (ONLY) relative to the predicate *sase* (CAUSE), as illustrated by the two repersentations in (46) below for (44):

(46) a. *Matrix Scope:* (ONLY > CAUSE)
ONLYx, x=beer, [**CAUSE** (I, DRINK (Taroo, x))]
b. *Lower Scope:* (CAUSE > ONLY)
CAUSE (I, ONLYx, x=beer [DRINK (Taroo, x)])

Roughly, the representation in (46a) is translatable into the reading "Only with respect to beer, I brought about a situation such that Taro drinks it," or more informally, "I admit that I gave beer to Taroo. Whoever gave whiskey to him, however, it is not me." The representation in (46b), on the other hand, is translatable into the reading "I brought about a situation such that Taro drinks only beer," or more informally, "I kept an eye on Taro so that he would not drink anything other than beer."[62] It is also worth mentioning here that the reading represented as (46b) seems to be a secondary, marked option for many speakers, although it clearly is regarded as a possible reading, once its existence is pointed out to them.

The observation here can be extended from the causative construction to the two passive constructions and the desiderative construction, as in (47)-(49) below:

(47) *Indirect Passive*:

    Hanako wa Taroo ni asi o   wazato-*sika*
            TOP   by foot ACC deliberately-but

    hum-are-*na*-katta
    step=on-PASSIVE-NEG-PAST

    'Hanako had her foot stepped on only intentionally by Taro.'

(48) *Direct Passive*:

    Hanako wa Taroo ni wazato-*sika*
            TOP   by deliberately-but

    butukar-are-*na*-katta
    bump-PASSIVE-NEG-PAST

    'Hanako was bumped into only intentionally by Taro.'

(49) *Desiderative*:

    ano ban kare wa mezurasiku biiru-*sika*
    that night he   TOP unusually beer-but

    nom-ita-gar-*an*a-katta
    drink-want-display-PAST

    'That night, he unusually showed his desire only for beer.'

All these examples exhibit a similar ambiguity which can be represented, again, as a scope ambiguity involving *sika na* (ONLY), as in (50)-(52) below:[63]

(50) *Indirect Passive*:

    a.   ONLYx, x=deliberately [RECEIVE (Hanako, STEP-ON (Taroo, foot), x)]

    b.   RECEIVE (Hanako, ONLYx, x=deliberately [STEP-ON (Taroo, foot, x)])

(51) *Direct Passive*:

    a. ONLYx, x=deliberately [RECEIVE (Hanako$_1$, BUMP (Taroo, e$_1$), x)]

    b. RECEIVE (Hanako$_1$, ONLYx, x=deliberately [BUMP (Taroo, e$_1$, x)])

(52) *Desiderative*:

    a. ONLYx, x=beer [DISPLAY (Taroo, WANT (e$_1$, DRINK (e$_1$, x)))]

    b. DISPLAY (Taroo$_1$, ONLYx, x=beer [WANT (e$_1$, DRINK (e$_1$, x))])

If the ambiguity just described is real, it will provide us with some interesting problems, and will motivate the Affix Raising Analysis of the *sika-na* (ONLY) construction.

The first question to be asked is how *sika na* in (44) (repeated below) can take scope over *sase* (CAUSE) (as shown in (46) repeated below) and at the same time satisfy the locality imposed by the licensing condition of negative polarity items. (Notice that the negative morpheme *na* in (44) is attached to the causative morpheme *sase* rather than to the verbal root *nom* (drink).)

(44) ano ban watasi wa Taroo ni biiru-*sika*
    that night I   TOP   DAT beer-but

    nom-ase-*na*-katta
    drink-CAUSE-NEG-PAST

    'That night, I made Taroo drink only beer.'

142

(46) a. *Matrix Scope*: (ONLY > CAUSE)

ONLYx, x=beer, [CAUSE (I, DRINK (Taroo, x))]

b. *Lower Scope*: (CAUSE > ONLY)

CAUSE (I, ONLYx, x=beer [DRINK (Taroo, x)])

In the Affix Raising Approach, we can provide an answer to this question by postulating the derivation in (53) below for (44): (Here, we begin with the pre-LF representation obtained after raising of the tense morpheme.)

(53) a. *Pre-LF₁*:   b. *Pre-LF₂*:

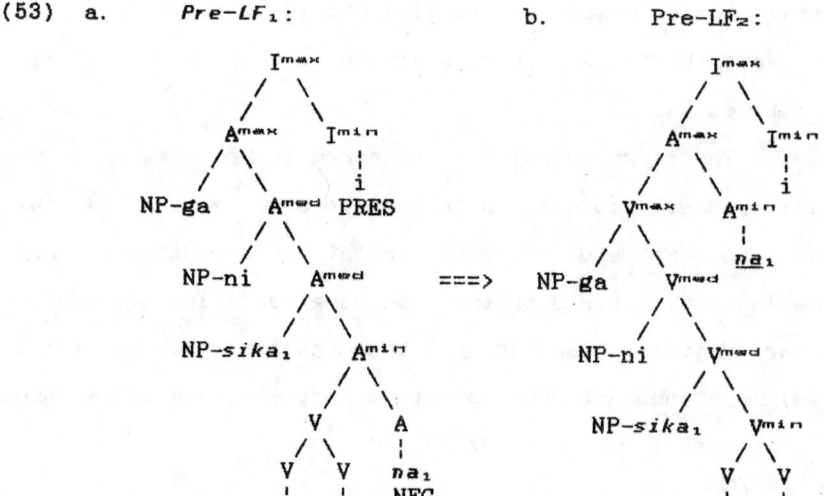

c.   LF:

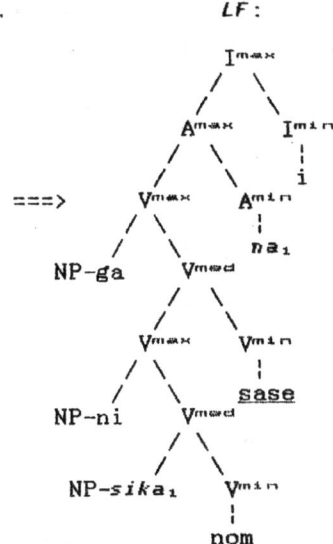

Here, the two instances of affix raising proceed quite straightforwardly. First, Move-alpha raises the outermost morpheme of the complex predicate, *na* (NEG), to satisfy its syntactic c-selectional property (+[V^{max} __]). Then, it raises *sase* (CAUSE) out of the complex predicate to satisfy the θ-Criterion. In (53a), the negative polarity item *sika* may be licensed by *na* under head-government, as indicated by the coindexation there. The resulting LF representation (53c), thus, can be considered to underlie the semantic representation in (46a), which exhibits the scope of *sika na* (ONLY) higher than *sase* (CAUSE).

The second question to be asked is how the lower scope reading of *sika na* ever becomes possible in (44), and the third question is why this reading is marked.

Notice that the **mere postulation of a complement** at whatever level of representation as in (54) below does not offer any immediate answer to these questions, since *na* (NEG) is not located within the complement:[64]

(54) watasi wa [Taroo ni biiru-*sika* nom] sase-*na*

In the Affix Raising Approach, the lower scope of *sika na* as in (46b) may be syntactically represented at LF if we assume a derivation as in (55) below: (Again, the tense morpheme has already been raised in (55a).)

(55) a.　　　　Pre-LF₁:　　　　b.　　　　Pre-LF₂:

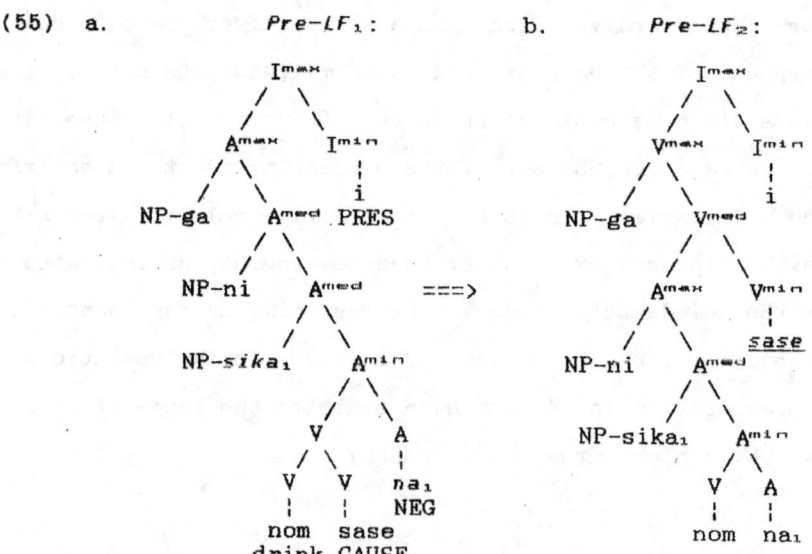

c.   LF:

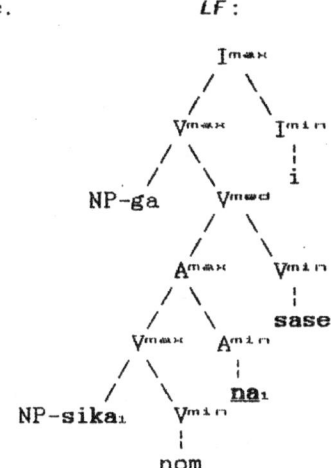

Again, the negative polarity item *sika* is licensed by *na* under head-government immediately after the tense morpheme has moved out in (55a). Crucially, however, this derivation involves the order of affix raising reversed to that in (53) above --- raising of *sase* (CAUSE) first, then *na* (NEG). The result is the LF representation in (55c), in which *sika na* (ONLY) takes scope lower than *sase*. The semantic representation in (46b), thus, can also receive its syntactic basis.[45]

2.4.3.1.3. **Non-string-vacuous Affix Raising**

The question to be raised here, of course, is whether the derivation in (55) should ever be allowed in the

grammar, given its deviation from the Mirror Image
Derivations (75) in 2.3.6.

The answer seems to be in the affirmative when we
make the following assumptions: (i) *na* (NEG) does not
have its own θ-marking property, (ii) the percolation of
features in morphology is allowed from the non-head as well
as the head morpheme if and only if the head morpheme fails
to provide them (Selkirk (1982)).

Selkirk's modification of Williams' (1981a) and
Lieber's (1981) percolation conventions has been proposed
on the basis of languages in which various inflectional
features are distributed among more than one affix but must
all be percolated up to the lexical node for the sake of
correct agreement, as illustrated in (56a) below:

(56) a. V^{min} [+**Tense**/+Plural/3 Person]   b. A^{min} [+θ]
         / \   / \
        V V_{af} [+Plural/3 Person]   V   A
       / \   / \ |
      V V_{af} [+**Tense**]   V   V na
                                                        | | NEG
                                                       tabe sase
                                                       eat CAUSE
                                                            [+θ]

The two assumptions we have just made interact with each
other and yield the non-head percolation of the θ-marking
properties illustrated in (56b).

With these assumptions in mind, recall now the pre-LF
representation (55a) (repeated below):

(55) a. $Pre\text{-}LF_1$:

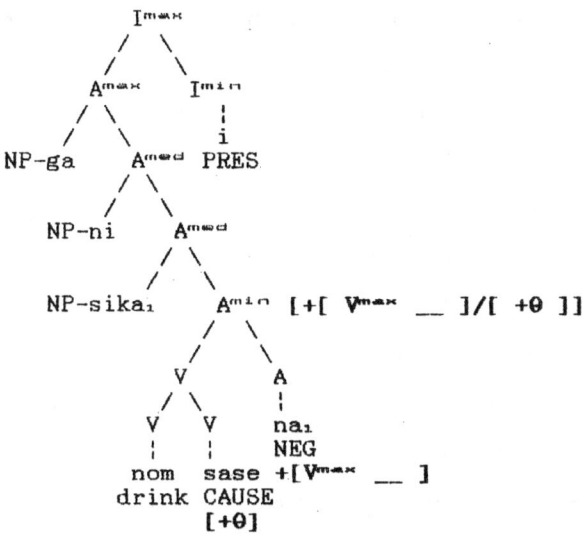

There are two principles of grammar yet to be satisfied in this representation --- c-selection checking and the θ-Criterion. Move-alpha, the remedy for such potential violations of grammatical principles, on the other hand, may affect only one item at a time. Suppose that the grammar chooses to satisfy c-selectional checking. It will, then, raise *na* (NEG) first, providing the derivation in (53) above, which is quite striaghtforward, as we have seen above, since the only c-selectional properties percolated up to the lexical node A^{min} is that of the head morpheme *na*, as illustrated in (55a) above.

Suppose, on the other hand, that the grammar chooses to satisfy the θ-Criterion first. This choice, presumably, will provide us with the derivation in (55). Given Selkirk's Percolation Conventions, this move should also be possible, since the head morpheme *na* (NEG) lacks its own θ-marking property. Syntax, therefore, may have access to the θ-marking property of the non-head *sase* (CAUSE) percolated up to the lexical node. Therefore, raising of *sase* may be triggered by a potential violation of the θ-Criterion there. There probably is a reason, however, to regard the derivation in (55) as a marked option, since it deviates from the Mirror Image Derivations, which holds in the majority of cases involving affix raising.

Thus, the crucial difference between a complex predicate allowing non-string-vacuous affix raising like V-*sase-na* (V-CAUSE-NEG) and a complex predicate rejecting it like V-*sase-rare* (V-CAUSE-PASSIVE) is that the percolation of the θ-marking properties from the non-head morpheme is permitted in the former, but not in the latter.

Let us recapitulate our proposal here in a more general way. We assume that, in principle, any affix contained in a complex predicate is subject to the application of Move-alpha. The Isomorphy Constraint, on the other hand, imposes a restriction on this syntactic rule such that it applies only when some violation of grammatical principles would otherwise arise. Raising of a particular affix, therefore, is triggered only when its properties are percolated up to the lexical node, creating some potential violation of grammatical principles detected by syntax. Selkirk's percolation convention gives priority to the head features of a complex predicate to percolate up to the lexical node (X^{min}). However, it also permits non-head features to percolate up to the lexical node when the head morpheme lacks those features. Selkirk's percolation convention, therefore, allows us to predict that raising of the head affix (= string-vacuous) and raising of non-head affixes (= non-string-vacuous) are both possible, but the former constitutes the unmarked case.

Thus, the Affix Raising Approach allows us not only to capture the scope ambiguity of *sika na* (ONLY) represented by the two semantic representations in (46), but also to provide a reason for the marked status of the lower scope reading represented by (46b).[66]

2.4.3.1.4. Alternatives

There exist at least two different syntactic analyses that may be proposed as an alternative to the **Affix Raising** Approach in accounting for the ambiguity detected in the examples like (44) and (45) (repeated below):

(44)　ano ban　watasi wa　Taroo ni　biiru-sika
　　　 that night I　　TOP　　 DAT beer-but

　　　 nom-ase-na-katta
　　　 drink-CAUSE-NEG-PAST

　　　 'That night, I made/let Taroo drink only beer.'

(45)　Rupan wa　tesita　ni　hooseki-sika
　　　 Lupin TOP follower DAT jewelry-but

　　　 nusum-ase-na-katta
　　　 steal-CAUSE-NEG-PAST

　　　 'Lupin made/let his followers steal only the
　　　 jewelry.'

Let us examine them here.

In the first alternative, the scope ambiguity in (44) is ascribed to the possibility for the *sika*-phrase to be ambiguously analyzed either as a matrix or complement element at the relevant level of representation, as in (57) below:

(57)　a.　*Matrix Scope*:

　　　　　ano ban watasi wa Taroo$_1$ ni biiru$_2$-sika

　　　　　[e$_1$ e$_2$ nom] ase-na-katta

　　　b.　*Lower Scope*:

　　　　　ano ban watasi wa Taroo$_1$ ni [e$_1$ biiru-sika

　　　　　nom-ana] sase-katta

According to this analysis, the matrix scope of *sika na* is made possible in the representation (57a), while the lower scope reading will be made possible by the application of the Negative Raising to (57b), as will be described further soon below.

We reject this approach on the grounds that it cannot account for the matrix scope of *sika na* (ONLY) in (58) below and also in (47) above, in which the *sika*-phrase is clearly located nowhere but within the complement, sitting between an internal argument and the lower predicate:

(58) Nobunaga wa wazato   [V^{max} tukaino-mono ni
      Nobunaga TOP deliberately   messenger   DAT
      Hideyosi ni tegami-*sika* todoke] sase-*na*-katta
      Hideyoshi DAT letter-but   deliver   CAUSE-NEG-PAST

   'Nobunaga deliberately made/let the messenger deliver only a letter.'

Also, this approach crucially relies on the "extra NP" analysis of causatives --- the causee *Taroo ni* in (57a) must be analyzed to be a matrix element. We have rejected this analysis, however, on the basis of adverbial interpretation.

The second alternative captures the scope ambiguity in (44) in terms of the rule called Negative Raising (or Negative Transportation).

Negative Raising, a device originally proposed in early studies of English (Fillmore (1963), Klima (1964), Lakoff (1969), etc.), has been extended to Japanese by McGloin (1972, 1976), based upon sentences like (59b) below:

(59) a. watasi wa sono e   wa *tittomo* okasiku-*na*-i
         I   TOP that picture TOP at=all   funny-NEG-PRES

   to   omo-u
   CCOMP think-PRES

   'I think that picture is not funny at all.'

b. watasi wa sono e   wa *tittomo* okasi-i
    I   TOP that picture TOP at=all   funny-PRES

   to   omow-*ana*-i
   COMP think-NEG-PRES

   'I don't think that picture is funny at all.'

   (McGloin (1976, 385))

Here, (59b) is claimed to be "semantically equivalent" to (59a), the negative polarity item *tittomo* (at all) licensed by the negative morpheme in the matrix clause. The licensing of an embedded negative polarity item in examples like these has been claimed to be made possible by the raising of the negative out of the complement clause. This raising is triggered by a small class of verbs including "verbs of thinking" like *omow* (think) and *kangaer* (think) (McGloin (Ibid.)). The licensing of the negative polarity item and also scope determination of the negative itself, in other words, are claimed to take place in the complement before the Negative Raising applies.

One possible move is to assume that the lower scope reading of *sika na* in (44) (repeated below) is made possible by the application of Negative Raising to the underlying representation in (60):[67]

(44) ano ban watasi wa Taroo ni biiru-*sika*
      that night I   TOP   DAT   beer-but

   nom-ase-*n*a-katta
   drink-CAUSE-NEG-PAST

   'That night, I made Taroo drink only beer.'

(60) ano ban watasi wa [Taroo ni biiru-*sika*

   nom-*(a)na*] sase-katta

Again, the licensing of the negative polarity item *sika* and the scope determination of the negative are claimed to take place before Negative Raising (and in this case Verb Raising as well) applies.

Exactly the same account may be offered to the licensing of the negative polarity item *itteki mo* (even a drop) in (61a) below by the negative morpheme *n*a attached to *sase* (CAUSE):

(61) a. ano ban watasi wa kare ni osake-o
         that night I   TOP he   DAT   liquor-ACC

   itteki-mo   nom-ase-*n*a-katta
   a=drop-even drink-CAUSE-NEG-PAST

   'That night, I did not make/let him drink even a drop of liquor.'

   b. ano ban watasi wa [kare ni osake-o *itteki-mo*

   nom-*ana*] sase-katta

However, there is good reason to question such an extension of the Negative Raising Approach to the complex predicate construction. The crucial observation comes from the comparison of (44) and (61) above with (62) and (63) below, respectively.

(62) *watasi wa [ano ban   kare wa biiru-*sika* non-da]
         I   TOP that night he   TOP beer-but   drink-PAST

   to   omow-ana-i
   COMP think-NEG-PRES

   '*I do not think that he drank but beer that night.'

(63) *watasi wa [ano ban   kare wa osake o   *itteki-mo*
         I   TOP that night he   TOP liquor ACC a=drop-even

   non-da] to   omow-ana-i
   drink-PAST COMP think-NEG-PRES

   'I do not think that he drank even a drop of liquor
    that night.'

Compare further (62) and (63) with (64) and (65), respectively, to confirm the ill-formed status of the former:

(64) watasi wa [ano ban   kare wa biiru-*sika*
        I   TOP that night he   TOP beer-but

   nom-ana-katta] to   omo-u
   drink-NEG-PAST COMP think-PRES

   'I think that he drank nothing but beer that night.'

(65) watasi wa [ano ban   kare wa osake o   *itteki-mo*
        I   TOP that night he   TOP liquor ACC a=drop-even

   nom-ana-katta] to   omo-u
   drink-NEG-PAST COMP think-PRES

   'I think that he did not drink even a drop of liquor
    that night.'

It is clear here that, for whatever reason, the application
of Negative Raising to (64) and (65) must be blocked.
Note, then, that, if the Negative Raising Approach were
truly extendable from the verbs of thinking like *omow*
(think) to the causative morpheme *sase*, we would
incorrectly predict that its application is also blocked in
(60) and (61a).

Note, incidentally, that it is **not** possible to assume
that Negative Raising may apply only when the complement is
tenseless. For instance, in (59b) above, which originally
motivated Negative Raising, or in the similar example (66)
below, the complement clause is clearly tensed.

(66) [kare no handan ga *sukosi-mo* matigattei-ta] to
      he GEN judgment NOM at=all   wrong-PAST   COMP

     omow-ana-i   hito
     think-NEG-PRES person

  'the person who does not think that his judgment
  was wrong at all'

Thus, whether or not Negative Transportation is motivated
independently (cf. (59b) vs. (63)), it does not seem to be
responsible for the ambiguity in (44). Recall also that we
have already seen many different reasons to reject the Verb
Raising Approach adopted in this alternative.

Furthermore, the Negative Raising Approach does not
explain how *sika na* in (44) can take scope over *sase* and at
the same time satisfies the locality imposed by the

licensing condition of negative polarity items. As we will see in 2.4.3.2. and 2.4.3.3. below, there also are other cases to which the Affix Raising Approach offers a simple solution without any additional cost, but the Negative Raising Approach has nothing to offer.[66]

2.4.3.2. Honorification

The following paradigms illustrate the basic properties of *sonkei-go* (respect language), a type of honorification in Japanese:[67]

(67) a. Sensei ga denwa o o-kake-ni-nat-ta
　　　Teacher NOM telephone ACC dial (HON)-PAST

　　　'Our teacher made a telephone call.'

　　b. *aitu ga denwa o o-kake-ni-nat-ta
　　　that=brat tel. ACC dial (HON)-PAST

　　　'That brat made a telephone call.'

(68) a. gakusei-tati ga [Sensei ga sonnani
　　　students　　　NOM Teacher NOM that=much

　　　o-okori-ni-nar-u] to omottei-na-katta (koto)
　　　get=angry (HON)-PRES COMP didn't=think　(fact)

　　　'The students did not expect that the teacher would get angry like that.'

　　b. *Sensei ga [gakusei-tati ga sonnani
　　　Teacher NOM　students　　　NOM that=much

　　　o-okori-ni-nar-u] to omottei-na-katta (koto)
　　　get=angry (HON-PRES COMP didn't=think　(fact)

　　　'The teacher did not expect that the students would get angry like that.'

c. Sensei ga [gakusei-tati ga sonnani okor-u]
   Teacher NOM students NOM that=much get=angry

   to o-omoi-ni-nar-ana-katta (koto)
   COMP didn't=think (HON)   (fact)

   'The teacher did not expect that the students
   would get angry like that.'

(69) a. Sensei ga sono otoko o o-tasuke-ni-nat-ta
        Teacher NOM that guy ACC help (HON)-PAST

   'Our teacher helped that guy.'

   b. *sono otoko ga Sensei o o-tasuke-ni-nat-ta
      that guy NOM Teacher ACC help (HON)-PAST

   'That guy helped our teacher.'

First, as (67a-b) illustrate, honorified verbs of the form
o-V-ni-nar must be licensed by what Harada (1976) refers to
as "a person socially superior to the speaker (SSS)" (e.g.,
Sensei (Teacher)).[70] Second, as (68a-c) as well as (67b)
illustrate, such licensing is clause-bound. Third, as
(69a-b) illustrate, the SSS as the licenser of o-V-ni-nar
must be the "subject" of a sentence. The last generalization has led Harada to label this type of honorification as
"subject honorification".[71]

Again, with an LF derivation in (70) below (for
(67a)) provided in the Affix Raising Approach, we can
capture these generalizations in terms of the notion
"licensing under head-government" represented in terms of
coindexation, as in (71) below:[72]

(70) a.   *S-str/Pre-LF₁:*   b.   *Pre-LF₂:*

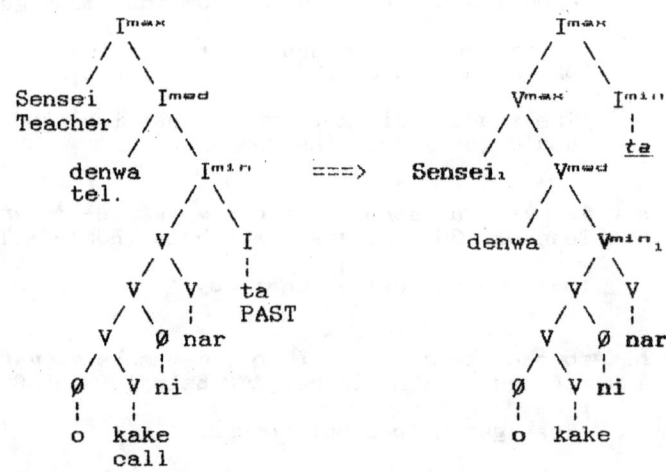

($\emptyset$ = null category, See footnote 37)

(71) *Subject Honorification Licensing Condition*:

An honorified verb of the form *o-V-ni-nar* must head-govern a subject SSS at LF.[73]

(subject = [N^{max}, X^{max}])

In (70b), the honorified verb *o-kake-ni-nar* (dial (HON)) head-governs the subject SSS *Sensei* (Teacher), hence the well-formedness of (67a) above.

When we extend this licensing analysis of honorifics to the complex predicate construction, it can capture the "cyclicity of honorification" observed by Harada, without any additional cost. We will see what this "cyclicity" consists of.

First, observe the examples in (72) below:

(72) a. Kootyoo-sensei ga syukutyoku-no yoomuin ni
    Principal   NOM on=night=duty janitor DAT

    keisatu o   o-yob-ase-ni-nat-ta   (koto)
    police   ACC call-CAUSE (HON)-PAST (fact)

    'The principal made/let the janitor on night duty
    call the police.'

b. syukutyoku-no yoomuin ga Kootyoo-sensei ni
   on=night=duty janitor NOM Principal   DAT

   yoomuin-situ   de sibaraku o-yasumi-ni-nar-ase
   night-duty=room at a=while rest (HON)-CAUSE

   -te sasiage-ta   (koto)[74]
   -GER respectfully=give-PAST   (fact)

   'The janitor on night duty let the principal take
   a rest in the night-duty room for a while.'

In (72a), the entire complex predicate *yob-ase* (call-CAUSE) is honorified, and it is licensed by the causer SSS *Sensei* (Teacher). In the Affix Raising Approach, this licensing may take place quite straightforwardly in the pre-LF representation (73) below, which we obtain after the tense morpheme *ta* (PAST) is raised to satisfy its syntactic c-selectional property (+[V^{max} __]):

(73)   Pre-LF:

In (72b), on the other hand, what is honorified is the verbal root *yasum* (rest) rather than the entire complex verb, and it is licensed by the causee SSS rather than the causer. In the Affix Raising Approach, this licensing as well may be carried out strightforwardly in the Pre-LF representation (74b), which is obtained **after** the raising of *sase* (CAUSE) is triggered by the θ-Criterion:

(74) a.   Pre-LF₁: b.   Pre-LF₂:

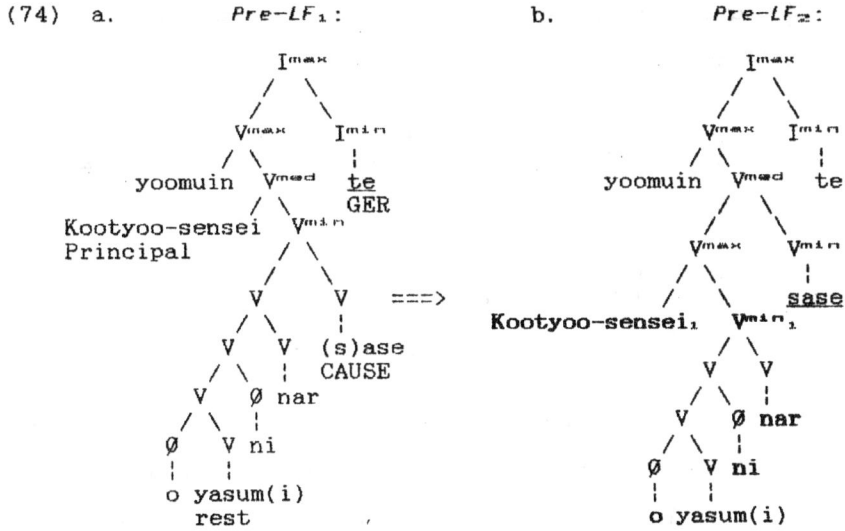

The "cyclicity" of honorification, thus, can be captured in the Affix Raising Approach in quite a simple way.

Let us here take up a dialectal variation of the honorification of the complex predicate.[75] Consider again (72a) (repeated below):

(72) a. Kootyoo-sensei ga   syukutyoku-no yoomuin ni
        Principal   NOM   on=night=duty janitor DAT

        keisatu o   o-yob-ase-ni-nat-ta (koto)
        police ACC   call (HON)-PAST   (fact)

        'The principal made/let the janitor on night duty
        call the police.'

Harada (1976, 551) reports that this and other similar sentences involving honorification of complex predicates as in (75)-(76) are acceptable to many speakers but are rejected in the "prescriptive accounts of Japanese honorifics":

(75) Sensei ga hon o o-kaki-hazime-*ni-nat*-ta (koto)
     Teacher NOM book ACC write-begin (HON)-PAST (fact)

   'Our teacher started writing a book.'

(76) Sensei ga sake o o-nomi-sugi-*ni-nat*-ta (koto)
     Teacher NOM liquor ACC drink-exceed (HON)-PAST (fact)

   'Our teacher drank too much liquor.'

Let us here label that dialect which accepts sentences like (72a), (75) and (76) as "Dialect A", and that which rejects them as "Dialect B". Adopting a version of the Verb Raising Approach to complex predicates, Harada proposes the following global constraint on the applicability of subject honorification (= a set of transformational rules for him), to account for this dialectal variation: (Dialect B is claimed to have this constraint.)

(77) Subject honorification is blocked on a certain cycle if:

   (a) the input structure is an output of predicate raising on the same cycle, and

   (b) subject honorification was applicable but did not apply, on the previous cycle.

We believe that the Affix Raising Approach can offer a simpler account. Recall, first, the pre-LF representation (73) (repeated below), which we have assigned to (72a):

(73) $Pre-LF_1$:

Although this representation permits the correct licensing of the honorified complex verb by the causer SSS, it still has to satisfy the θ-Criterion (see below), hence has to be mapped onto the pre-LF representation as in (78) below, involving non-string-vacuous raising of *sase* (CAUSE):

(78)   Pre-LF$_2$:

Let us assume that the honorific markers *ni* and *nar* have syntactic c-selectional properties (+[V^{max} __]) but **no θ-marking properties**. The mapping between (73) and (78) then follows naturally from the system of affix raising we have adopted above --- given Selkirk's Percolation Conventions, the first θ-marking morpheme visible to syntax, hence subject to affix raising, is *sase* (CAUSE).

Paying attention to this point, we can now offer the following account for the dialectal variation in question.

In one dialect of present-day Japanese (Dialect A), syntax is allowed to affect a word-internal non-head morpheme when principles of grammar require it. As a result, Dialect A permits the mapping of (73) onto (78), hence the honorification of complex predicates as in (72a), (75) and (76).

In another dialect (Dialect B), on the other hand, it is absolutely prohibited for syntax to affect the interior of a word. As a result, Dialect B does not permit the mapping of (73) onto (78), hence rules out the sentences (72a), (75) and (76).

The crucial distinction, therefore, can probably be reduced to whether the grammar permits the limited non-head feature percolation as determined by Selkirk's Percolation Conventions (Dialect A) or permits only the head-feature percolation (Dialect B). The Affix Raising Approach supplemented by Selkirk's Percolation Conventions, thus, permits us to offer a simple account of the dialectal variation reported by Harada.

The Affix Raising Approach, in fact, makes an even more interesting prediction concerning honorification. Consider again the example (72a) and its LF derivation repeated below:

(72) a. Kootyoo-sensei ga syukutyoku-no yoomuin ni
       Principal   NOM on=night=duty janitor DAT

   keisatu o   o-yob-ase-ni-nat-ta (koto)
   police ACC   call (HON)-PAST   (fact)

   'The principal made/let the janitor on night duty call the police.'

(79) a. Pre-LF₁:

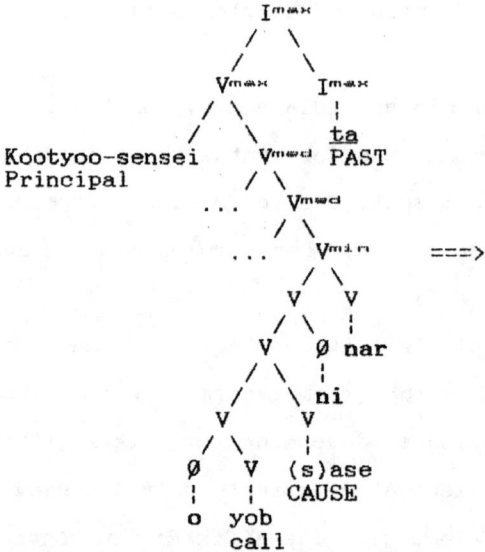

===>

b. Pre-LF₂:

Although we have mentioned above only the possibility for the honorified verb *o-yob-ase-ni-nar* (call-CAUSE (HON)) to be licensed by the subject SSS *Kootyoo-sensei* (Principal) in (79a), in principle, nothing in our analysis precludes the honorified verb *o-yob(i)-ni-nar* (call (HON)) in (79b) from being licensed by a subject SSS within the complement of *sase* (CAUSE) when such licensing has not yet taken place. (In this particular example, it simply is the case that the complement to *sase* lacks a legitimate SSS.) Put another way, the Affix Raising Approach predicts that an honorified verb of the surface form $o-V_1-sase-ni-nar$ (V_1-CAUSE (HON)) as in (72a) may sometimes be interpreted as $o-V_1-ni-nar$ (V_1 (HON)), provided that the sentence contains a causee that can behave as a legitimate licenser of honorified verbs.

This prediction, in fact, seems to be borne out. Thus, it makes perfect sense to many speakers for a father to scold his child with a sentence in (80) below:

(80) omae wa watasi ga rusu-no-aida-ni *O-zii-sama*
 you TOP I NOM while=absent Grandfather (HON)

 ni keisatu-made *o-yob-ase-ni-nat*-ta soo
 DAT police-even call-CAUSE (HON)-PAST hearsay

 zya-nai-ka
 isn't=it

 'I heard that you made Grandfather call even the police while I was away.'

In this sentence, the interpreted honorified verb is clearly *o-yob(i)-ni-nar* (call (HON)), which is licensed by *O-zii-sama* (Grandfather (HON)). In our analysis, this licensing can be properly represented in the pre-LF-representation resulting from the raising of *sase* (CAUSE), as in (81b) below:

(81) a. *Pre-LF₁*:   b.   *Pre-LF₂*:

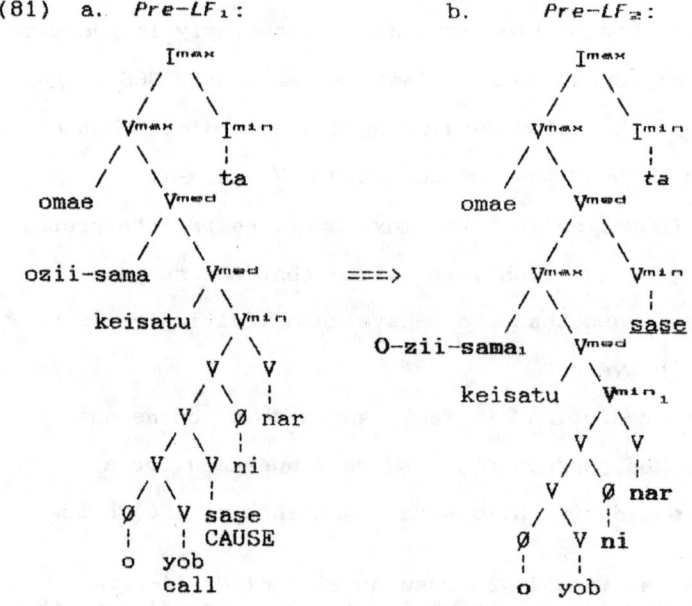

(82)-(83) below provide further examles:

(82) isya wa *Sensei* ni bansyaku-made
      doctor TOP Teacher DAT daily=drink-even

      o-yame-sase-*ni-nat*-ta soo   da-na
      stop-CAUSE (HON)-PAST hearsay is

      Sonnani   owaru-i   no   ka?
      that=much ill-PRES NMNL Q

      'I heard that the doctor made our teacher quit even
      his daily drink at dinner. Is he that ill?'

(83) keisatu wa *Sensei* ni nanto simatusyo   o
      police TOP Teacher DAT alas written=apology ACC

      o-kak-ase-*ni-nat*-ta   to   iu-de-wa-nai-ka
      write-CAUSE (HON)-PAST   COMP I=heard

      'I heard that the police made our teacher write,
      I can't believe it, even a written apology.'

In the exmples like (84) and (85) below, where two potential licensers are found, it seems to be the case that either the entire complex predicate (*o*-V₁-*sase-ni-nar*) or the verbal root (*o*-V₁-*ni-nar*) may be interpreted as an honorified verb:

(84) *O-zii-sama*   ga *O-baa-sama*   ni keisatu
      Grandfather (HON) NOM Grandmother (HON) DAT police

      -made o-yob-ase-ni-nat-ta   (koto)
      -even call-CAUSE (HON)-PAST (fact)

      'Grandfather made Grandmother call even the police.'

(85)   O-isya-sama ga Sensei ni bansyaku-made
       doctor (HON) NOM Teacher DAT daily=drink-even

       o-yame-sase-ni-nat-ta (koto)
       stop-CAUSE (HON)-PAST (fact)

       'The doctor made our teacher quit even his daily
       drink at dinner.'

In these ambiguous cases, however, the interpretation involving the honorification of the entire complex predicate seems to be the preferred, primary reading. This asymmetry in fact makes perfect sense in our analysis.

Note, first, that the primary reading in (84) corresponds to the reading in (72a) (repeated below), and the secondary reading in (84) corresponds to the reading in (80) (repeated below), as indicated by the coindexation:

(72) a. $Kootyoo\text{-}sensei_1$ ga   syukutyoku-no yoomuin ni
        Principal   NOM on=night=duty janitor DAT

        keisatu o   o-yob-ase-$ni\text{-}nat_1$-ta   (koto)
        police ACC call-CAUSE (HON) -PAST (fact)

        'The principal made/let the janitor on night duty
        call the police.'

(80) omae wa   watasi ga   rusu-no-aida-ni $O\text{-}zii\text{-}sama_1$
     you TOP I   NOM while=absent   Grandfather (HON)

     ni keisatu-made o-yob_1-ase-$ni\text{-}nat$-ta   soo
     DAT police-even call -CAUSE (HON)-PAST hearsay

     zya-nai-ka
     isn't=it

     'I heard that you made Grandfather call even the
     police while I was away.'

In Dialect B, which absolutely prohibits non-head feature percolation, hence non-string-vacuous affix raising, neither (72a) nor (80) are acceptable sentences. This is so because non-string-vacuous affix raising is required in both these sentences by the θ-Criterion. (See the derivations in (73)/(78) and (81) above.)

In Dialect A, on the other hand, the percolation of the θ-properties of *sase* (CAUSE) is permitted in both these examples due to the lack of θ-marking properties in the honorific markers *ni* and *nar*. Therefore, both (72) and (80) are well-formed sentences even if they involve non-string-vacuous affix raising.

Crucially, however, a deviation from the Mirror Image Derivations is "visible" with respect to honorification in (80) but not in (72). The language learners, in other words, must confront a clear morphology-syntax mismatch in the examples like (80) --- the surface string of morphemes gives an impression that the entire complex predicaet *o-V-sase-ni-nar* is honorified, whereas only the portion of it, *o-V-ni-nar*, is actually licensed at LF. In a case like (72), on the other hand, no such morphology-syntax mismatch is confronted --- the entire complex predicate as observed at surface, *o-V-sase-ni-nar*, is licensed at LF as a single honorified verb. If we assume that a "visible" deviation from the Mirror Image Derivations -- what we have just labeled as a "morhology-syntax mismatch" -- induces the markedness of sentences, we make a prediction as summarized in (86) below, and we have just seen that this prediction seems to be borne out:

(86)   In Dialect A   In Dialect B
   (72a) :   ok   *
   (80) :   (ok)   *

Thus, the Affix Raising Approach predicts not only the possibility of licensing the honorification within the complement of the examples in (80)-(85), but also the marked status of the interpretation deriving from such licensing.[76]

One might question our interpretation of the examples in (80)-(85) above. For example, Susumu Kuno (personal communication) has pointed out to me that the example (82) is well-formed simply because the honorification there is licensed by the causer *isya* (doctor).

There are several reasons, however, to believe that this is not the case. First, a plain form *isya* (doctor) does not license honorification in a simple case like (87a) below. Compare it with (87b), which contains an honorified form *o-isya-sama* (doctor (NOM)):

(87) a. *sono *isya*   ga   uti-no musuko o *o-sirabe-ni-nat*-ta
         that doctor NOM my   son   ACC examine(HON)-PAST
   'That doctor examined my son.'

b. sono o-isya-sama   ga uti-no musuko o
    that doctor (HON) NOM my   don   ACC

   o-sirabe-ni-nat-ta
   examine (HON)-PAST

   'That doctor examined my son.'

Notice also that the exmaple (80) contains a vulgar form
omae (you) as the causer. Omae, however, can never license
subject honorification in other simple cases like (88)
below:[77]

(88) *omae ga denwa   o   o-kake-ni-nat-ta (koto)
     you NOM telephone ACC dial (HON)   (fact)

   'You made a telephone call.'

Finally, if we change the causee in (80) from the SSS
O-zii-sama (Grandfather (HON)) to a non-SSS otooto (younger
brother), as in (89) below, the sentence becomes completely
unacceptable. This verifies our observation that the
honorification in (80) is licensed by the causee SSS:[78]

(89) *omae wa watasi ga rusu-no-aidani otooto   ni
     you TOP I   NOM while=absent   y. brother DAT

   keisatu-made o-yob-ase-ni-nat-ta   soo
   police-even call-CAUSE (HON)-PAST hearsay

   zya-nai-ka
   isn't=it

   'I heard that you made your younger brother call even
   the plice while I was away.'

2.4.3.3. Reciprocalization

The third argument of ours for the LF-derivation of the complementation in the complex predicate construction concerns the verbal reciprocal suffix *aw*. With or without being accompanied by the reciprocal anaphor *otagai* (each other), this suffix exhibits basic properties quite comparable to those of subject honorification, as illustrated in (90)-(92) below:[77]

(90) a. *Taroo to Ziroo ga saigo-ni-nokotta itimai-no*
          and   NOM remaining   one

    moohu   o   ubai-at-ta   (koto)
    blanket ACC deprive-RECIP-PAST (fact)

    'Taro and Ziro scrambled for the last remaining blanket.'

b. *Yamada-kyoozyu to Tanaka-kyoozyu ga tyoosyuu ni*
        Prof.   and   Prof.   NOM audience DAT

    (otagai   no) gyooseki   o
    each=other GEN academic=records ACC

    syookaisi-at-ta   ato ...
    introduce-RECIP-PAST after ...

    'After Profs. Yamada and Tanaka introduced each other's scholarly records to the audience, ...'

c. **Taroo ga saigo-ni-nokotta itimai-no*
        NOM remaining   one

    moohu   o   ubai-at-ta   (koto)
    blanket ACC deprive-RECIP-PAST (fact)

    'Taro scrambled for the last remaining blanket.'

(91) a. Taroo ga [Ziroo to Hanako ga (otagai   ni)
         NOM   and   NOM each=other DAT

         aisi-at-te-iru]   to   omoikondei-ru (koto)
         love-RECIP-GER-PROG COMP convinced   (fact)

         'Taro is convinced that Ziro and Hanako love
         each other.'

   b. *Taroo ga [Ziroo to Hanako ga (otagai   ni)
         NOM   and   NOM each=other DAT

         aisiteiru] to   omoi-at-te-iru   (koto)
         loving   COMP convince-RECIP-GER-PROG (fact)

         '*Taro is mutually convinced that Ziro and Hanako
         love each other.'

(92) a. *hutari-no kisi* ga oozyo o   kisoi-at-ta
         two   knight NOM princess ACC compete-REC-PAST

         'Two knights competed for the princess.'

   b. *sono kisi ga *hutari-no oozyo*   o
         that knight NOM two   princesses ACC

         kisoi-at-ta
         compete-RECIP-PAST

         'That knight competed for two princesses.'

First, the examples (90a-c) illustrate that a verb headed by *aw* must be licensed by some plural (or distributive) NP. Second, as has been pointed out by Abe (1982), such licensing is clause-bound. This point is illustrated by (91a-b) and (90c)). Finally, the examples (92a-b) illustrated that the licenser of the "reciprocalized" verb must be the subject of the sentence.

Just as in the case of honorification, we can capture these constraints on the reciprocalized verbs in terms of

the notion "licensing under head-government", and offer an
LF licensing condition in (93) below:

(93) *Reciprocalized Verb Licensing Condition*:

At LF, a reciprocalized verb (V-aw) must head-govern
a plural or distributive subject NP.

(subject = [N^{max}, X^{max}])

Let us assume again that the licensing here is formally
represented as the coindexation between the subject NP and
the reciprocalized verb.

The LF derivation in the Affix Raising Approach, for
(92a) for example, will provide us with a syntactic basis
for this licensing, as the coindexation in (94b)
illustrates:

(94) a. *S-str/Pre-LF$_1$*:   b.   *Pre-LF$_2$*:

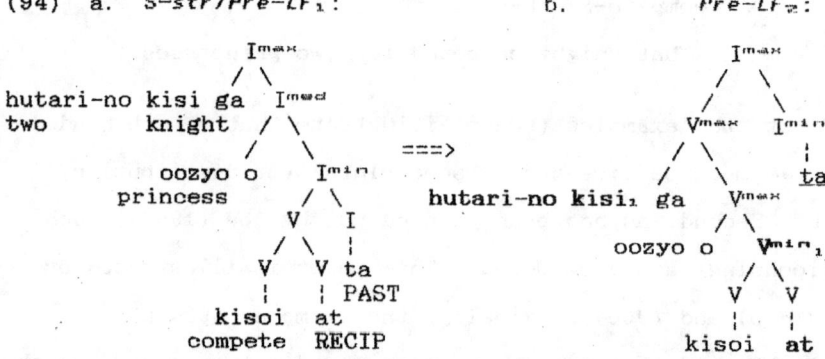

Let us now extend our investigation to the complex
predicate construction, and make an observation (perhaps

novel in the literature) that such "reciprocalization" of verbs may be "cyclic" as in (95) below:

(95)
a. [~NP~ e] nantoka [*ano   hutari* o   igami-*aw*]-ase-ru
              somehow those two   ACC hate-RECIP-CAUSE-PRES

   te wa naimono-ka
   way TOP doesn't=exist-I=wonder

   'I wonder whether there is any way to somehow make those two hate each other.'

b. *CIA to KGB* ga [sono nizyuu-supai ni (otagai   no)
       and   NOM   that double-spy   DAT each=other GEN

   senryoku   o   sagur]-ase-at-te-i-ta (koto)
   fighting=strength ACC search-CAUSE-RECIP-GER-PROG

   'CIA and KGB made that double spy search each other's war potential.'

Interestingly, a dialectal variation quite comparable to that in honorification seems to exist with respect to (95b). For example, Abe (1982) finds an example similar to (95b) rather unacceptable.

With the LF derivations in (96) and (97) below for (95a) and (95b), respectively, we will capture the cyclicity and the dialectal variation here in the way comparable to our account of honorification:

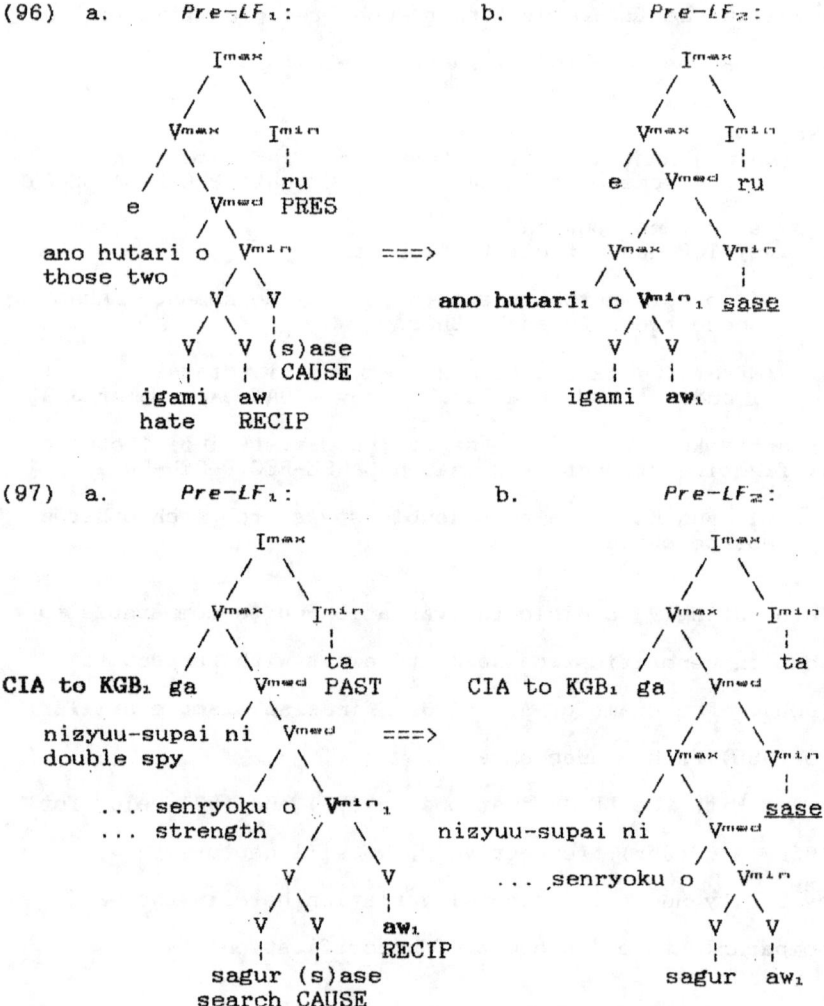

In (96b), the reciprocalized verbal root *igami-aw* (hate-RECIP) is licensed by the causee NP *ano hutari o* (those two ACC). In (97a), on the other hand, it is between the reciprocalized complex verb *sagur-ase-aw* (search-CAUSE-RECIP) and the causer NP *CIA to KGB ga* (CIA and KGB NOM) where the licensing takes place. Thus, the Affix Raising Analysis permits us to capture the "cyclicity" of reciprocalization.

In our analysis, the marked status of the reciprocalized complex predicate in (95b) is also predicted. The crucial assumption here is that the reciprocal suffix *aw* lacks a θ-marking property, which permits the marked application of Move-alpha to *sase* (CAUSE) in (97), given Selkirk's Percolation Conventions. We may, thus, ascribe the dialectal variation concerning (95b), again, to the choice of Selkirk's Percolation Conventions.[30]

An even more interesting observation has been brought into our attention by Nobuko Hasegawa (personal communication). As illustrated by the exmaples in (98) and (99) below, a reciprocalized causative complex verb (e.g., *raibarusis-ase-aw* (regard=as=a=rival-CAUSE-RECIP in (98)) at S-structure may sometimes be licensed at LF by a causee NP and receives an interpretation such that what is reciprocalized is the verbal root rather than the complex predicate:

(98) zurugasikoi Tanaka ga   kakusakusi-te [*waka-i*
     cunning   NOM maneuver-and   young

     hutari ni raibarusi-s]-ase-*at*-ta   (koto)
     two   DAT regard=as=a=rival-CAUSE-RECIP-PAST   (fact)

     'Cunning Tanaka maneuvered the two young people into
     regarding each other as a rival.'

(99) [NP e] [*aaiu gorotuki-domo* wa itido kinosumu-made
              such hoodlums   TOP once until=satisfied

     nagur]-ase-*at*-tara   iindesuyo
     punch-CAUSE-RECIP-COND   advisable

     'It is advisable to let those hoodlums punch each
     other until satisfied.'

The presence of such an interpretation, again, is predicted in the Affix Raising Approach, which provides the LF derivation (100) below for (98):

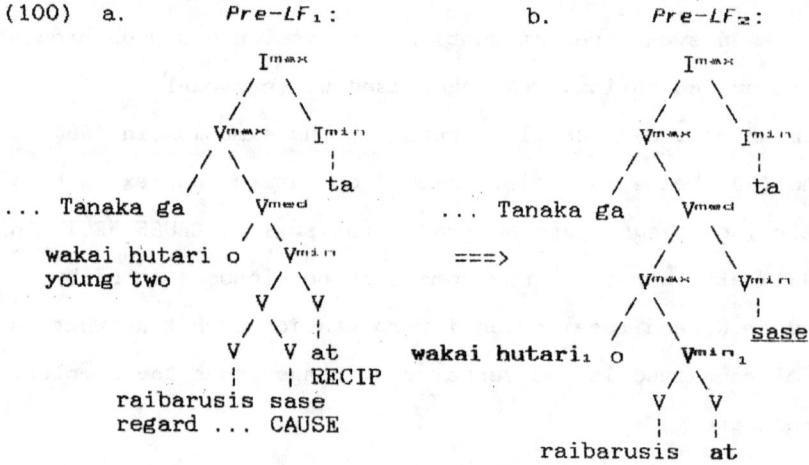

In (100b), the reciprocalized verbal root *raibarusis-aw* (regard=as=a=rival-RECIP) is licensed by head-governing the causee NP *wakai hutari* (young two).

Again, the derivation in (100), hence the resulting interpretation in (98), represents a marked case, involving "visible" deviation from the Mirror Image Derivations, i.e., the morphology-syntax mismatch between the surface string *raibarusis-ase-aw* (regard=as=a=rival=-CAUSE-RECIP) and its interpretation as [*raibarusis-aw*] *sase* ([regard =as=a=rival-RECIP]CAUS). This point can be confirmed when we find a similar reading in (101) below to be secondary to the reading involving the licensing of the reciprocalized complex predicate. Note that, in (101), we find two potential licensers of reciprocalized verbs --- both the causer and the causee:

(101)   *karera* ga *hutari* ni (otagai   no) waruguti o
        they   NOM two   DAT each=other GEN slander ACC

        iw-ase-at-ta   (koto)
        say-CAUSE-RECIP-PAST   (fact)

        'They made the two speak ill of each other.'

We thus have another case supporting the non-string-vacuous application of affix raising at LF.[91]

2.4.4. Summary

To sum up the entire section, we have argued, first, that the complementation involved in the complex predicate construction is syntactic in nature, and it takes place at the level of Logical Form. The relevant observations reported to support this claim are: (i) that certain quantifiers exhibit the (ambiguity of) scope narrower than the scope of some complex-predicate-forming suffixes, and (ii) that the quantifier-like expressions *onazi* (same) and *tigaw* (different) exhibit readings that represent the scope higher and lower than the scope of such suffixes.

We have also argued that the LF complementation in the complex predicate construction is derived by the application of affix raising. This claim has been supported by the observations concerning negative polarity, honorification and reciprocalization, which sometimes require an LF derivation as schematized in (102) (=(1) above):

(102)

```
           C^max                              /\
          /  \                               /  \
  ...    C^min     ===>                     /    B
        /  \                              C^max
       /\   \                    ...      /  \
     [ A  B  C ]                         C^min
                                         /  \
                                       [ A   C ]
```

(C = negative, honorific or reciprocal suffix)

Let us emphasize here that it is highly unlikely that the Verb Raising Approach discussed above can offer any non-ad hoc account for these phenomena, which require a non-string-vacuous reanalysis of the complex predicate construction at LF.

The phenomena we have dealt with in the last three subsections will also force us to reject the Coanalysis Approach to Japanese causatives proposed by Williams (1984b), as an alternative to the Affix Raising Hypothesis. In this approach, the causative construction (98), for example, is assigned two **simultaneous** analyses, presumably as in (103) below --- one syntactic (upper half) and the other **morphological and syntactic** (lower half):

(103)

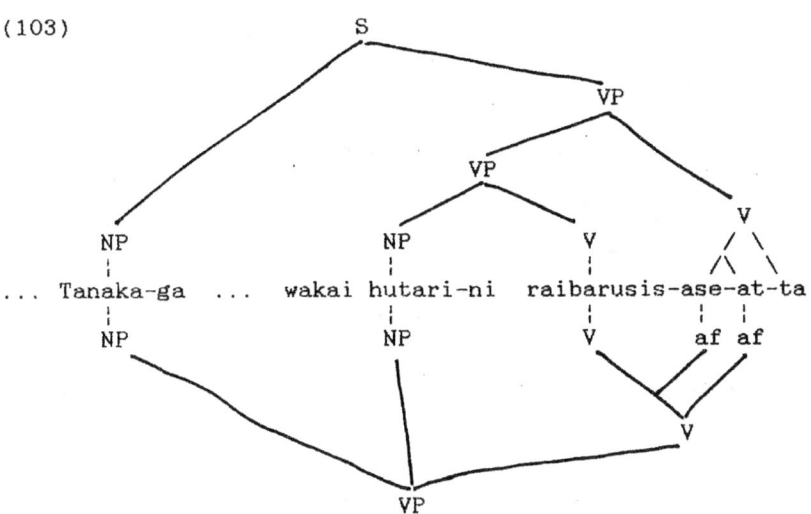

The representation in (103), however, does not allow us to explain how the reciprocalization in the "complement" becomes possible in example (98), precisely because it cannot handle any non-string-vacuous morphology-syntax mismatches.

2.5. Arguments against Lexical Derivation

Kuroda (1981) offers some conterarguments to the lexical derivation of "V + *sase*". The logic of his main argument proceeds as in (1) below:

(1)   (i) If any **syntactically-inserted** item intervenes between the two morphemes making up a complex predicate, the latter must also have been syntactically rather than lexically derived.

       (ii) The negative morpheme *na*, various supplementary particles (*huku-zyosi*) such as *wa* (CONTR), *sae* (even) and *dake* (only), the desiderative morpheme *ta*, and honorific marker *o ... ni nar* are **syntactically** introduced.

      (iii) The items mentioned in (ii) may intervene between a verb and *sase* that make up a complex predicate.

      (iv) Therefore, V-*sase* must be syntactically rather than lexically derived.

Some of the relevant examples from Kuroda are cited in (2)-(5) below.

(2) watasi wa Taroo ni tabako   o   suw-*anaku*-sase-ru
    I   top   DAT cigarette ACC inhale-*NEG*-Cause-PRES

    'I will make Taro not smoke.'

(3) a. watasi wa Taroo ni LI o yomi-*wa*   sase-ru
        I   top   DAT LI ACC read-*CONTR* CAUSE-PRES

        'I will make/let Taro at least read LI.'

    b. watasi wa Taroo ni LI o yomi-*sae* sase-ru
                                     even

        'I will make/let Taro even read LI.'

    c. watasi wa Taroo ni LI o yomi-*dake* sase-ru
                                     only

        'I will make/let Taro only read LI.'

(4) watasi wa Taroo ni tabako   o   sui-*taku*-sase-ru
    I   top   DAT cigarette ACC smoke-*want*-Cause-PRES

    'I will make Taro feel like smoking.'

(5) o-yasumi *ni nari* ta-i dake   o-yasumi *ni nar*-ase   te
    rest   want extent rest   CAUSE and

    o-oki-sita hoo   ga ii-no-de-wa-nai-desu ka
    leave   option nom may=be=good   Q

    'Is it not better to let *pro* rest as much as *pro* wants?'

In (2), (a)*naku* intervenes between V and *sase*.[82] *Naku* is a *renyoo* (sequential-verbal) form of the negative morpheme *na*, and -a- is an augment morpheme inserted between a consonant-ending verbal stem and *na*. In the traditional grammar of Japanese, an adjective is said to take a *renyoo* form when it is followed by a *yoogen* (verb or adjective).

In (3a-c), supplementary particles *wa*, *sae*, and *dake* intervene between V and *sase*.

In (4), *ta* (want) in its *renyoo* form may intervene between V and *sase*.

Finally, in (5), which Kuroda attributes to Susumu Kuno, *ni nar* intervenes between V and *sase* (and in fact V and *ta* (want) also) in the honorified complex predicate.

This is the only **empirical** argument I have found which might lead one to the conclusion that causative complex predicates **cannot** be lexically derived. Let us refer to this argument as the "Intervention" Argument. In what follows, we will reject the Intervention Argument, questioning the validity of its premises (1-ii) and (1-iii).[83] Let us begin with (1iii).

2.5.1. Intervening Negative Morpheme

Our objection to the Intervention Argument starts with the observation Kuroda himself makes: the surface string of the verbal expression in the example (2) (repeated below), may be analyzed not only as in (6a) but also as in (6b) below:[84]

(2) watasi wa Taroo ni tabako   o   suw-*anaku*-sase-ru
    I   top   DAT cigarette ACC inhale-*NEG*-Cause-PRES

   'I will make Taro not smoke.'

(6) a. suw-anaku-sase
        inhale-NEG-CAUSE

    b. [... suw-anaku] *s*-ase   (< s-sase)
                          do-CAUSE

In (6b), *sase* is attached not directly to the negative morpheme but to an irregular verb *s* (do), which in turn selects a complement containing *suw-anaku* (inhale-NEG). (Due to the application of Consonant Deletion, the initial consonant in *sase* drops.) If this surface ambiguity indeed exists, it significantly undermines the Intervention Argument, since the well-formed verbal expression in (2) may now be considered to be an instance of (6b) rather than (6a). The surface ambiguity described in (6), in other words, gives rise to a possibility that the allegedly "syntactically-inserted" negative morpheme does not actually intervene between the verb and *sase* that make up a complex predicate. Let us refer to the analysis in (6) as the "Surface Identity" Analysis.

Kuroda is careful enough to prepare a counterargument to this possibility. He argues that (7) below, a non-causative counterpart of (2), is ungrammatical, and that this discrepancy is good enough to show that the causative expression in (2) cannot be analyzed as in (6b).

(7) Taroo ga tabako   o   suw-anaku su-ru
     nom cigarette ACC smoke-NEG do-PRES

   'Taro tries not to smoke.'

The judgment here, however, is not as clearcut as Kuroda claims. I find the example in (7), for instence, as grammatical and awkward (cf. footnote 82) as (2). The sentence improves with a topic marker *wa* (which often makes a sentence sound more natural in Japanese), and improves still more with a punctual tense and a little more context, as in (8) below:

(8) Taroo wa tutomete   tabako   o   suw-anaku si ta
     top effortfully cigarette ACC smoke-NEG do-PAST

   'Taro tried hard not to smoke.'

Observe also that "*renyoo* form + *s* (do)" is clearly an available option for adjectives in general, as illustrated in (10) below:

(10) ore ga tyotto yasasiku su-ru   to   sugu
     I   nom little gentle do-PRES and moment
     tukeagariyagatte
     puffed=up

   'The moment I show my gentleness, you take advantage of it!'

The negative morpheme *na* behaves as an adjective with respect to conjugation, taking the adjectival tense morphemes *i* (PRES) and *katta* (PAST). There is nothing remarkable, therefore, about the possibility of the expression "*naku* (=*renyoo* form) + *s* (do)" as in (8) above.

In what follows, we will support the Surface Identity Analysis in (6) by further demonstrating that (6b) should be an available option as a possible analysis of the surface string in question.

Our argument for the Surface Identity Analysis (6) comes from the comparison of the categorial selectional properties of *sase* and *rare*.

To begin with, let us take a look at the following paradigm:

(11) a. suw-are   (< suw + rare)
        inhale-PASSIVE

b. suw-ase   (< suw + sase)
        CAUSE

(12) a. *yasasi-rare
        gentle-PASS

b. *yasasi-sase
        CAUSE

Whatever analysis of complex predicates one may adopt, the contrast between (11a-b) and (12a-b) must be somehow accounted for. One possibility is to capture the contrast in terms of the selectional properties of *rare* and *sase*, paying attention to the categorial distinction between *suw* (V) and *yasasi* (A). In any of the approaches we have dealt

with above, the contrast can be captured by saying that
rare and *sase* **morphologically** select only a verb.

If we adopt such a selectional account, we can also
predict the contrast between (11a-b) above and (13a-b)
below: (Recall that the negative morpheme *na* is an
adjective.)

(13)   a.   *suw-ana-rare
            inhale-NEG-PASS

       b.   *suw-ana-sase
            NEG-CAUSE

Crucially, however, an unexpected discrepancy arises
between *rare* and *sase*, when we change the adjectives in
(12) and (13) above into a *renyoo* (*-ku*) form, as in (14)
and (15) below:

(14)   a.   *yasasi*ku*-rare
            gentle-PASS

       b.   yasasi*ku*-sase
            CAUSE

(15)   a.   *suw-ana*ku*-rare
            inhale-NEG-PASS

       b.   suw-ana*ku*-sase
            CAUSE

Note that the contrast between (14a) and (14b) as well as
that between (15a) and (15b) suggests that it is a mistake
to ascribe the ill-formedness of (12a-b) and (13a-b) to the
mere lack of a *renyoo* form in these examples.

One possible way to account for this contrast is to
say that *sase* selects either a verb or an adjective,
whereas *rare* selects only a verb. In this account,
however, it must be additionally stated that when *sase*
selects an adjective, the adjective must be in a *renyoo*
form. Otherwise, the contrast between *yasasi-sase ((12b))
and *yasasiku-sase* ((14b)), and that between *suw-ana-sase
((13b)) and *suw-anaku-sase* ((15b)), would be left
unaccounted for.

A more careful examination of the paradigms in
(14)-(15), however, would allow us to retain the original
account, in which we assumed that both *rare* and *sase*
morphologically select nothing but a verb. There are
two crucial observations involved here.

First, not only *sase* but also *rare* becomes compatible
with a *renyoo* form of an adjective when it is attached not
directly to the adjective but to the irregular verb *s* (do),
which in turn selects a complement containing an adjectival
predicate, as in (16) and (17) below:

(16) a. [... yasasiku] *s*-are   (< yasasiku s-rare)
              gentle   *do*-PASS

      b. [... yasasiku] *s*-ase   (< yasasiku s-sase)
                          do-CAUSE

(17) a. [... suw-anaku] *s*-are   (< suw-anaku s-rare)
              inhale-NEG   *do*-PASS

      b. [... suw-anaku] *s*-ase   (< suw-anaku s-sase)
                            do-CAUSE

Second, the surface strings of (14b) and (17b) (= Adj-*sase*) are identical with those of (16b) and (17b) (= Adj-*s-ase*), respectively, due to the application of the phonological rule of Consonant Deletion in the latter. The claim is, then, that the acceptability of the surface strings *yasasikusase* and *suwanakusase* can be accounted for by the existence of the well-formed analyses of these surface strings as in (16b) (*yasasiku s-ase*) and (17b) (*suw-anaku s-ase*), respectively, even if we label the examples in (15b) (*yasasiku-sase*) and (15b) (*suw-anaku-sase*) ill-formed with the given analysis there, i.e., as a sequence "[-V] + *sase*". In other words, we can account for all the examples in (11)-(17) with a simple and uniform assumption that both *rare* and *sase* select only a verb, when we adopt the Surface Identity Analysis proposed above.

Thus, we have good reason to consider that what the negative morpheme *(a)naku* separates in the surface strings of (2) is a sequence of two independent verbs *suw* (smoke) and *s* (do) rather than a morphologically complex verb *suw-(s)ase* (smoke-CAUSE).

Recall that the Intervention Argument directed against the lexical derivation of complex predicates holds only if the negative morpheme *na(ku)* and other items intervene in a complex predicate (= premise (1 iii)). Since the Surface Identity Analysis supported above casts doubt on the truth of this premise, the validity of the conclusion must also be questioned.

Although we have dealt with only (2), the same objection holds also with (3a-c) and (4) (cf. Kuno (1980)). (3a) and (4) are repeated below as (18) and (19), respectively with our analysis:

(18)   watasi wa Taroo₁ ni [e₁   LI o   yomi-wa]   s-ase-ru
       I   top   DAT   LI ACC read-$CONT$] do-CAUSE

       'I will make/let Taro at least read LI.'

(19)   watasi wa Taroo₁ ni [e₁ tabako   o   sui-taku]
       I   top   DAT   cigarette ACC smoke-want

       s-ase-ru
       do-CAUSE-PRES

       'I will make Taro feel like smoking.'

2.5.2. Intervening Honorific Marker

Let us now turn to Kuroda's example (5), whose relevant portion is repeated below in (20):

(20)   a. o-yasumi ni nari-ta-i
           rest   want-PRES

       b. o-yasumi ni nar-ase-ru
           rest   CAUSE-PAST

Unlike in the other examples we have dealt with above, the right-end honorific markers *ni nar* seem to be truly intervening in the complex predicates here. These examples, therefore, seem to be much more relevant than other examples to the argument against the lexical derivation of complex predicates.

Recall that Kuroda bases his argument on the assumption that the honorific marker in question is **syntactically** (or more precisely **transformationally**) introduced (= premise (1 ii)). The strongest basis for this assumption is Harada's (1976) observation that honorification proceeds cyclically. This, however, does not necessarily argue for the transformational status of honorification since the "cyclicity effects" can be captured also by the Affix Raising Analysis, as we have seen in 2.4.3.2. above. In what follows, we will pursue an alternative view of honorification, that it is basically a **lexical** process.

We make the following proposals concerning subject honorification:[85]

(21) *Subject Honorification*:

    (i)   Subject honorification involves the prefixation of *o-* and the suffixation of *-ni* and *-nar* to a verbal root or stem in the lexicon.[86]

    (ii)   These affixation processes take place at the same level as other complex predicate forming affixation (i.e., at Level *i*, cf. 2.2.2.) in the lexicon.

    (iii) An honorified verb must be licensed at LF by head-governing an SSS (= Subject Honorification Licensing Condition (71) in 2.4.3.2.)

(iv)   One of the honorific markers, *nar*, is
       "accented", i.e., it has an underlying floating
       high tone, as indicated below:
       (See 2.2.4. above.)

/nar/

H

As we have seen in 2.4.3.2. above, the licensing condition (21iii) combined with the Affix Raising Approach allow us to account for the cyclicity effects in honorification and more.

The level-ordering proposed in (21ii) allows us to predict that the right-end honorific markers *ni nar* may freely intervene in a complex predicate as long as their selectional constraints ((21i)) are satisfied, i.e., as long as they are attached to a verbal root or stem. Thus, there is nothing remarkable about the examples like (20a-b) above as well as the ones in (22)-(25) below in this analysis:

(22)   *o*-nomi-*ni*-*nar*-u
          drink

(23) a. *o*-nomi-*ni*-*nar*-ase-ru
          drink   CAUSE

      b. *o*-nom-ase-*ni*-*nar*-u
          drink-CAUSE

(24) a. *o-nom-ni-nari-ta-gar-u*
        drink   want-display

   b. *o-nomi-ta-gari-ni-nar-u*
        drink-want-display

(25) a. *o-nom-ni-nar-ase-ta-gar-u*
        drink   CAUSE-want-display

   b. *o-nom-ase-ni-nari-ta-gar-u*
        drink-CAUSE   want-display

   c. *o-nom-ase-ta-gari-ni-nar-u*
        drink-CAUSE-want-display

Second, the level-ordering in (21ii) combined with the accentedness of the honorific marker ((21iv)) allows us to account for the fact that the honorified verbs exhibit a different accent pattern from phrases, as illustrated in (26)-(28) below:

(26) o-nomi-ni-nar-u
      drink

(27) o-nom-ase-ni-nar-u
          CAUSE

(28) imoya-ni   nar-u
      potate=peddler-DAT become

Compare also the pitch track diagrams of the honorified verbs in Table 3 and Table 4 below with that of a phrasal expression in Table 5:

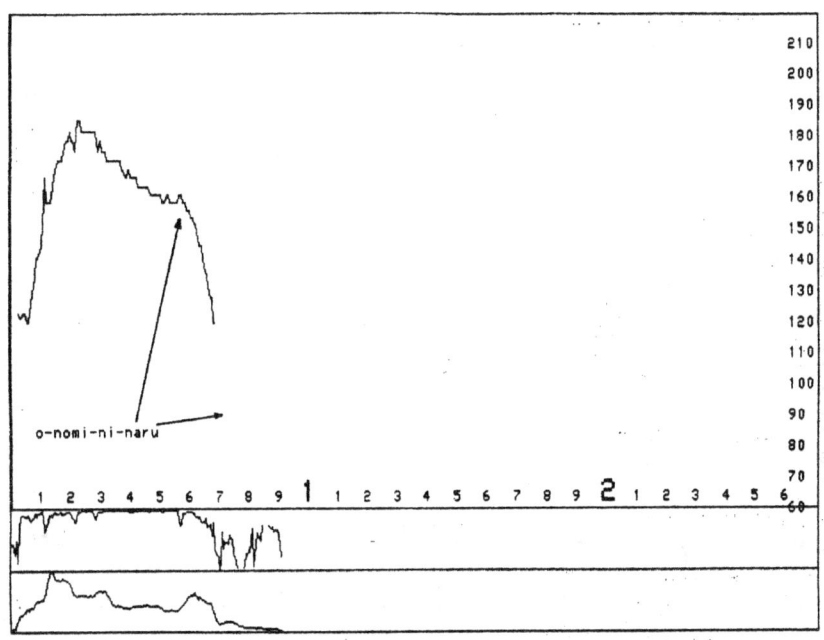

Table 3. Pitch track diagram of o-no'mi-ni-na'r-u

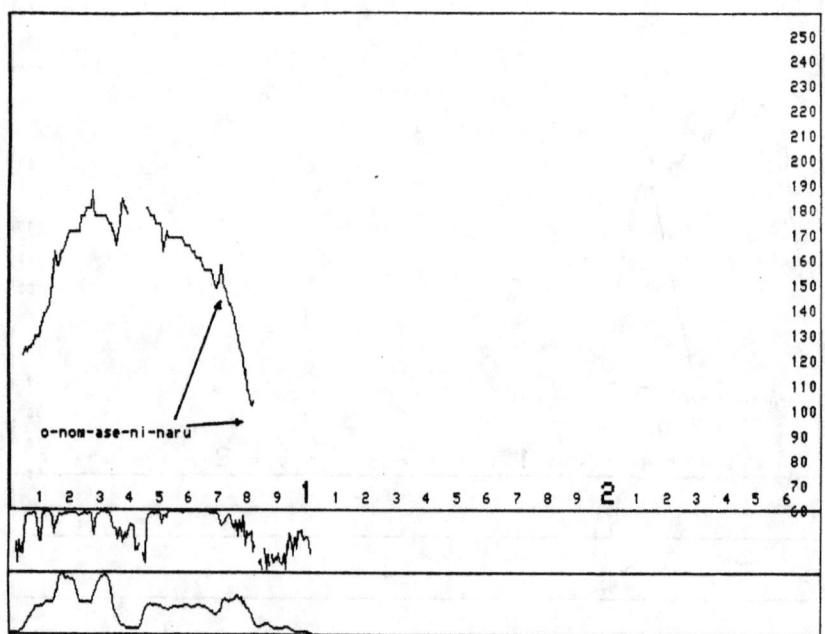

Table 4. Pitch track diagram of o-no'm-ase-ni-na'r-u

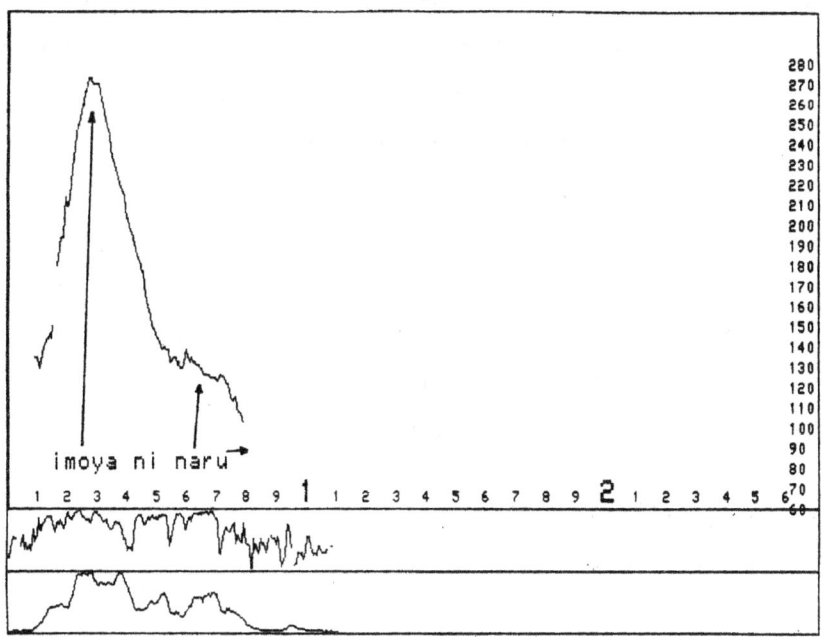

Table 5. Pitch track diagram of imo'ya-ni na'r-u

The honorified verbs in (26) and (27), both of which contain two "accented" items (nom and nar) and the present tense morpheme ru, exhibit a clear lexical pattern with a penultimate accent. Note also that it is a whole complex predicate that is honorified in (27) despite its lexical accent patterned.

The phrasal expression in (28), on the other hand, exhibits downdrift at the second of the two accented items (imoya and nar), which manifests itself as a brief plateau in the middle of the lowering of the pitch.

The contrast here is exactly as we predict if the former, but not the latter, involves the lexical derivation as proposed in (21ii). The underlying accent (floating high tone) of the verbal root *nom* (drink) in (27) is subject to High Tone Deletion (29) below in the lexicon, whereas that of the noun *imoya* (potato=peddler) in (28) is not. Therefore, at the time when Downdrift takes place in the post-lexical phonology, the two examples are represented differently, as in (30) below. (Recall our arguments concerning downdrift in 2.2.4. above.)

(29) *High Tone Deletion*:

   H H ===> ∅ H

(30) a. o-nom-ase-ni-nar-u
           ∅   H

   b. imoya-ni nar-u
          H   H

Thus, (30b), but not (30a), may exhibit downdrift.

Third, the level-ordering (21ii) and the accentedness of the honorific marker (21iv) will also allow us to predict that an honorified verb exhibits a penultimate accent with the present tense (*ru*) and an antepenultimate accent with the past tense (*ta*) even when *nar* is embedded in the middle of an unaccented complex predicate, as illustrated in (31) below: (Recall that ta (PAST) is not introduced at the same level as ru (PRES). See 2.2.2.)

(31) a. o-yame-ni-nar-sase (yame 'stop') ===>

                    H

      o yame-ni-nar-ase'-ru
                  |
                  H

b. o-yame-ni-nar-sase ===>

                H

      o yame-ni-nar-a'se-ta
                |
                H

This also argues for the lexical derivation of honorified verbs as proposed in (21ii).

Finally, the Lexical Analysis of honorification combined with the Surface Identity Analysis of negated causatives will allow us to predict that all the honorified verbs in (32a-c) below are well-formed, whereas that in (33) is not:

(32)
a. Sensei wa gakusei ni rooka   de tabako   o
    Teacher top student DAT corridor in cigarette ACC

    o-suw-ase-ni-nat-ta
    smoke-CAUSE   PAST

    'Our teacher made/let the students smoke in the
    corridor.'

b. Sensei wa gakusei₁ ni [e₁ kyoositu de tabako o
   Teacher top student DAT   classroom in cigarette ACC

   suw-anaku] o-s-ase-ni-nat-ta
   smoke-NEG   do-CAUSE   PAST

   'Our teacher made/let the students not smoke in
   the classroom.'

c. isya no keikoku ga Sensei₁ ni [e₁ tabako o
   doctor GEN warnings NOM Teacher DAT   cigarette ACC

   o-suii-ni-nar-anaku] s-ase-ta
   smoke   NEG   do-CAUSE-PAST

   'The doctor's warnings made our Teacher not smoke.'

(33) *Sensei wa gakusei₁ ni [e₁ kyoositu de
     Teacher top student DAT   classroom in

     tabako   o   o-suw-anaku] s-ase-ni-nat-ta
     cigarette ACC smoke-NEG   do-CAUSE   PAST

     'Our teacher made/let the students not smoke in
     the classroom.'

Note that, in (33), two independent verbs are honorified at a time, hence the ungrammaticality there. Compare (33) with (32a).[87] Thus, both the Lexical Analysis of Honorification and the Surface Identity Analysis for *nakusase* (NEG (do) CAUSE) receive further support.

In conclusion, there is good reason to question the premise (1 ii) in the Intervention Argument with respect to the honorific markers *ni naru*.

2.5.3. Summary

To sum up, we have argued that Kuroda's counterargument to the lexical derivation of complex predicates cannot be accepted at its face value. In 2.5.1., we have argued that a negative morpheme *na(ku)* and other allegedly "syntactically-inserted" items are not actually intervening in a complex predicate in any of Kuroda's examples (2)-(4). In 2.5.2., we have argued that, although the honorific markers *ni nar* do intervene in a complex predicate, this fact does not argue against the lexical derivation of complex predicates, since honorification itself is a lexical process taking place at the same level as various complex predicate formations.[88]

Footnotes to Chapter II

1. The verb *gar* is difficult to translate into English. The best translation I know of is Kuno's (1973) "show a sign of". In this thesis, I will provide "display" as its gloss mainly for ease of presentation. It reflects Martin's (1975) translation "display an emotion or attitude".

2. Hasegawa (1980) is unique in that she takes the positions (2i-ii) but not (2iii-iv). Miyara (1981) also rejects (2iii). We will return to these works in 2.3.5. below.

3. *Sase* becomes *ase* when it follows a consonant-final stem.

4. For (4i), see Kuroda (1965a, 1978), Kuno (1973), Farmer (1980), Miyagawa (1980) and Saito (1982) to name only a few. For (4ii) and (4iii), see Kuroda (1965b), Shibatani (1973, 1974), Harada (1973), C. Kitagawa (1974), Inoue (1976), Tonoike (1978), Y. Kitagawa (1979), Miyara (1981), and Abe (1985), among others, in addition to the above mentioned works.

5. Shibatani (1973, 1976) also claims that a pro-sentence *sore* (it) may ambiguously refer to a "matrix" clause or the "complement" of *sase*. I find it difficult, however, to detect this ambiguity.

6. Although we will concentrate on these two works, there are other important works that also argue for the lexical derivation of (at least some of the) complex predicates. See, for example, Miyara (1981) and Abe (1985).

7. An important assumption underlying this analysis is that Japanese lacks VP as a constituent (Hinds (1973)).

8. The notion "blocking", in other words, is equivalent to "not allowed to enter the PDS". Miyagawa assumes that whether or not blocking entails non-occurrence of the blocked item in the language is a separate issue.

9. Farmer later modifies (19) to deal with a passive construction. (p.136)

10. Hasegawa's (1981) approach with "functional structures" is also subject to the same criticism.

11. We are not here concerned with the "metrical clash".

12. Siegel has also shown that Degemination, Destressing and Velar Softening are triggered by Class I affixation but not by Class II affixation.

13. Selkirk (1982), on the other hand, offers a "syntactic" approach to level ordering, claiming that the lexical levels can be understood as category levels in an X-bar theory of word structure. In this approach, word-internal categories serve as the characteristic domains of the rules of lexical phonology. Nothing in our discussion below hinges on the choice of these two alternatives.

14. It was later pointed out that the boundary symbols "+" (associated with Class I morphemes) and "#" (associated with Class II morphemes) proposed in Chomsky ans Halle (1968) can be eliminated from phonological representations when we introduce level-ordering (Pesetsky (1979), Selkirk (1982), Mohanan (1982), Kiparsky (1982), etc.)

15. At least in some versions of this theory (e.g., Kiparsky (1985)), the same rule is allowed to apply both as a lexical and a post-lexical rule. It should be kept in mind, however, that when a rule has such a dual function, it exhibits a completely distinctive set of properties, depending on its mode of application.

See also Pulleyblank (1983) for a nice summary of the distinction between lexical and post-lexical phonology.

16. To be precise, "on the syllable containing the stem-final mora" (McCawley (1968)).

17. To be more precise, Haraguchi assigns an accent diacritic marker (*), which is later linked with a high tone. We have also slightly modified the rules in order to incorporate Haraguchi's assumption that the rules apply only to "accented" adjectives. These changes, however, do not affect our discussion below.

18. The vowel in the environment here must be specified to be optional in order to account for the accents in the examples like:

(i) no'n-da
     drink-PAST

(ii) ka'n-da

19. See Hayes (1981) for the notion "extrametricality", and Pulleyblank (1983) for its extension to tones.

20. We will disregard the initial lowering effect in the Tokyo dialect. See Haraguchi (1977), Clark (1983), Archangeli and Pulleyblank (1984) and the references cited there for discussion.

21. Note the contrast between this conclusion and Farmer's and Miyagawa's assumptions concerning the status of tense morphemes introduced in 2.1.2. above.

22. Kurata argues that the proposed level-ordering can be motivated independently of accentuation. The following paradigm suggests that Level i suffixation triggers Consonant Deletion, whereas Level j suffixation triggers Consonant Assimilation, when they create a sequence of two consonants:

(i)   a.   but + sase ===> but-ase
            hit   CAUSE

        b.   but + rare ===> but-are
                PASSIVE

        c.   but + ru ===> but-u
                PRES
        ----

        d.   but + ta ===> but-ta
                PAST

(ii)   a.   tomar + sase ===> tomar-ase
            stop

        b.   tomar + rare ===> tomar-are

        c.   tomar + ru ===> tomar-u
        ----

        d.   tomar + ta ===> tomat-ta

(iii) a.   kaw + sase   ===>   kaw-ase
            buy

       b.   kaw + rare   ===>   kaw-are

       c.   kaw + ru   ===>   ka(w)-u

       ----

       d.   kaw + ta   ===>   kat-ta

   This present-past asymmetry also follows straightforwardly if we extend the proposed level-ordering to cover Consonant Deletion and Consonant Assimilation, as in (iv) below:

(iv)   morphological rules   phonological rules

Level i: -ru (PRES)
            -sase (CAUSE)   ===>   Penultimate Accent
            -rare (PASIVE)   Assignment (9)
                                      Consonant Deletion

Level j: -ta (PAST)   ===>   **Consonant Assimilation**

23. One logical possibility left unexamined so far is that *sase* in (14b) independently undergoes accentuation rule, and is later attached to *ta* in the lexicon, and then to *tabe* in syntax, as in (i) below:

(i) sase   ===>   sa'se   ===>   sa'se-ta   ===>   tabe-sa'se-ta
                                                    eat-CAUSE-PAST

   It is quite difficult to maintain this analysis, however, since the accent on *sase* is most likely to originate in the verbal root *tabe* in (i). The lack of an accent in (iia) below, which contains an unaccented verbal root (cf. (iib)), confirms this point:

(ii)   a.   <u>ake</u>-sase-ru   (open-CAUSE-PRES)

       b.   <u>ake</u>-ru   (open-PRES)

24. Coda Nasalization changes the first member of a voiced geminate into a nasal. As pointed out by Ito and Mester, this rule is responsible not only for the surface absence of voiced geminates in Japanese but also for the sequence of a nasal and a voiced obstruent in Intensive Infixation as in (i) below:

(i) a. yokotobi ===> yokottobi 'stepping aside'

b. togaru ===> tongaru 'sharpen'

25. See Ito and Mester (1986) for a treatment of nasal consonants.

26. Ito and Mester also argue that the cyclic application of Voicing Spread within nominal compounds makes it possible to eliminate Otsu's (1980) Right Branch Condition on *Rendaku* voicing in Japanese. This also suggests that Voicing Spread is a lexical process.

27. We assume that underlying accents for most adjectives and all verbs in Japanese are represented as "floating" high tones.

Despite the popular assumption, we must specify the location of underlying accent for at least those adjectives which always exhibit a stem-final accent, as in (i) below:

(i)   a. surudo'-i   b. surudo'-katta
         sharp-PRES   PAST

(ii) a. kawai'-i   b. kawai'-katta
         cute

(iii) a. mizika'-i   b. mizika'-katta
         short

(iv) a. kitana'-i   b. kitana'-katta
         dirty

The desiderative suffix *ta* also seems to belong to this class:

(v)   a. yame-ta'-i
         quit-want-PRES

      b. yame-ta'-katta
                  PAST

Following Pulleyblank (1983), we will assume that the accents of these adjectives are represented as prelinked high tones on the final mora, as in (vi):

(vi) a. surudo   b. ta
            | |
            H   H

28. An augment morpheme -*i*- is inserted between a consonant-ending verb and an adjective.

29. The contrast in (i) below suggests that -*gar* (display) is accented:

(i) a. k̄anasi-i
       sad-PRES

    b. k̄anasi-ḡar-u
              display-PRES

30. It will be made clear below why a phonetically empty argument *e* should be assumed for (3b) but not for (3a).

31. For example: (cf. Sugioka (1984))

(i) a. siryo (N) + huka (A) ==> siryo-buka-i (A)
       thought   deep   thoughtful-PRES

    b. awa (N) + tat (V) ==> awa-dat-u (V)
       suds   stand   foam-PRES

    c. yasasi (A) + sa (N-Affix) ==> yasasi-sa (N)
       gentle   ness   gentleness

32. Kratzer (1984) proposes that a finite sentence in German is the maximal projection of a predicate of the form V-INFL. She further makes an interesting distinction between finite and non-finite sentences.

33. For the arguments that phrase structure in Japanese is configurational, see the works cited in 2.1.2.1. above. We will also provide further motivation for such a configurational analysis in 2.3.5.3. below with respect to adverbial interpretation.
34. See 2.4.3. below for a slight modification and cases involving non-string-vacuous affix raising.

35. This rule voices the initial obstruent of the second member in a morphologically derived word. See Otsu (1980) and Ito and Mester (1986) for the details of this rule.

36. Note that the bracketing paradox here cannot be handled by the "redefinition of relatedness" in Williams' (1981) sense, since this process is restricted to heads.

37. Ø here indicates that the prefix *ko* belongs to a "null category class" (Lieber (1981, p.50)). We assume that this makes it possible for the categorial feature [+V] to percolate up from the VP in (10b). See 2.3.4. and 2.4.3. for related discussions.

38. Lebeaux proposes that the nominal derivational affixes in general subcategorize for a level-neutral projection, e.g., V^{ered}, rather than a category of any specific "bar-level" like V^{min}, V^{med} or V^{max}. He also proposes certain modification of the θ-Criterion. See Lebeaux (1984b) for details.

39. Following Kuroda (1965a), I am assuming here a "uniform" analysis of direct and indirect passives. See 2.3.5.3. below for a brief discussion in the light of adverbial interpretation.

40. This is meant to be the thematic representation of the notion "event-type", which is expressible informally as in (i) below for the sentence (ii):

(i) λe [eat (e) & Agent (e,h) & Theme (e,s)]

(ii) Hanako ga susi o   tabe-ta
     　　　 nom   ACC   eat-PAST

We will provide a syntactic basis for this claim in Chapter Three. See also Williams (1984b) for a similar claim.

41. See Bresnan (1978, 1982), Bach (1983) and Abe (1985), among others, for a different view.

42. See Pesetsky (1982) for the claim that even c-selection is derivative.

43. Although the subject antecedent condition is not exceptionless (cf. Miyagawa (1980), C. Kitagawa (1981)), it is probabaly safe to say that it is a valid descriptive generalization for the core cases of the binding of *zibun*. See 4.3.2.1. below for more details of *zibun*.

44. Hasegawa (1980) proposes an alternative analysis like (i) below, in which *sase* (CAUSE) takes a VP-complement:

(i)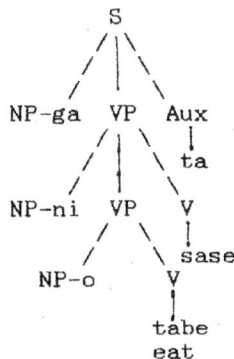

This analysis, however, has some problems. For example, whether the NP-*ni* in (i) is θ-marked by *sase* or *tabe* (eat), violation of the θ-Criterion seems to be unavoidable, since NP-*ni* is analyzed as the internal argument of *sase* and the external argument of *tabe* at the same time, in the sense of Williams (1981b).

Since (i) is assumed to be a D-structure representation, our arguments in 2.2. for the lexical derivation of complex predicates also run counter to it.

Miyara (1981) also claims that the complement in the *ni*-causative (but not in the *o*-causative) is a clause without tense and COMP, which he labels as "S'".

45. The parallelism between (39a-b) and (40a-b) supports Kuroda's (1965) claim that direct and indirect passives uniformly involve syntactic complementation, contra N. McCawley (1972b) and Kuno (1973). See Howard and Niyekawa-Howard (1976) for a nice summary of discussion.

46. Abe (1985) regards the adverbial in (49b) as unambiguous, and offers an analysis within a version of categorial grammar.

47. We have already seen above that the Affix Raising Approach incorporating FI will provide us with a simple account of the bracketing paradox in Japanese ((8)-(9)).

48. We will assume that the indexing on V^{main} percolates down to its head item *sase* (cf. Williams (1981a)).

49.   Although the adverb could be immediately dominated by the I^{max} node in (62a) and (63a), it will not affect our arguments. Rather, what is truly at stake is that the linear position of the adverb in this sentence allows it to be dominated by the lower V^{max} node in (63c) after *sase* moves out of the complex predicate. In the other examples below as well, we will be concerned only with the adverbial appearing in the relevant position in a tree.

50.   This is one interpretation of Willimas' (1984a) "Atomicity Thesis" in syntax, which disallows sentence grammar rules to refer to the interior of words.

51.   In May (1985, 34), Aoun and Sportiche's (1983) rather than Reinhart's definition of "c-command" is used.

52.   See Postal (1971), Wasow (1974), Chomsky (1976), Reinhart (1976), Koopman and Sportiche (1982), Higginbotham (1983), Safir (1984), Saito and Hoji (1983), among others, for discussions of "crossover" phenomena.

53.   The example (13) is more than two-ways ambiguous. We will concentrate here, however, on the readings indicated in (14).

54.   I believe that the reading in (16a) is available independent of the specificity of *dokokano hakubutukan* (somewhere museum), hence represents the scope relation indicated there. Hoji (1985), on the other hand, claims that quantified adverbs in Japanese never exhibit scope ambiguities. If this claim is correct, we cannot rely on the exmaple (15a). The example (15b), which involves scrambling of quantified arguments, however, still demonstrates the point at issue.

55.   As we will discuss in Chapter Three, quantifiers may also have scopes relative to Aux. This also poses a significant problem for the PAS Approach to quantification.

56.   See also Haïk (1985) and references cited there.

57.   To be more precise, Carlson considers that a plural/distributive NP is only one instantiation of "plural eventuality", which is the crucial licensing factor.

58.   * here is meant to indicate the unavailability of the intended S-internal comparison.

59.   *Betuno* (distinct/another) also seems to exhibit a similar behavior.

60.   See McGloin (1976), Muraki (1978), Kuno (1983), etc., and references cited there for a more extensive study of negation in Japanese.

See also Ladusaw (1979) and Linebarger (1980), among others, for discussions of semantic versus syntactic treatments of negative polarity items.

61.   See McGloin (1972, 1976) for discussion as to what counts as the legitimate negative environment to license negative polarity items in Japanese.

62.   The scope ambiguity of *sika na* exists independent of the lexical ambiguity of *sase* (CAUSE) between "coercive" and "permissive" readings. This point can be verified when we turn to other complex predicate constructions directly below. McCawley and Momoi (1986) make a similar observation concerning the *-te* construction.

63.   In the semantic representations in (50)-(52):   (i) I am rather loosely mixing arguments and adverbs, (ii) I have translated the passive morpheme *rare* into "RECEIVE", following Makino (1973), and (iii) the control property between arguments is indicated by the coindexation.

64.   We will deal with two alternative syntactic approaches to this problem in 2.4.3.1.4. below.

65.   After *na* (NEG) is raised out of (55b), it also has a choice of adjoining to the V^{max} headed by *sase* (CAUSE). This choice, however, will lead us to an LF representation identical to (53c), hence does not add anything new to our analysis.

66.   A similar marked application of affix raising as in (i) below would yield a representation in which the θ-Criterion is violated. We thus correctly predict that the verb may not take scope over tense here:

(i)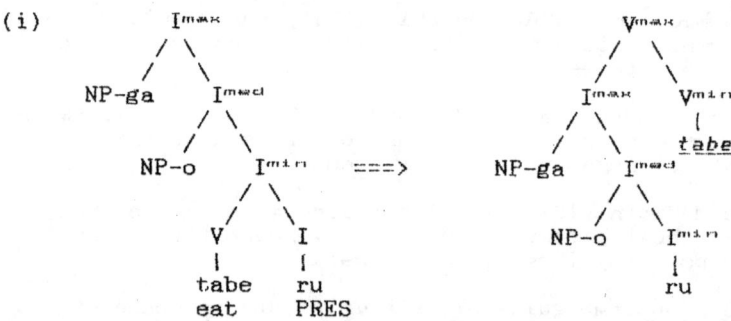

67. McGloin also proposes such an extension. Her analysis is more complicated, involving the lowering of *sika-na* as an underlying predicate in an abstract logical structure.

68. One potential problem to the Affix Raising Approach is that the example (49) (repeated below) is only two-ways, not three-ways, ambiguous despite the fact that it involves two derivational suffixes *ta* (want) and *gar* (display)

(49) ano ban   kare wa mezurasiku biiru-*sika*
      that night he   TOP unusually beer-but

      nom-ita-gar-ana-katta
      drink-want-display-PAST

      'That night, he unusually showed his desire only for beer.'

In particular, it lacks the reading represented as (i) below:

(i) WANT (Taroo$_1$, ONLYx, x=beer [DISPLAY (e$_1$, DRINK (e$_1$, x))])

In fact, more generally, a multiply-suffixed complex predicate involving *sika na* is predicted to exhibit a multiple scope ambiguity, if non-string-vacuous affix raising is freely permitted.

Recall, however, that we have adopted a position such that non-string-vacuous affix raising is regulated by Selkirk's percolation convention. The affix raising as in (ii) and (iii) below, therefore, can be blocked due to the presence of the θ-marking properties of the suffixes to the right of the moved suffixes:

(iii) ... nom-(i)ta-gar-ana ===> ... nom-gar-ana] ta

(iv) .. tabe-sase-ta-gar-ana ==> .. tabe-ta-gar-ana] sase

I am grateful to Hajime Hoji for bringing this issue into my attention.

69. A phonological rule of Consonant Assimilation changes *nar* into *nat* before another consonant. See 2.2. above.

70. We will disregard honorification of adjectives in this thesis.

71. See Saito (1982) for some exceptions to this generalization.

72. I am assuming here that honorified verbs, tensed or untensed, are derived in the lexicon. This assumption is in line with the conclusion in 2.2. above. We will further argue for the lexical derivation of honorified verbs in 2.5. below.

Following Harada (1976), we tentatively assume that an honorified verb has an internal structure as indicated in (70b). Another good possibility is to assume that it involves nominalization by a phonetically-null suffix (indicated by *e*), as illustrated in (i) below:

(i)
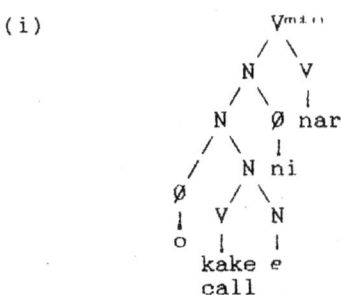

73. To be more precise, we should probably consider that the coindexation at LF serves **only as a basis for** the licensing of honorification which takes place in a later level of representation. In other words, the notion SSS probably becomes relevant in a more semantic and/or pragmatic interpretation of honorified expressions. We will continue to assume (71), however, for simplicity.

74. The example (72b) becomes somewhat awkward without *sasiage-ta* (respectfully=give-PAST). It seems to be generally disallowed to license a surface honorified verb with an SSS, and at the same time make this SSS causee of causation without indicating deference on the part of the causer. Pragmatically, this constraint makes sense.

75. The term "dialect" here is not intended to represent a variety of a language in different geographical areas or social groups. Perhaps, a more precise labeling of what we will be dealing with is "groups of idiolects". We will continue to use the term "dialect", however, for ease of reference.

76. As has been pointed out to me by Hajime Hoji (personal communication), we also predict that the speakers of Dialect B disallow the lower scope reading of *sika na* ((46b)) for the example (44). (Recall that this reading is made possible by non-string-vacuous affix raising, as illustrated in (55) above.) I have been unable to attest this prediction.

77. One potential problem here is the ill-formedness of the example like (i) below, in which the causer is the first person pronoun *watasi* (I):

(i) *watasi ga Sensei ni bansyaku-made
     I   NOM Teacher DAT daily=drink-even

    o-yame-sase-*ni-nat*-ta (koto)
    stop-CAUSE (HON)-PAST (fact)

'I made my teacher quit his daily drink at dinner.'

Note that this sentence cannot be ruled out in our analysis presented above.

    One possibility is that the first person subject is special in that the sentence becomes ungrammatical if an honorified verb head-governs it at any stage of derivation.

    I am grateful to Susumu Kuno for bringing this issue into my attention.

78. For some reason, neither indirect nor direct passives exhibit a similar maked interpretation with the honorified verbal root:

(i) *aitu   wa *Sensei* ni sakuhin o
    that=brat TOP Teacher   by work   ACC

   o-home-rare-*ni-nat*-ta
   praise-PASSIVE (HON)-PAST

   'That brat had his work praised by our teacher.'

(ii) *aitu₁   wa *Sensei* ni e₁ *o*-nagur-are-*ni-nat*-ta
     that=brat TOP Teacher   by   punch-PASSIVE (HON)-PAST

    'That brat was punched by our teacher.'

Observe, however, that even the surface honorified verbal root cannot be licensed in the passive examples (cf. (72b)):

(iii) *aitu   wa Sensei   ni sakuhin o
      that=brat TOP Teacher by work   ACC

     o-home-*ni-nar*-are-ta
     praise (HON)-PASSIVE-PAST

     'That brat had his work praised by Our teacher.'

(iv) *aitu₁   wa Sensei   ni e₁ *o*-naguri-*ni-nar*-are-ta
     that=brat TOP Teacher by   punch (HON)-PASSIVE-PAST

    'That brat was punched by our teacher.'

   Although Susumu Kuno (personal communication) has provided me with (v) below as a counterexample, this example seems to involve honorification of an adjective rather than a verb (cf. *o-genki-ni-nar* 'become high-spirited'):

(v) *Sensei* ni hara no soko-made
    Teacher by belly GEN bottom-even

    o-mitoosi-*ni-nar*-are-te   wa tamarimasen
    see=through (HON)-PASSIVE-GER TOP intolerable

    'I must surrender, having my real intention read by you, my teacher.'

79. Again, Consonant Assimilation changes *aw* to *at* before another consonant.

80. Again, we predict, but have been unable to attest, that those who do not accept the honorification of complex predicates will disallow the reciprocalization of complex predicates as well.

81. While it is relatively harder to find relevant examples, at least indirect passives seem to allow a similar marked interpretation of reciprocalized verbs, as illustrated by (i) below:

(i) kokono zinusi-san wa [hutari-no kosakunin   ni
    this   landlord   TOP   two   tenant=farmer by

    kenkas]-are-at-te   oozyoositeiru
    quarrel-CAUSE-RECIP-and   in=trouble

    'The landlord here is suffering from two of his
     tenants' quarreling with each other.

82. Following Kuroda, we regard (2) as a basically grammatical sentence although it is slightly awkward for some reason. See Kuroda for discussion.

83. As has been pointed out to me by David Pesetsky (personal communication), the validity of (1-i) is not so clearcut, either. Some of the verb-particle constructions in English, for example, may count as lexically-derived expressions with an intervening lexical item:

(i) a. **turn** the light **on**

    b. **look** it **up**

84. Kuno (1980) also makes this observation concerning examples similar to (3a-c).

85. Again, we are concentrating on the honorification of verbs.

86. The interdependence among the three instances of affixation (*o-*, *-ni* and *-nar*) should probably be captured in terms of the morphological licensing condition for the suffix *nar* as in (i) below, extending the notion "head-government" from syntax to morphology:

(i) *-nar* must head-govern *o-* and *-ni*.

87. Presumably, (i) below is ill-formed because the honorification marker is attached to an adjective rather than a verb:

(i) *o-suw-anaku-*ni*-*nar*
    inhale-NEG

88. In fact, it is not at all clear whether the negative morpheme *na* and various *hukuzyosi* like *wa* (CONT), *sae* (even) and *dake* (only) are truly introduced transformationally or otherwise syntactically.

The appearance of *na* to the left of *i* (PRES) and *katta* (PAST) in a word, for example, suggests that it be also lexically introduced. Although a word containg *na* shows an irregular accent pattern (cf. McCawley (1968)), a slight complication of an analysis will still allow us to make it fall under a lexical pattern.

CHAPTER III
DERIVING SUBJECTS

3.1. Subjects in Japanese

In the previous chapter, we have argued that complex predicates like V-*sase-ru* (V-CAUSE-PRES) and V-*ta-i* (V-want-PRES) are derived in the lexicon and inserted into a syntactic structure as a coherent lexical item. In particular, we have argued that not only the derivational suffixes like *sase* (CAUSE), *rare* (PASSIVE) and *ta* (want) but also the inflectional suffixes like *ru/i* (PRES) and *ta/katta* (PAST) are also lexically introduced and derive a word. Once this position is taken, there is in fact no reason not to assume that a "simplex" predicate as in (1a) below is also derived in the lexicon and introduced into a syntactic structure as a derived word, as in (1b):

(1) a. Nihonzin ga sasimi o   tabe-ru
        Japanese NOM   ACC eat-PRES

   'Japanese people eat sashimi (= sliced raw fish).'

   b. D-/S-str:

$$
\begin{array}{c}
I^{max} \\
/\ \ \backslash \\
NP\text{-}ga \quad I^{med} \\
\phantom{NP\text{-}ga\ }/\ \backslash \\
\phantom{NP\text{-}ga\ }NP\text{-}o \quad I^{min} \\
\phantom{NP\text{-}ga\ NP\text{-}o\ }/\ \backslash \\
\phantom{NP\text{-}ga\ NP\text{-}o\ }V \quad I \\
\phantom{NP\text{-}ga\ NP\text{-}o\ }|\quad\ | \\
\phantom{NP\text{-}ga\ NP\text{-}o\ }tabe\ \ ru
\end{array}
$$

Since we have also argued that the tense morpheme *ru*, for example, is raised out of the predicate to satisfy its syntactic c-selectional property (+[V^{max} __]), what our analysis amounts to is the claim that the subject of a sentence in Japanese is first generated as the subject of I^{max} ([N^{max}, I^{max}]) at D-structure but (typically) turns into the subject of V^{max} ([N^{max}, V^{max}]) at LF due to the application of affix raising, as in (2) below:

(2)   *LF*:

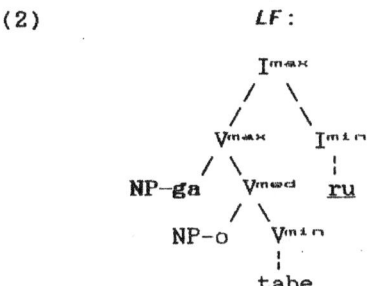

Borrowing from Borer (1986), let us refer to the subject of I^{max} as "I-subject" ("I" for "Inflectional"). Moreover, let us extend this terminology, and refer to the subject of V^{max} as in (2) above and the subject of A^{max} as in (4) below as "T-subject" ("T" for "Thematic"): ((4) represents (3b).)

(3) a. atama ga ita-i
head NOM hurt-PRES

b. Yamada-san ga rekisi ni kuwasi-i
NOM history DAT knowledgeable-PRES

'He is very knowledgeable about history.'

(4)   LF:

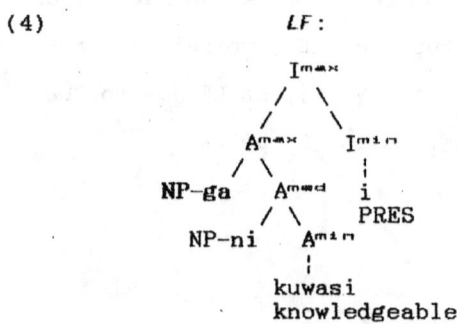

Our proposal is, in other words, that, in Japanese, T-subjects are derived at LF from the base-generated I-subjects.

One immediate motivation for this analysis, particularly for the postulation of T-subjects at LF, comes from the simplification it brings to the Theta Theory. Up to now in the literature of Government and Binding Theory, the θ-marking of objects and that of subjects have always been treated separately. Objects are θ-marked under government by a lexical head within its maximal projection. Subjects, on the other hand, are assumed to be θ-marked by VP.

Several attempts have been made to justify this
dichotomy of θ-marking. For example, it has been argued
that the "compositionality" of the θ-role assigned to
subjects requires VP to be the θ-marker (Marantz (1981),
Hasegawa (1981), Aoun and Sportiche (1981), etc.). It has
also been pointed out that θ-marking by VP can perhaps be
mediated by "predication" even if the structural relation
"government" does not hold (Travis (1984)).

While these approaches are not out of the question,
it will be simpler if both subjects and objects can be
θ-marked under government. Given the T-subject Analysis as
in (2) above, such a simplification of the Theta Theory
will be made possible. Notice that, in (2) above, the
T-subject "NP ga" can be θ-marked under head-government
either by V^{min} or V^{max}, whichever may turn out to be the
correct θ-assigner. In 3.2. below, we will argue that
exactly the same story holds in English with an analysis we
will offer there.

The T-subject Analysis of LF representations in
Japanese may also be motivated in the light of the Empty
Category Principle (ECP) as stated in (5) below
(cf. Chomsky (1981), Lasnik and Saito (1984), etc.)

(5) a. *Empty Category Principle*:

    A nonpronominal empty category must be properly
    governed at LF.

b. *Proper Government*:

   A properly governs *B* if *A* governs *B* and

   (i) *A* is a lexical category X^0 (Lexical Government)
   or
   (ii) *A* is coindexed with *B*, and no NP or S' node intervenes between the two (Antecedent Government)

It has been proposed by Huang (1982) and Lasnik and Saito (Ibid.) that the INFL in languages like Chinese and Japanese must be stipulated to be a proper governor, in contrast to languages like English and French. The crucial observation is that the sentence in (6) below may be interpreted as in (7): (This observation was originally made by Huang (1982) concerning Chinese.)

(6) zeimusyo   wa [*dare ga nani o* katta ka]
    revenue=office TOP who NOM what ACC bought COMP[+WH]

    sirabeteiru   no
    investigating Q

(7) who is the person *x* such that the revenue office is investigating what *x* bought

The fact that (6) can be interpreted as (7) suggests that Japanese permits the following LF representation:

(8) *LF*: [s· dare₁ ga [s· zeimusyo wa [s· nani₂ o [s· t₁ t2
         katta ka]] sirabeteiru no]]

Since *dare ga* (who NOM) cannot antecedent govern its trace due to the intervening S-bar nodes, it has been concluded that this trace must be lexically governed, hence the stipulation that INFL in languages like Japanese and Chinese counts as a lexical governor.

In the T-subject Analysis as in (2) above, on the other hand, no such extra assumption is necessary to account for the absence of ECP violations in (6). The T-subject there is lexically governed by the verbal head within its projection, just as the object is. This is a significant simplification of the theory of government.

A piece of confirmation of this analysis can be obtained when we examine how the "major subjects" in Japanese interact with the ECP.

"Major subject"[1] refers to one (or more) sentence-initial ga-marked NP(s) followed by another full clause. Yamada-san ga (the Yamadas NOM) in (9) below is an example of a major subject:

(9) Yamada-san ga go-tyoonan   ga daigaku ni
                NOM HON-eldest=son NOM college DAT

    gookakus-are-ta
    pass-HON-PAST

    'Yamada-san's eldest son passed the entrance
    examination for a college.'

Since the verb gookakus (pass) in (9) is a two-place predicate and the tense morpheme ta (PAST) syntactically c-selects V^{max}, the Affix Raising Approach will provide us with the derivation at LF as in (10) below:[2]

(10) a. $S\text{-}str/Pre\text{-}LF_1$:   b. $Pre\text{-}LF_2$:

```
         I^max                                I^max
        /    \                               /    \
 Yamada-san ga  I^med                  Yamada-san ga  I^med
              /    \                               /    \
       gotyoonan ga   I^med    ===>          V^max         I^min
                    /    \                  /    \          |
            daigaku ni    I^min       gotyoonan ga  V^med   ta
                         /   \                    /    \
                        V     I              daigaku ni   V^min
                        |     |                            |
                     gookakus ta                        gookakus
```

Notice that, in the pre-LF representation (10b), the T-subject *gotyoonan ga* (HON-eldest=son NOM) is lexically governed by the verb but the major subject *Yamada-san ga* (the Yamadas NOM) is not. One possible prediction that the T-subject Analysis makes, then, is that the LF-extraction of a major subject out of certain domains --- for example, out of a complex NP --- will yield a violation of the ECP, just as the extraction of an adjunct from the same domains does (Lasnik and Saito (1984)), as illustrated in (11) below:

(11) *anata wa [$_{NP}$ [$_{S}$ kare ga *naze* e_1 oti-ta] daigaku$_1$]
      you TOP   he NOM why   fail-PAST college

     o   zyukennasaru otumori   desu ka?
     ACC apply (HON) intention is   Q

     '*Why$_1$ are you applying to the college which$_2$ he
       failed to get in e_2 t_1?'

This prediction seems to be borne out --- for many speakers, (12c) below is significantly worse than (12a-b) unless it is uttered as an echo question:

(12)
a. watasi mo [$_{NP}$ [$_{Imax}$ Yamada-san ga [$_{Vmax}$ gotyoonan ga
    I   also   NOM   eldest=son NOM

    e$_1$ gookakusare]-ta] daigaku$_1$] o zyukensuru tumori
          pass   PAST college   ACC apply=to   intention

    desu
    is

    'I also intend to apply to the college Yamada-san's
    eldest son got in.'

b. anata wa [$_{NP}$ [$_{Imax}$ Yamada-san ga [$_{Vmax}$ *nanbanme-no*
    you   TOP   NOM   which=order-GEN

    musukosan ga e$_1$ gookakusare]-ta] daigaku$_1$] o
    son   NOM   pass   PAST college   ACC

    zyukennasaru otumori   desu ka
    apply=to   intention is   Q

    '*Which son of Yamada-san's do you intend to apply to
    the college which he succeeded to get in?'

c. *anata wa [$_{NP}$ [$_{Imax}$ *donata*   ga [$_{Vmax}$ gotyoonan ga
    you   TOP   which=person NOM   eldest=don NOM

    e$_1$ gookakusare]-ta] daigaku$_1$] o
          pass   PAST college   ACC

    zyukennasaru otumori   desu ka
    apply=to   intention is   Q

    'Which person is such that you intend to apply to the
    college which his eldest son has succeeded to get in?'

A similar ECP violation arises when the major subject is extracted from a *wh*-island at LF:

(13) a. zeimusyo   wa [ɪmax Yamada-san ga [vmax okusan
         revenue=office TOP   NOM   wife

   ga sono hooseki o   ikura-de   kat]-ta] ka
   NOM that jewel   ACC how=much-for buy PAST COMP

   sirabeteiru
   investigating

   'The revenue office is investigating how much
   Yamada-san's wife paid for that jewel.'

b. zeimusyo   wa [ɪmax Yamada-san ga [vmax okusan
   revenue=office TOP   NOM   wife

   ga *nani o   ikura   de* kat]-ta] ka
   NOM what ACC how=much for buy PAST COMP

   sirabeteiru   no
   investigating   COMP

   'What is the revenue office investigating how much
   Yamada-san's wife paid for?'

c. *zeimusyo   wa [ɪmax dare ga [vmax okusan ga
   revenue=office TOP   who NOM   wife   NOM

   nani o kat]-ta] ka   sirabeteiru   no
   what ACC buy PAST COMP investigating COMP

   '*Who is the revenue office investigating
   what his wife bought?'

For many speakers, (13b) may be interpreted as in (14)
below, whereas (13c) may never be interpreted as in (15),
with the major subject *dare ga* (who NOM) taking the matrix
scope:

(14) what is the thing *x* such that the revenue office is
     investigating how much Yamada-san's wife bought *x* for

(15) who is the person *x* such that the revenue office is
     investigating what *x*'s wife bought.

The judgments just reported concerning the examples (12c) and (13c), thus, suggest that major subjects are not lexically governed.

While examining these examples with my informants, on the other hand, I have noticed that a rather clear dialectal split exists in the native speakers' judgments --- one group of speakers clearly recognize the distinction, for example, between (12b) and (12c) as reported above, whereas another group of people do not detect any significant distinction between the two.

One possible source of this dialectal variation may lie in the way major subjects are θ-marked. While it has been pointed out by Kuno (1973), Saito (1982) and C. Kitagawa (1982), among others, that a certain semantic or pragmatic relation must hold between the major subject and the rest of the sentence, the source of its θ-role seems to have been left unidentified in the literature. In order to retain the universality of the θ-Criterion, however, we must assume that major subjects do receive a θ-role. We therefore tentatively propose that major subjects are θ-marked by I^{max} under head-government (cf. (10b)). It may be the case, then, that the grammar of one dialect identifies only **lexical** θ-markers (X^{min}) as possible lexical governors, whereas the grammar of another dialect permits **any** θ-markers, whether lexical or non-lexical, to behave as lexical governors. The results will be that the former dialect recognizes the ECP violations in (12c) (and (13c)), while the latter dialect does not. If this account has any plausibility, the dialectal variation in question does not necessarily undermine the T-subject Approach to the ECP phenomena in Japanese.

There seems to be another complication. Hajime Hoji and Nobuko Hasegawa (personal communication) have reported to me that the ECP violation we have observed above disappears when the *wh*-phrase in a major subject position "inalienably possesses" a regular subject, as in (16) below:

(16) a. Keioo-byooin de wa [NP [Imax Yamada-san ga
       hospital   at TOP   NOM

   [Vmax *dotirano me ga* mienakunat]-ta] gen'in] ga
         which   eyes NOM lost=sight-PAST cause   NOM

   kaimei-deki-na-katta no-desuka
   could=not=figure=out Q

   'At Keio Hospital, which eye of Yamada-san's
    couldn't they figure out the cause for losing
    sight?'

b. Keioo-byooin de wa [NP [Imax *dare ga* [Vmax *me ga*
      hospital   at TOP   who NOM   eye NOM

   mienakunat]-ta] gen'in] ga kaimei-deki-na-katta
   lost=sight-PAST   cause   NOM could=not=figure=out

   no-desuka
   Q

   'At Keio Hospital, about who couldn't they figure
    out the cause for his eyes's losing sight?'

If this indeed is the case generally, it requires some extra explanation. Although we do not have any definite answer to this question at this moment, one possibile move to take is to ascribe the special status of the examples like (16b) to the "inalienable possession" holding between the major subject and the regular subject. For example, it may have an effect of making the V^{max} transparent so that the G-root for the head-government by the verbal head will be the I^{max}, as illustrated in (17) below: (Let us express the inalienable posession in terms of coindexation here. The diagram is simplified for ease of exposition.)

(17)
```
                    Iᵐᵃˣ = G-root
                   /  \
           dare₁ ga    Iᵐᵉᵈ
                      /  \
                     /    \
                   (Vᵐᵃˣ)  Iᵐⁱⁿ
                   /  \      |
               me₁ ga  Vᵐⁱⁿ  ta
                        |
                    mienakunar
```

3.2. Subjects in English

Suppose that the postulation of the Logical Form T-subjects (e.g., V^{max}-internal subjects) is not limited to the grammar of Japanese but is extendable to the grammar of other languages. An immediate objection to this move may come from English, in which subjects may precede various auxiliary elements at S-structure, as exemplified by (1) below, hence are unlikely to become located within V^{max} at LF:

(1)
```
            I^max
           /    \
         you    I^med
               /    \
            I^min    V^max
              |     /    \
             can  V^min   it
                    |
                   do
```

The purpose of this section is to propose and motivate an analysis that allows us to neutralize such discrepancies between Japanese and English. If successful, such an attempt will permit us to extend the T-subject Analysis of Logical Form representations from Japanese to English, and take a significant step toward the reduction of the language-particular variations of the basic features of Logical Form.

3.2.1. Subject Raising Approach

We propose the following syntactic analysis for English, which we will refer to as the "Subject Raising" Approach:

(2) *Subject Raising Approach*:

   (i) At D-structure, the subject of a sentence in English is generated under V^{max}.[3]

   (ii) At S-structure, Move-alpha raises the subject out of V^{max}, and places it under I^{max}, leaving a trace behind.[4]

   (iii) At LF, the trace left behind behaves as a T-subject.

This analysis can be illustrated by the derivation in (3) below:

(3)

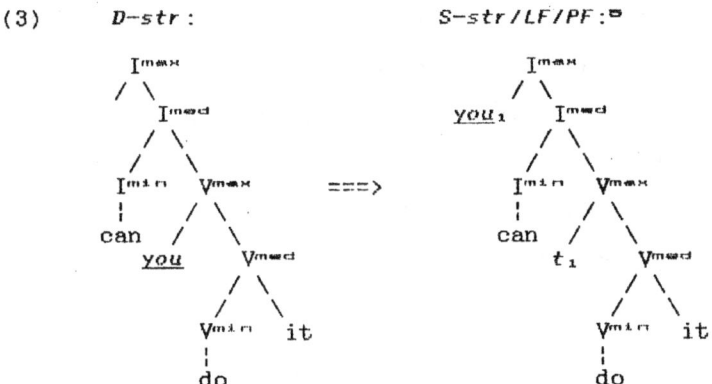

In a sense, we are proposing an analysis for English that is opposite to the one we have offered for Japanese --- I-subjects are derived at S-structure from the base-generated T-subjects.[6]

One crucial feature to be emphasized here is that this analysis retains the base-generated T-subject in the form of a trace even at the level of LF. This is precisely

what allows us to assimilate the analysis for English to
that for Japanese. Thus, we can motivate this analysis
exactly in the same way as we motivated the T-subject
Analysis for Japanese in the light of the Theta Theory.
The θ-marking of subjects can now be done within the
maximal projection of the θ-marker under head-government
--- no complication of the theory is necessary.

Notice that this simplification of the Theta Theory
does not preclude us from accounting for subject-object
asymmetries in English using the ECP. Even if the subject
is θ-marked and lexically governed at the base-
generated position within V^{max}, the intermediate trace (t')
left by the movement of the I-subject as in (4b) below is
still subject to the ECP. As a result, the "*that*-trace
effect" as in (4a) below shows up:[7]

(4) a. *who₁ do you think that t₁ can do it?

b. LF:

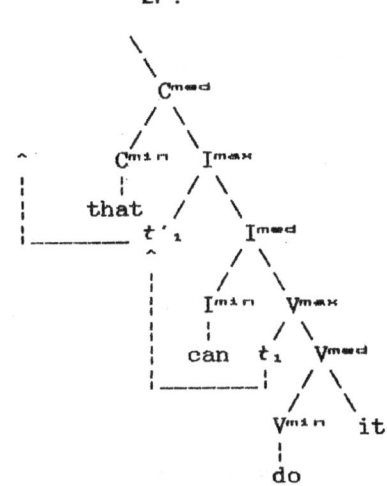

One important question yet to be answered in the Subject Raising Approach is what triggers the application of Move-alpha for the derivation of I-subjects in English. In providing an answer for this question, we assume that two principles of grammar independently fulfill this task in the way described below.

First, we will assume that there is a principle that requires the presence of a pleonastic element in a sentence like (5) below. This principle triggers Subject Raising when the pleonastic element fails to be base-generated, as illustrated in (6).

(5) *It* seems that he is honest

(6) a. D-str: ___ can [$_{Vmax}$ you do it]

    b. S-str: you$_1$ can [$_{Vmax}$ t$_1$ do it]

Chomsky (1982) makes the following stipulation and identifies it as the principle under consideration. This stipulation is known as the "Extension" of the Projection Principle:

(7) *Extension of the Projection Principle*:

    A sentence (= our I^{max}) must have a subject
    (at S-structure).

Although we tentatively adopt (7), we believe that this stipulation should eventually be derived from more general aspects of the grammar. In Borer (1986) and Kitagawa (1984), for example, it is independently claimed that (7) follows from the obligatoriness of number-person (and gender) agreement between subject and INFL.[a] Fabb (1984) and Kuroda (1985) derive (7) from the theory of Case, and Rothstein (1983) from the theory of Predication.

    The stipulation in (7), however, is still insufficient to provide the full account of the triggering of Subject Raising in English. For example, it would incorrectly allow the non-application of Subject Raising in (8) below, in which (7) has been satisfied by the lexical insertion of a pleonastic element *it*. This representation, however, may never surface as a well-formed sentence:

(8) *It* can [∨max *you* do it]

Note, however, that the representation in (8) can be ruled out by the Case Filter, if we assume that verbs do not assign Case to T-subjects. This assumption, we believe, is plausible, as demonstrated by the examples in (9) below, where the subject of an identical verb is assigned different Cases depending on its S-structure environments:

(9) a. I believe that *he* will *come* with us
 b. I expect *him* to *come* with us
 c. He condescended *PRO* to *come* with us

The variety of Case in (9a-c) suggests that the verb is **not** the source of Case. We thus assume that the Case Filter is also partially responsible for the triggering of Subject Raising in English.

It should probably be mentioned here that the idea of deriving surface I-subjects from underlying T-subjects is by no means novel (although the inheritence of "T-subjecthood" by a trace has never been proposed before). For example, Subject Raising in simplex sentences has been proposed in the framework of Case Grammar (Fillmore (1968), Stockwell, Schachter and Partee (1973)), and Generative Semantics (McCawley (1970)). It should also be pointed out that an analysis similar to ours has been independently developed also in the framework of Government and Binding Theory by Kuroda (1985) and Sportiche (1986).

3.2.2. Arguments for the Subject Raising Approach

It seems to us that there exist at least three different ways to motivate the Subject Raising Approach to English, as summmarized in (10) below:

(10) (i) By providing an independent motivation for the existence of the base position of a T-subject.

(ii) By showing that the trace of the subject indeed exists within the V^{max} after Subject Raising takes place.

(iii) By showing that V^{max} including a T-subject functions as a constituent.

In what follows, we will attempt to achieve (10 i-iii).

3.2.2.1. Base-generation of T-subjects

In the previous subsection, we have proposed that the Subject Raising in English is triggered by the extension of the Projection Principle ((7)) and the Case Filter. If this approach is basically correct, it will make a prediction that certain base-generated T-subjects may surface in their original positions (i.e., within V^{max} or A^{max}) in the following way.

Suppose that a sentence is base-generated with a pleonastic element *it* in its I-subject position. Suppose, moreover that the same sentence contains an element that does not require Case, as its base-generated T-subject. Obviously, this may give rise to a situation in which nothing triggers the application of Subject Raising, since this sentence has no potential violation of either (7) or the Case Filter.

A candidate for such a case, we believe, is the "extraposition" construction[9] exemplified by (11) below, in which the sentence-final clausal subject corresponds to what we have referred to above as "non-Case requiring T-subject":[10]

(11) a. It [$_{Vmax}$ turned out *that he was a spy*]
 b. It [$_{Vmax}$ bothers me *that he hasn't called us yet*]
 c. It is [$_{Amax}$ likely *that he will arrive late*]

This analysis is tantamount to the claim that the basic underlying word order in English is Verb-Object-Subject (VOS). Although the VOS hypothesis for English has been less explored compared to the VSO hypothesis (McCawley (1970a), Muraki (1974), Bach (1971a,b), etc.), nothing in fact precludes us from adopting this purely head-initial base configuration for English. In fact, it will allow the uni-directional head-government of internal and external arguments, which has some significance according to Horvath (1981), Stowell (1981), Travis (1983), Koopman (1984), Chomsky (1986a), etc. Moreover, if it turns out that the underlying analysis of the extraposition construction as in (11a-c) has any plausibility, it will provide us with an independent motivation for the existence of the base position of a T-subject, hence for the Subject Raising Approach as well. Keeping this goal in mind, let us explore this hypothesis.

The first thing we would like to establish is that the sentential T-subjects in (11a-c) are truly located within the V^{max} or A^{max} there. Since this position has already been argued for by various researchers, let us simply introduce the essence of their arguments. All the arguments presented below will suggest that the extraposed clause is located within the V^{max} or A^{max} at least at the levels of D-structure and S-structure. The first two arguments below have been proposed by Reinhart (1976).

First, when the V^{max} or A^{max} is preposed in this construction, the extraposed clause can accompany it, as illustrated by the contrast in (12) and (13):

(12) *VP-preposing*:

I warned you that it would upset Rosa that you smoke, and [$_{Vmax 1}$ upset her *that you smoked*] it certainly did t_1.

(13) *Though-movement*:

[$_{Amax1}$ Unlikely *that she would pass*] though it was t_1, Rosa still decided to take the exam.

This suggests that the extraposed clause is located within the V^{max} or A^{max}, making up a single constituent.

Second, whether the sentential subject is in the extraposed position (= our T-subject position) or in the intraposed position (= our I-subject position) **may affect** the possibility for an R-expression (*Rosa*) within the sentential subject to be bound by an object pronoun (*her*), as illustrated in (14) below:

(14) a. *It (should have) [$_{Vmax}$ bothered *her*$_1$ that *Rosa*$_1$ has failed]

    b. [$_{CP2}$ That *Rosa*$_1$ has failed] (should have) [$_{Vmax}$ bothered *her*$_1$ t_2]

Reinhart accounts for the contrast in (14) in terms of the constraint in (15) and the analysis in (16) for (14a):

(15) a. Two NPs cannot be coreferential if one is in the syntactic domain of the other and is not a pronoun. (p.125)

    b. The domain of a node *A* consists of *A* together with all and only the nodes c-commanded by *A*. (p.33)

    c. Node *A* c-commands node *B* if neither *A* nor *B* dominates the other and the first branching node which dominates *A* dominates *B*. (p.32)

(16)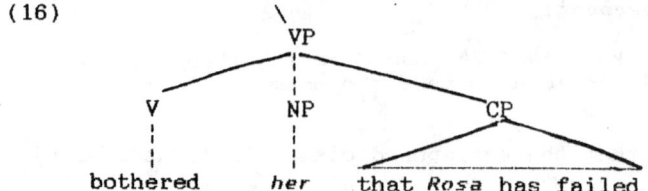

What is crucial in (16) is that *Rosa* is located within the syntactic domain of *her*, namely, VP, hence the prohibition against the coreference between *her* and *Rosa* in (14a).[11]

The third argument comes from Baltin (1978), who points out that the extraposed clause deletes under VP/AP-deletion --- i.e., the extraposed clause in the antecedent phrase must be interpreted as part of the reading of the deleted (or empty) V^{max}/A^{max} (= $\emptyset$) in (17a-b) below. This again argues that the extraposed sentential subjects are indeed located within V^{max} or A^{max}:

(17) a. It used to [$_{V^{max}}$ bother me *that people smoke in this room*]; with this big fan installed, however, it never will $\emptyset$ again.

b. Ten years ago, it was [$_{V^{max}}$ impossible *for anyone to beat him*], but after all these years, it probably is not $\emptyset$ any more.

Once it is established that the extraposed clause is located in V^{max} or A^{max} at D- and S-structures, the remaining task for us is to show that it has been base-generated there rather than moved from elsewhere. In

other words, we would like to argue for the intraposition
analysis (cf. Emonds (1970)) over the extraposition
analysis (cf. Rosenbaum (1967)) of the construction in
question.[12]

A crucial argument has been provided to us by David
Pesetsky (personal communication). Observe the following
paradigm:

(18) a.   [That he knows the truth] is significant.
   b.   ??We consider [that he knows the truth] to be
        significant.
   c.   *It was considered [that he knew the truth]
        to be significant.
   d.   *It seems [that he knows the truth] to be
        significant (to them).

While the example (18b) is less than perfect,[13] it is
unmistakably better than examples like (18c-d), which are
completely intolerable. We therefore regard (18b) as a
basically grammatical sentence, leaving its awkwardness
unexplicated at this moment. (We will return to this
topic when we deal with Emonds' (1976) and Koster's (1978)
claim that sentential subjects are all instances of
sentential topics.)

The paradigm in (18), then, seems to provide us with
a rather clear generalization --- the sentential I-subject
is permitted only in the position where Case is available.
The examples in (19) below show that the sentential

I-subjects in (18a) and (18b) are in a Case position, whereas those in (18c) and (18d) are not. Note the possibility of phonetically non-empty NPs in such positions:

(19) a. *The difference* is significant.
  b. We consider *the difference* to be singnificant.
  c. *It was considered *the difference* to be significant.
  d. *It seems *the difference* to be significant.

Suppose, now, that sentential I-subjects and T-subjects at surface are both **base-generated** in the V^{max}-final T-subject position, as we have claimed. Recall also that the Isomorphy Constraint permits the application of Move-alpha if and only if principles of grammar, for example, the Case Filter, require it. Then, with the assumption in (20) below, the statements in (21) will follow as a theorem in the Subject Raising Approach, leading us to the explication of the paradigm in (18) above:

(20) Sentential subjects are either nominal ([+N]) or non-nominal.[14]

(21) a. **Nominal** sentential subjects **undergo** Subject Raising.
  b. **Non-nominal** sentential subjects **do not undergo** Subject Raising.

The implicit assumptions here are: (i) the Case Filter
requires sentential subjects to receive Case if and only if
they are nominal in nature, and (ii) verbs do not assign
Case to T-subjects.

According to (21a), then, those sentential subjects
which have undergone Subject Raising, namely sentential
I-subjects, are nominal. All sentential I-subjects in
(18a-d), therefore, must be also nominal.[15] From this, it
follows that (18a-b) are well-formed whereas (18c-d) are
not, since sentential I-subjects appear in a Case position
in the former but not in the latter examples. The Subject
Raising Approach thus can offer a quite simple acount for
the paradigm in (18) above.

The correctness of (21a-b) can be verified in the
light of the following two generalizations.

First, Rosenbaum (1967) observes that gerunds do not
undergo the rule of extraposition (save in a few
exceptional cases), as illustrated by the contrast in (22)
below:

(22) a. *His arriving late* was likely at that time.

b. *It was likely at that time *his arriving late*.

Second, as pointed out by Emmon Bach (personal
communication), there seems to be a one-to-one correlation
between the possibility for a predicate to take a

that-clause as an I-subject and for it to take a gerund as an I-subject. We therefore obtain a contrast between (23)-(24) and (25)-(26) below:

(23) a. [That he would arrive late] was *likely* at that time.
 b. [His arriving late] was *likely* at that time.

(24) a. [That he was found guilty] was *tragic*.
 b. [His being found guilty] was *tragic*.

(25) a. *[That he would arrive late] was *sure*.
 b. *[His arriving late] was *sure*.

(26) a. *[That he is innocent] *seems*.
 b. *[His being innocent] *seems*.

Given the Case Filter, the Isomorphy Constraint and the base-generation of V^{max}-final T-subjects, we can straightforwardly capture both these generalizations in the Subject Raising Approach.

Let us begin with Rosenbaum's observation. As is well-known, gerunds give every indication of being nominal clauses. The contrast in (22), then, is exactly as predicted in our Subject Raising Approach --- gerundive T-subjects base-generated within V^{max} or A^{max} must undergo the Subject Raising since they are nominal, hence must receive Case to satisfy the Case Filter.

Suppose that this account is on the right track. We then have good reason to assume that the predicates in (23) and (24) may select a nominal element as their T-subject. The possibility of a clearly non-sentential NP subject (= [+N]) with these predicates supports this assumption:

(27) [NP The loss of a loved one] is { likely / tragic }.

The ill-formedness of (28) below, on the contrary, suggests that the predicates in (25) and (26) **do not** select a nominal T-subject.

(28) *[NP The loss of a loved one] { is sure / seems }.

With this contrast in selectional properties, we can account for the paradigm in (23)-(26) in the following way.

In (23) and (24), nominals base-generated as T-subjects successfully receives Case as the result of Subject Raising. In (25a) and (26a), on the other hand, Subject Raising has applied to the non-nominal T-subjects, violating the Isomorphy Constraint. This accounts for the ungrammaticality of these sentences.[16]

In (25b) and (26b), neither the Case Filter nor the Isomorphy Constraint is violated. These sentences, however, are ruled out since the predicates there must select non-nominal T-subjects, which gerunds are not.[17]

We thus have seen that the theorem in (21) and one of its underlying assumptions, i.e., that subjects are base-generated in the V^{max}-final position, are empirically motivated.[16]

Recall here the paradigm in (18) (repeated below) again:

(18) a. [That he knows the truth] is significant.
   b. ??We consider [that he knows the truth] to be significant.
   c. *It was considered [that he knew the truth] to be significant.
   d. *It seems [that he knows the truth] to be significant (to them).

When this paradigm was introduced above, we mentioned that the example (18b) is much more tolerable than (18c-d), but is still awkward compared to (18a).

Modifying Emonds' (1976) proposal, Koster (1978) claims that sentences like (18b) and (29)-(31) below are awkward[17] because the sentential subjects in these examples are not located in what he calls a "satellite" position (= topic position), where they should be base-generated:

(29) *Subordinate Clause*:

   a. ??That [for Bill to smoke] bothers the teacher is quite possible.
   b. ??Although [that the house is empty] may depress you, it pleases me.

(30)　*Subject-Aux Inversion:*

　　a. ??Did [that John showed up] please you?

　　b. ??What does [that he will come] prove?

(31)　*Topicalization:*

　　??Such things₁, [that he reads so much] doesn't prove t₁.

Adopting the essence of this approach, Stowell (1981) ascribes the awkwardness of (29)-(31) to the Case Resistance Principle (CRP) in (32) below:

(32)　*The Case-Resistance Principle:*

　　Case may not be assigned to a category bearing a Case-assigning feature.

Stowell assumes that tensed clauses and infinitival clauses bear a Case-assigning feature. Therefore, when they are generated in a Case position as in (18b) and (29)-(31) above, they move to the topic position to avoid a violation of the CRP. From the topic position, they bind a trace in the subject position, which receives Case.

This is one possible account of the awkwardness of (18b) and (29)-(31) also in our Subject Raising Approach. We should perhaps assume, then, that the violation of the Case Filter will lead sentences into a higher degree of ungrammaticality than that of the CRP, in order to account for the contrast between (18b) (and (29)-(30)) and the much more intolerable (18c-d).[20]

Finally, let us point out that the Subject Raising Approach to the extraposed construction solves certain problems posed by the Extraposition Approach such as the movement of a sentential I-subject to a position from which it does not c-command its trace, the replacement of such an offending trace by a pleonastic element *it*, and the co-superscripting between the inserted *it* and the extraposed clause to retain the proper thematic relation between the predicate and the sentential subject.[21] This seems to us to be a significant improvement of the analysis of extraposition from a theoretical point of view.

In this regard, it may also make sense to extend the VOS-cum-Subject Raising Approach to the analysis of the "inverted" subject construction in Romance languages, for example in Italian. Rizzi (1982) ascribes the lack of an ECP violation in the subject extraction as in (33) below to the availability of the derivation as in (34):

(33) Chi credi che verrà?

'*Who$_1$ do you believe that t_1 will come?'

(34) [$_{COMP}$ *chi*$_1$] credi che [$_{Imax}$ t_1 INFL [$_{Vmax}$ verrà t'_1]]

The essence of this analysis is that subject inversion yields an extraction site of the subject that is lexically governed within the (derived) V^{max}, hence there is no ECP violation.

Our point is that, by adopting the Subject Raising Approach, we can provide the derivation in (35) below, and achieve the same effect with respect to the ECP:

(35) [$_{COMP}$ chi$_1$] credi che [$_{Imax}$ verrà-INFL t_1]
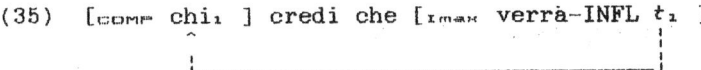

Crucially, this approach allows us to avoid various undesirable features of the Subject Inversion Analysis, which are quite comparable to those required in the Extraposition Analysis in English just mentioned above. Similar but slightly different proposals have been made independently by Safir (1982) and Borer (1986). See also Contreras (to appear) and Westphal (1985) for a similar claim for Spanish.[22]

A piece of support for this analysis may come from Burzio's (1986) observation that the sentence in (36) below constitutes a possible counterexample to the principle that each chain contains exactly one θ-position, and each such position appears in one and only one argument chain (Chomsky (1981, 1986a)). (From this principle, it follows that movement must always be to a non-θ-position):

(36)   alcuni articoli si leggeranno

   'One reads some articles.'

If we adopt Burzio's analysis (adopted from earlier work by Luigi Rizzi) as in (37) below, the two chains created by the movement of the impersonal subject clitic *si* (one) and the object phrase *alcuni articoli* (some articles) will contain an overlapping θ-position (**A**) as illustrated by the two chain representations in (38):

(37) D-str: <u>si</u> ___ leggeranno <u>alcuni articoli</u>
                 A **B**   **C**

   Pre-S-str: <u>t</u>$_1$ <u>si</u>$_1$ leggeranno <u>alcuni articoli</u>
                 A **B**   **C**

   S-str: <u>alcuni articoli</u>$_2$ <u>si</u>$_1$ leggeranno <u>t</u>$_2$
                        A   **B**   **C**

(38) si: (**B, A**)

   alcuni articoli: (**A, C**)

We can dismiss this counterexample, on the other hand, if we adopt the Subject Raising Analysis as in (39) below:

(39) [$_{NP_1}$ *alcuni articoli*] *si*$_2$ [$_{V_{max}}$ leggerano t_1 t_2]

Notice that the derivation now involves no movement to a θ-position. Thus, while its full evaluation must await further investigation, the extension of the Subject Raising

Approach to the inverted subject construction in Italian seems to be a desirable move to take.

To sum up, we have argued that the Subject Raising Approach to English proposed in 3.2.1. can and in fact should be extended to the so-called extraposition construction in English and possibly to the inverted subject construction in Romance languages like Italian. Several different motivations have been provided for this claim based upon the ovservations made by Pesetsky ((18a-d)), Rosenbaum ((22)), Bach ((23)-(26)), Rizzi ((33)), and Burzio ((36)).

If this approach is basically correct, sentences containing an extraposed sentential subject in English (and sentences with the inverted subject in Romance languages) will provide us with a case in which T-subjects surface in their base-generated position, hence an independent motivation for postulating such base positions in the Subject Raising Approach to English (and Romance languages).

3.2.2.2. Trace in V^{max}

Pursuing further the VOS hypothesis coupled with the Subject Raising, we now argue that the S-structure and LF representations of an English sentence contain a

V^{max}-internal trace of the raised subject, as schematized in (40) below:

(40)
```
           I^max
          /    \
        NP₁    I^med
              /    \
           I^min   V^max
                  /    \
               V^med    t₁
              /    \
           V^min   NP
```

The first argument for this is based upon Carlson's (1985) observation we took up in 2.4.2.2. above. That is to say, the sentence in (41) below exhibits two distinct interpretations --- wide scope and narrow scope readings of *different*:

(41) John and Bill₁ want [PRO₁ to live in different cities]

In Carlson's analysis, which we have adopted, it was considered that the narrow scope reading of *different* (= scope lower than *want*) in (41) is licensed by the PRO as the complement subject. Carlson further argues that a trace left behind by syntactic movement may also behave as a licenser of *same* and *different*, as illustrated by the possibility of the narrow scope readings of *different* in (42a-b) below:

(42) a. Which kids$_1$ does the hurried baby sitter want
 [to send t_1 to *different* rooms]

 (Carlson (1985, 24))
 b. Starsky and Hutch$_1$ were expected [t_1 to arrest
 different gangsters]

He then makes an observation crucial to us --- *same* in (43) below exhibits not only a wide scope reading but also a narrow scope reading, i.e., lower scope than the VP adverb *reluctantly*:[23]

(43) John and Mary *reluctantly* moved to the *same* city.

This fact clearly suggests the existence of a phonetically empty licenser of *same* below the scope of the VP-adverb *reluctantly*, i.e., within the VP.[24] Again, the Subject Raising Approach provides us with a simple account of this otherwise puzzling observation --- the trace of the raised subject behaves as the licenser of *same* within the V^{max}, as illustrated in (44) below:[25]

(44) John and Mary$_1$ [$_{Vmax}$ reluctantly moved to the *same* city t_1]

We thus have good reason to postulate the V^{max}-internal trace of the raised subject for a sentence in English.[26]

The essence of the second argument has been provided to us by Barbara Partee (personal communication).[27] Observe, first, the example in (45) below:

(45)   Someone must love her.

This sentence is ambiguous with respect to the scope of the subject NP *someone* relative to the auxiliary *must*, as illustrated in (46) below:

(46) a. *Higher Scope*:

   There exists at least one person who the speaker believes loves her.

   b. *Lower Scope*:

   The speaker believes that there exists at least one person who loves her.

The ambiguity here is reminiscent of the ambiguity in the raising construction (47) discussed by May (1977, 1985):

(47) $[_{Imax}$ someone$_1$ is likely $[_{Imax}$ t_1 to love her]]

(48) a.   *Higher Scope*:

   There is at least one person who is likely to love her.

   b.   *Lower Scope*:

   It is likely that there is at least one person who loves her.

In the Subject Raising Approach, we can assimilate (45) to (47), postulating the following S-structure representation:

(49) $[_{Imax}$ someone$_1$ must $[_{Vmax}$ love her t_1]]

In both (47) and (49), the trace of the raised subject

plays a crucial role in supplying the lower scope of *someone* when scope determination of QPs takes place at the level of Logical Form, no matter how it may be done (cf. May (1977, 1985), Burzio (1981), etc.)[28]

One might attempt to account for the contrast in (45) by claiming that a modal there is optionally raised at LF as illustrated in (50) below:

(50) a. LF: [$_{IP}$ must$_1$ [$_{IP}$ someone t_1 love her]]

b. LF: [$_{IP}$ someone [$_I$ · must love her]]

Although this is an interesting alternative sufficient to account for the contrast in (45), it dissimilates the facts in (45) from those in (47) (repeated below), where the QP has a scope lower than a predicate rather than a modal:

(45)   Someone *must* love her.

(47)   Someone is *likely* to love her.

Moreover, it requires a still different account for (43) repeated below, despite its similarity to the facts in (51) (= (i) in footnore 25). Note that the QP in (43) has a scope narrower than a VP-adverb rather than a modal:

(43)   John and Mary *reluctantly* moved to the *same* city.

(51)   Starsky and Hutch *must* arrest *different* gangsters.

On the other hand, the Subject Raising Approach can offer a
unified account to all the facts in (45), (51), (47) and
(43), ascribing the lower scope readings there to the
presence of a trace below a modal, a predicate and an
adverb, as in (52)-(55) below:

(52) $[_{Imax}$ someone$_1$ *must* $[_{Vmax}$ love her t_1]]
(53) $[_{Imax}$ Starsky and Hutch$_1$ *must* $[_{Vmax}$ arrest different gangsters t_1]]
(54) $[_{Imax}$ someone$_1$ is *likely* $[_{Imax}$ t_1 to love her]]
(55) $[_{Vmax}$ John and Mary$_1$ $[_{Vmax}$ *reluctantly* moved to the same city t_1]]

Thus, on the basis of its broader empirical coverage, we
will choose the Subject Raising Approach over the Modal
Raising Approach.

Moreover, as has been pointed out to me by David
Pesetsky (personal communication), if modals truly undergo
QR, they are expected to exhibit the properties and
restrictions found in other instances of such a process.
The facts, however, seem to be the contrary. For instance,
despite the claim by Quine (1960), May (1977) and others,
there do exist speakers who find it at least marginally
possible to detect a scope ambiguity between the two QPs
in (56) below:

(56) *Some politician* expected [John to address *every rally*]

For some speakers, in other words, the application of QR is not absolutely clause-bound. When it comes to Modal Raising, on the other hand, even these speakers find it absolutely impossible to apply it across the clause boundary, as illustrated by the impossibility of interpreting (57) below as represented in (58):

(57) Someone believes that John must love her.

(58) LF: [$_{IP}$ must$_1$ [$_{IP}$ someone believes [$_{CP}$ that [$_{IP}$ John t$_1$ love her]]]]

It is also unclear why QR would become optional only in the case of modals.

Thus, there seem to be good reasons not to adopt the QR approach to modals.

To sum up, we have argued for the postulation of the V^{max}-internal trace of the raised subject in English sentences, based upon the scope readings of various quantified elements below the scope of modals and VP-adverbs.

3.2.2.3. V^{max} as a Constituent

As the final piece of support for the Subject Raising Approach, we will provide motivations for assuming that V^{max} containing a T-subject makes up a constituent at various levels of representation. Let us emphasize here that what we here refer to as V^{max} is not equivalent to the traditional notion of VP, which corresponds to the V^{med} in below:

(59)
```
         V^max
         /  \
        /    \
     V^med    NP
     /  \
    /    \
  V^min   NP
```

Let us first point out that Reinhart's and Baltin's arguments for the V^{max}-internal location of the extraposed clauses presented in 3.2.2.1. above also serve as arguments for the constituency of V^{max} and A^{max} containing such T-subjects.

For example, the facts in (12) and (13) (repeated below) suggest that the preposed V^{max}/A^{max} containing a T-subject (henceforth simply V^{max} or A^{max}) makes up a constituent at D- and S-structures:

(12) *VP-preposing*:

I warned you that it would upset Rosa that you smoke, and [$_{Vmax1}$ upset her *that you smoked*] it certainly did t_1.

(13) *Though-movement*:

[$_{Amax1}$ Unlikely *that she would pass*] though it was t_1, Rasa still decided to take the exam.

The facts in (17a-b) repeated below also suggest the constituency of V^{max} and A^{max} --- the extraposed sentential subject in the first clause is obligatorily interpreted as part of the deleted (or empty) VP/AP (or rather V^{max}/A^{max}) in the second clause:

(17) a. It used to [$_{V^{max}}$ bother me *that people smoke in this room*]; with this big fan installed, however, it never will ∅ again.

b. Ten years ago, it was [$_{V^{max}}$ impossible *for anyone to beat him*], but after all these years, it probably is not ∅ any more.

If one adopts a deletion analysis of this construction (cf. Sag (1976)), (s)he will be led to conclude that such constituency holds at PF. If one adopts an interpretive analysis (cf. Williams (1977)), on the other hand, (s)he will conclude that such constituency holds at LF.

The LF constituency of V^{max} seems to receive support also in the light of semantics. Observe first the following examples:

(60) a. *John* will *talk to Mary*, which usually makes her happy.

b. *Bill* was *talking to Mary*, which usually is the sign of upcoming trouble.

As David Pesetsky (personal communication) has pointed out to me, each relative pronoun in (60) takes not the entire sentence but the sentence minus tense and aspect as its

antecedent. The possibility of such an interpretation
clearly suggests that a sentence may denote not only a
particular event (cf. Davidson (1976=1967)) but also an
event-type, which can be characterized as a generic event
(or a set of events).

It seems to us that the Subject Raising Approach can
provide us with a syntactic analysis in which we can
ascertain exactly which constituent at LF corresponds to
such an interpretation, namely, the V^{max}, as illustrated in
(61) below:

(61)   LF:

```
           I^max
          /  \
      John₁   I^med
             /  \
          I^min   V^max
                 /  \
              V^med   t₁
              /  \
           V^min   to us
             |
            talk
```

Note the crucial role played by the trace of the raised
subject, which permits us to obtain a constituent
consisting of the subject and VP (in the traditional
sense).[27]

Thus, there seems to exist a good semantic basis for
assuming the LF constituency of V^{max} containing a

T-subject, whether this T-subject is phonetically empty or not.[30]

Finally, let us point out that the constituency of V^{max} seems to be motivated also in the light of idioms. Observe, first, the so-called "sentential" idioms from English in (62)-(64) below:

(62) The cat will get out of the bag.
 'The secret will be revealed.'
(63) The axe fell.
 'We got caught.'
(64) The shit hit the fan.
 'A problem started.'

In these idioms, not only tense but also aspects and modals can alternate rather freely, as illustrated in (65)-(67) below:

(65) Make sure that the cat *doesn't* get out of the bag.
(66) The axe *will* fall someday.
(67) When those guys arrive, the shit *will* really hit the fan.

These facts suggest to us that what truly makes up an idiom in these examples is not the entire sentence but "the sentence minus an auxiliary element", i.e., "the subject plus VP".

Again, the Subject Raising Approach can properly supply a syntactic constituency for such idioms, i.e., the V^{max}, as illustrated in (68) below:

(68)   The shit$_1$ INFL [$_{Vmax}$ hit the fan t_1]

With the crucial use of a coindexed trace, we are, in a sense, assimilating (68) to the cases like (69) and (70) below:[31]

(69)   The cat$_1$ seems [t_1 to have gotten out of the bag]
(70)   How much advantage$_1$ did he [take t_1 of you]?

We thus have seen another piece of motivation for postulating V^{max} as a constituent at the level where idioms are interpreted --- presumably at LF (cf. Pesetsky (1985)).[32]

3.3. Summary

In this Chapter, we have introduced the notions "I-subject" and "T-subject" as the subcategories of "subject" defined as [N^{max}, X^{max}]. It has been argued that, in Japanese, T-subjects are derived from I-subjects by way of affix raising at the level of LF, whereas, in English, I-subjects are derived from T-subjects by way of the Subject Raising at S-structure. In either case, the formal grammatical device that fulfills this task is Move-alpha, whose application is triggered if and only if principles of grammar require so, in accordance with the Isomorphy Constraint. It has also been pointed out that the trace of the raised subject in English plays a crucial role in retaining the constituency of the V^{max} at the level of Logical Form.

Footnotes to Chapter III

1. This name is due to Kuroda (1984).

2. Let us here disregard the honorification of the verb.

3. Although we will deal mostly with verbal predicates below, we believe that a similar analysis can be offered for nominal and adjectival predicates as well.

4. From now on, the expression "Subject Raising in English" strictly refers to this process.

5. It is quite possible that this process involves adjunction rather than substitution.

6. One possibility is that affix raising applies even in English. The presence of various auxiliary elements, however, makes it difficult to pursue this line.

7. See Lasnik and Saito (1984) for the arguments that intermediate traces are subject to the ECP. We assume that the presence of the I-subject trace (t') here is required at LF to supply Case to the chain.

8. Kitagawa (1984) further proposes that the agreement-requiring property of INFL be parametrized, hence that (7) not to be considered absolutely universal.

9. We are using the terms "extraposition" and "extraposed clause" simply to indicate the position of a sentential subject, without adopting the analysis involving rightward movement. It should also be emphasized here that we are dealing strictly with the extraposition of **sentential subjects**, not other elements such as relative clauses, appositive clauses, result clauses and PPs.

10. Another candidate for the construction in question involves an empty pronominal anaphor (PRO) as a base-generated T-subject, as in (i) below:

(i) *it_1 INFL [$_{Vmax}$ love you PRO_1]

We will assume that such sentences will be ruled out due to the anomalous interpretation of PRO resulting from the obligatory coindexation between PRO behaving as an anaphor and the pleonastic *it*. We will deal with the control of PRO in Chapter Four.

11. The contrast in (14) also forces us to reject the
following analysis for (14b) (and other regular English
sentences):

(i)   *D-str/S-str/LF*:   *PF*:

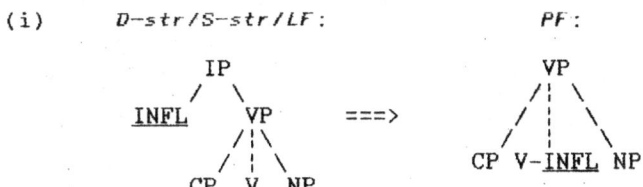

In this analysis, the coreference between *Rosa* and *her*
would incorrectly be predicted to be impossible, since the
sentential subject containing *Rosa* (CP) remains in the
syntactic domain of the object NP (*her*) at every syntactic
level.

12. Koster (1978) also proposes the base-generation of
extraposed clauses, but without assuming intraposition.
See below for his analysis of sentential I-subjects.

13. This observation led Rosenbaum (1967) to consider that
the application of Extraposition is obligatory in the
embedded context. There seems, in fact, to be a rather
clear dialectal split here --- while one group of speakers
find (18b) only slightly awkward, another group of speakers
find it much less acceptable. Even the latter group of
speakers find it, however, much better than the examples
(18c-d). I am grateful to David Pesetsky for providing
me with this information.

14. This assumption is by no means novel, but has been
often proposed in the literature. See, for example,
Rosenbaum (1967) and Emonds (1970, 1976).

15. In this regard, the PP-subject as in (i) below
(Stowell (1981, 225)) may be regarded as a type of nominal
expression:

(i) [Under the stars] is a nice place to sleep.

The contrast in (ii) supports this idea:

(ii) a. ?I consider [under the stars] to be a wonderful
         place to sleep.

     b. *It seems [under the stars] to be a wonderful
         place to sleep.

Note that the PP-subject requires Case.

16. Suppose, on the contrary, that the Extension of the Projection Principle ((7)) has triggered the Subject Raising of the sentential T-subject in (25a) and (26a), assuming that no pleonastic element has been base-generated in the D-structure I-subject positon. Since the moved T-subject is a **non-nominal** clause, however, it can neither carry the Case assigned by the INFL nor can it supply relevant number and person features to the INFL to satisfy (7). Thus, (25a) and (25b) can be ruled out even under this assumption.

17. It seems also possible to ascribe the ill-formedness of the double extraposition construction as illustrated in (i) below to the selectional properties of the predicate there such that it must select a nominal subject:

(i) a. That John has blood on his hands proves (that) Mary is innocent.

    b. *It proves (that) Mary is innocent that John has blood on his hands.

       (Emonds (1970, 1976), who ascribes the observations to Edward Klima)

18. Kiparsky and Kiparsky (1971, 346) consider that extraposition is optional for factive predicates, but is obligatory for non-factive predicates, based upon the contrast between (i-b) and (ii-b) below:

(i) *Factive Predicate*:

    a. *It* makes sense *to me that there are porcupines in our basement*.

    b. *That there are porcupines in our basement* makes sense *to me*.

(ii) *Non-factive Predicate*:

    a. *It* seems *to me that there are porcupines in our basement*.

    b. **That there are porcupines in our basement* seems *to me*.

       They also consider that gerundive subjects may be

selected only by factive predicates, based upon the
contrast in (iii) below:

(iii)   a.   *Factive Predicate*:

             His being found guilty is tragic.

        b.   *Non-factive Predicate*:

             **His being found guilty* seems.

Note that what their claims amount to is the
generalization that sentential I-subjects are always
interpreted as factive, whereas sentential T-subjects may
be interpreted as either factive or non-factive.

In the Subject Raising Approach to extraposition, we
can capture this generalization by assuming (iv) below:

(iv)   a.   **Nominal** clauses are interpreted only as factive.

       b.   **Non-nominal** clauses are interpreted as either
            factive or non-factive.

We analyze the sentential subjects in (i-a), (ii-a) and
(ii-b) as non-nominal clauses and those in (i-b), (iii-a)
and (iii-b) as nominal clauses. The well-formedness of
(i-a), (i-b) (ii-a), (iii-a) and the position of their
sentential subjects are straightforwardly accounted for in
the light of the Case Filter.

The ill-formed status of the example (ii-b), on the
other hand, can be accounted for in the way analogous to
our account of (25a) and (26a) in the text. ((iii-b) is
basically an identical sentence to (26b).)

As the examples in (23) illustrate, however, there
are exceptions to Kiparsky and Kiparsky's generalizations.
That is, some sentential I-subjects are interpreted as
non-factive.

19. Koster (1978) (and Stowell (1981) -- see below) labels
the examples in (29)-(31) as ungrammatical (*), following
Rosenbaum's (1967) and Emonds' (1970) original
observations. However, as we have pointed out above, most
speakers find these examples much more tolerable than
(18c-d), just as (18b) is. Thus, we assume that (29)-(31)
have roughly the same status as (18b).

20. Another candidate for the explanation is the difficulty of parsing. Note that the intraposed sentential subject in (18b), for example, is highly likely to be processed as the complement of the matrix verb *consider* in the initial parsing of this sentence.

21. Our analysis also differs crucially from Emonds' (1970) intraposition analysis, which involves replacement of *it* in the I-subject position with the sentential T-subject only when the two items are coindexed.

22. Stowell (1978) also offers a similar analysis for the *there* construction in English.

23. That *reluctantly* is a VP-adverb rather than an S-adverb can be demonstrated by the interpretation of the following sentences involving VP-deletion:

(i)   John *reluctantly* came to the party, and Bill (*reluctantly) did ∅, too.

(ii) *John *reluctantly* came to the party, but Bill did ∅ *enthusiastically*.

(iii) John and Mary reluctantly moved to the same city, and Bill and Susan did ∅ also.

In (i), the repetition of *reluctantly* in the second clause makes the sentence unacceptable. In (ii), the presence of *enthusiastically*, an adverb incompatible with *reluctantly*, in the second clause makes the sentence unacceptable. In (iii), the narrow scope reading of *same* is possible also for the second clause. Both these facts suggest that *reluctantly* in the antecedent clause is interpreted as part of the VP. See Thomason and Stalnaker (1973) for further arguments.

24. See 2.3.5.3. for the determination of adverbial scope.

25. Edwin Williams (personal communication) has pointed out to me that a similar scope ambiguity can be detected in a sentence involving a modal as in (i) below:

(i) Starsky and Hutch *must* arrest *different* gangsters.

We will deal with modals directly below.

26. In order to account for the facts in (43), Carlson makes an appeal to the Derived VP Rule proposed by Partee (1975). In the Subject Raising Approach, we can subsume

this translation rule under the more general process of
Move-alpha. Put into different words, this approach lets
Move-alpha fulfill the Lambda-abstraction in syntax. The
coindexation between the raised subject and its trace,
then, may be considered to carry out the task of
Lambda-conversion.

27. An almost identical argument has been independently
offered by Sportiche (1986).

28. One possibility is that the S-structure representation
(49) is mapped onto either of the two LF representations in
(i) below:

(i) a. *Higher Scope*:

  $[_{Imax}$ *someone*$_1$ $[_{Imax}$ must $[_{Vmax}$ love her t_1]]]

  b. *Lower Scope*:

  $[_{Imax}$ must $[_{Vmax}$ *someone*$_1$ $[_{Vmax}$ love her t_1]]]

This analysis crucially differs from a similar analysis
proposed by May (1977, 1985), in that the moved quantifier
phrase does not leave a trace behind. This is a natural
consequence of the Subject Raising Approach, in which any
I-subject position is analyzed to be a non-argument
position. There exist no principles of grammar, in other
words, that require the moved I-subject *someone* to leave a
trace behind at LF. Thus, the resulting LF representation
in (ib) does not contain any non-c-commanded variable even
after the QP is lowered from the S-structure I-subject
position.

29. Lebeaux's (1984b) Affix Raising Approach
(cf. 2.3.2.) combined with our proposal that V^{max} at LF
supplies the event-type interpretation permits us to
explain how such an interpretation arises not only in
sentences but also in derived nominals in English, as
illustrated in (i) below. Note the derived V^{max} in (ib):

(i) a.   S-str: b.   LF:

```
          N^max                                      N^max
         /    \                                     /     \
the enemy's  N^med              ===>              /        \
            /    \                              V^max       N^min
          N^min  of the city          the enemy's  V^med     ion
         /    \                                   /     \
        V      N                                V^min   of the city
        |      |                                  |
     destruct  ion                             destruct
```

30. Note that this analysis treats "subject" strictly as an argument rather than a functor. Although it goes far beyond the scope of this thesis, this may have some non-trivial implication to the theory of semantic compounding. See, for example, Partee (1975) for a relevant discussion.

31. One might insist that the idiom in (64), for example, is a sentential idiom of the form (i) below, where x indicates a blank to be filled freely:

(i)   [$_{IP}$ The shit [$_{INFL}$ x] hit the fan]

There in fact exist many such idioms with blanks, as exemplified in (ii) below:

(ii)   a.   take advantage of x

        b.   pull x's legs

It seems to be the case, however, that such blanks allowed in idioms must always be non-head items except in the case like (i). This fact casts some doubt on this alternative approach.

32. Sportiche (1986) offers a similar argument.

CHAPTER IV
BINDING THEORY

4.1. Introduction

It is hardly deniable that native judgments on the binding of anaphors and pronominals result from the interaction of syntactic, semantic, pragmatic and other factors that dominate the competence and/or performance of language. Nevertheless, it seems reasonable to assume that the core part of such binding is governed by certain formal principles that are syntactic in nature.

For example, one recent approach in the generative tradition assumes that the Nominative Island Condition (NIC: Chomsky (1980)) accounts for the contrast between (1a) and (1b) below, and that the Specified Subject Condition (SSC: Chomsky (1973)) accounts for the contrast between (2a) and (2b).

(1) a. They$_1$ believe [(that) { *each other / they$_1$ } will win]

b. They$_1$ believe [{ each other$_1$ / *them$_1$ } to have won]

(2) a. They$_1$ expected [Mary to like { *each other / them$_1$ }]

b. They$_1$ expected [PRO$_1$ to like { each other$_1$ / *them$_1$ }]

This approach, however, is somewhat unsatisfactory, in that the binding theory must refer to the totally independent and (in principle) unrelated notions "Nominative Case" and "subject".

The first serious attempt to eliminate this unattractive feature from the binding theory was made by Chomsky (1981). In that work, the NIC was reduced to the SSC, with the claim that AGR functions as a type of subject ("SUBJECT") with respect to binding of anaphors and pronominals.[1]

In this chapter, we will challenge this approach. In fact, we will follow exactly the opposite direction, and propose that it is the SSC that is reduced to the extended version of the NIC. First, we question the validity of the notion "SUBJECT", drawing mostly on Portuguese. We then will attempt to unify the two types of binding conditions (NIC and SSC) in terms of "Case" and "head-government", eliminating the reference to either "SUBJECT" or "subject". This proposal will be mostly based upon the data from Japanese and English. In the course of discussion, it will also be pointed out that this unification of the binding conditions is made possible only when we incorporate into the theory the notion V^{max}-internal subject, i.e., the subject head-governed by a predicate. We will provide, in other words, another piece of motivation for the two hypotheses argued for in the previous chapters, i.e., the Affix Raising Hypothesis for Japanese and the Subject Raising Hypothesis for English, demonstrating that they will allow us to straightforwardly capture the phenomena of binding under the notion "government".

4.2. SUBJECTS

4.2.1. AGR as a "SUBJECT"

The unification of the binding conditions in terms of the notion "SUBJECT" crucially depends upon the assumption that AGR ("agreement features") contained in the INFL of the finite clause, may function as a subject with respect to binding. More precisely, it is assumed that AGR is nominal in character, hence may function both as an antecedent and an opacity-creating element for the binding of anaphors and pronominals, just as structural subjects may. In this sense, it is essential in this approach that AGR, rather than either Tense or the Nominative Case assigning property ([+NOM]) of the INFL is identified as a SUBJECT, since the latter two are assumed to be non-nominal in nature, hence are highly unlikely to form a natural class with structural subjects. One important task to be fulfilled in this approach, therefore, is to demonstrate that there indeed exists a clear correlation between AGR and referential opacity, independent of the existence of Tense and [+NOM].

However, since AGR, Tense and the Nominative Case assigning property ([+Nom]) in INFL cannot be dissociated from one another in the finite clause of English, we cannot rely on English to evaluate this proposal. Inflected infinitives in Portuguese and gerunds in Turkish, on the other hand, do show such a dissociation: AGR is present independent of Tense. Some data have been presented by Rouveret (1980), Zubizarreta (1980) (from Portuguese) and by George and Kornfilt (1978) (from Turkish) to show that these constructions are opaque domains for binding. Such data naturally led them to claim that it is AGR rather than Tense that creates opacity for binding. As has been mentioned above, this claim was adopted by Chomsky (1981) in what became the "SUBJECT" approach to binding theory.

In a more recent work, Chomsky (1986a) discards the idea that AGR as a potential binder creates opacity, calling it "somewhat artificial assumption" (p.176). While this conclusion is reasonable, it is desirable to provide it with an empirical basis by showing that AGR **must not** be considered to create opacity. In 4.2.2. below, we will attempt to supply this "missing argument". We will claim that it is a mistake to regard AGR as responsible for the opacity even in Portuguese.

4.2.2. Opacity in Portuguese²

4.2.2.1. Inflected Infinitivals

As illustrated by (1a-b) below, inflected infinitivals in Portuguese exhibit overt subject-verb agreement without any tense morpheme.

(1) a. O João disse para [tu   não *saires*   de
       the João told for   you=NOM not *to=leave=2=SG* of

       casa]
       house

       'João told you not to leave home.'

    b. O João lamenta [tu   *teres*   gasto
       the João regrets   you=NOM *to=have=2=SG* spent

       esse dinheiro]
       that money

       'João regrets you to have spent that money.'

Moreover, as illustrated in (2) below, a lexical anaphor in general may not appear in the subject position of an inflected infinitival.

(2) *Eles lamentam [*um ao outro* terem   gasto
     they regret   each other   to=have=3=PL spent

     esse dinheiro]
     that money

Based upon this fact, Rouveret (1980) and Zubizarreta (1980;1982), among others, conclude that it is AGR rather than tense that makes the subject position of an embedded sentence inaccessible from the matrix with respect to binding.

A closer examination of inflected infinitivals, however, immediately suggests a different possibility: it might be significant that the subject in the inflected infinitival is marked with Nominative Case. There still is a possibility, in other words, that neither AGR nor Tense creates opacity, but that opacity is created by **the Nominative Case assigning property ([+Nom])** of INFL. In the remainder of this section, I will argue for this possibility. With this claim, we will naturally predict, contra Rouveret and Zubizarreta, that when AGR is present independently of [+Nom], the embedded subject will be accessible from the matrix with respect to binding. In 4.2.2.3. below, we will present a construction in European Portuguese in which AGR can be dissociated from both Tense and [+Nom]. This construction will permit us to evaluate our prediction.

4.2.2.2. Lexical Anaphors in Portuguese

Let us start our discussion with an examination of the general properties of lexical anaphors in Portuguese. The behavior of the "strong" (=non-clitic) reflexive pronoun *si* in (3) and (4) below clearly indicates that it behaves as an anaphor with respect to Principle A of the

Binding Theory (Binding Theory (A)). Its binding is both "local" (in the relevant sense), as illustrated in (3), and "obligatory", as illustrated in (4).

(3) a. Os alunos$_1$ gostam de si$_1$.
the students like of themselves

'The students like themselves.'

b. Os alunos$_1$ supõem [que os professores$_2$
the students suppose that the teachers

gostam de si$_{2/*1}$]
like of themselves

'The students suppose that the teachers like themselves.'

(4) a. *Si gostam dos alunos.
themselves like of=the students

'Themselves like the students.'

b. *Eu gosto de si.[3]
I like of himself/themselves

'I like himself/themselves.'

The situation is the same when this reflexive pronoun is contracted with a preposition like com (with) (and go):[4]

(5) a. Os esquizofrênicos$_1$ sonham sempre consigo$_1$
the schizophrenics dream always with=themselves

'The schizophrenics always dream of themselves.'

b. Os esquizofrênicos$_1$ supõem [que os paranóicos$_2$
the schizophrenics suppose that the paranoiacs

sonham sempre consigo$_{2/*1}$ (próprio)][5]
dream always with=themselves

'The schizophrenics suppose that the paranoiacs always dream of themselves.'

Um ao outro (each other) and its various forms are used usually as a supplement to weak reflexive pronouns (clitics) in order to disambiguate the reciprocal from the reflexive interpretation, both of which are possible with *si*. *Um ao outro*, however, may be used as a reciprocal pronoun by itself independent of a reflexive pronoun. When it is used this way, it also behaves as an anaphor with respect to the Binding Theory (A):

(6) a. Ele supõe [que eles$_1$ gostam *um do outro*$_1$]
       he supposes that they like each other

 b. *Eles supõem [que ele gosta *um do outro*]
       they suppose that he likes each other

4.2.2.3. Gerundive Infinitivals

Having examined lexical anaphors, let us now turn to the construction in Portuguese that is directly relevant to our argument. The examples (7) and (8) below show subject-verb agreement without either tense or a nominative subject:

(7)   Eu sonhei contigo   a roubares   galinhas
      I dream   with=you=ACC   at stealing=2=SG   chickens

      'I saw you stealing chickens in my dream.'

(8)   Eu deparei contigo   a beijares
      I found   with=you=ACC   at kissing=2=SG

      a   professora
      the teacher=F

      'I found you kissing the teacher.'

In both (7) and (8), we have a combination of a preposition
a (at) and an inflected infinitival, which is used as a
(somewhat colloquial) free variation of (uninflected)
gerund by the native speakers of European Portuguese (but
rarely by those who speak Brazilian Portuguese). I will
refer to this construction as a "**gerundive infinitival**".
Note the lack of both tense and a nominative subject in the
gerundive infinitivals in (7) and (8).

Before proceeding further, we must show that a
complement with a gerundive infinitival is indeed a
construction appropriate to our argument, i.e., S' rather
than a sequence of NP-S', PP-S' (two complement
constituents of a three-place predicate), or NP (a head
noun modified by a gerundive infinitival). We can
demonstrate that our construction is S' with the following
facts.

First, just as NP can be focused in a pseudocleft
construction, as in (9a) below, a complement with a
gerundive infinitival (GI) can also be focused in this
construction as in (9b). (This has been pointed out to me
by João Peres.)

(9)   a.   Ele não deparou com uma mina de outro,
           he not found with a mine of gold

           o que ele deparou foi [NP uma mina de água]
           the that he found was a mine of water

           'He didn't find a gold mine. What he found was
           a well.'

b. Ele não deparou contigo   a   roubares
       he not found   with=you=ACC at stealing=2=SG

       galinhas, o   que ele deparou foi
       chickens the that he found   was

       [s: contigo   a   comeres   galinhas]
            with=you=ACC at eating=2=SG chickens

       'He didn't find you stealing chickens. What he
       found was you eating chickens.'

This shows that the complement in question makes up a single constituent.

To make the point even clearer, compare (9a-b) with the pseudocleft constructions involving predicate *persuadir* (persuade), which may take as its complement either a sequence NP-S' (as a three-place predicate) or S' alone (as a two-place predicate). First, when the NP-S' complement is focused, as in (10a) below, the pseudocleft construction is ill-formed:

(10) Ele não persuadiu a   Maria a ser examinada
     he not persuaded the Maria to be examined

     pelo   especialista,
     by=the specialist,

     'He didn't persuade Maria to be examined
     by the specialist.'

     a. *o   que ele persuadiu foi [NP a Maria]
         the that he persuaded was   the Maria

        [s. PRO a ser examinada pelo   médico]
                to be examined by=the doctor

        'what he persuaded was Maria to be examined
        by the doctor.'

b. o   que ele persuadiu foi [s′- que a   Maria
    the that he   persuaded was   that the Maria

    fosse   examinada pelo   médico]
    be-SUBJUNCTIVE examined by=the doctor

    'what he persuaded was that Maria be examined
    by the doctor.'

c. ?o   que ele persudiu a   Maria foi [s′- a   ser
    the that he persuaded the Maria was   to be

    examinada pelo   médico]
    examined by=the doctor

    'what he persuaded Maria was to be examined
    by the doctor.'

When only a single constituent S' is focused as in (10b) and (10c), on the other hand, the construction becomes acceptable, although (10c) is slightly less than perfect for some reason. Thus, the contrast between (9b) and (10a) on the one hand and the well-formedness of both (9b) and (10b-c) on the other, suggest that the gerundive infinitival construction should be analyzed as a single constituent.

Second, a proper noun can be a subject in this construction as shown in (11) below, suggesting that it would be a mistake to analyze the whole complement as an NP containing a gerundive infinitival as the restrictive modifier of the head N.

(11) Eu deparei com *Pedro e Maria* a roubarem
      I found   with Pedro and Maria at stealing=3=PL

   galinhas
   chickens

   'I found Pedro and Maria stealing chickens.'

Finally, the "cognitive synonymy" of the active-passive pairs in (12) and (13) below also argues against all the NP-S', PP-S', and NP analyses of this construction.

(12) a. Eu sonhei com os alunos a roubarem
        I dreamed with the students at stealing=3=PL

   galinhas
   chickens

   'I saw the students stealing chickens in my dream.'

   b. Eu sonhei com galinhas a serem   roubadas
      I dreamed with chickens at being=3=PL stolen

   pelos alunos
   by=the students

   'I saw chickens being stolen by the students in my dream.'

(13) a. Eu deparei com os alunos a beijarem
        I found   with the students at kissing=3=PL

   as professoras
   the teachers

   'I found the students kissing the teachers.'

b. Eu deparei com as professoras a serem
   I   found   with the teachers=F at being=3=PL

   beijadas pelos alunos
   kissed   by=the students

   'I found the teachers being kissed
   by the students.'

Compare now (12a-b) and (13a-b) with (14a-b) below.

(14) a. O João persuadiu o especialista a examinar
       the João persuaded the specialist to examine

      a Maria
      the Maria

      'João persuaded the specialist to examine Maria.'

   b. O João persuadiu a Maria a ser examinada
       the João persuaded the Maria to be examined

      pelo especialista
      by=the specialist

      'João persuaded Maria to be examined
      by the specialist.'

   (Quicoli (1976), with slight modification)

Again, since *persuadir* (persuade) in (14) is a three-place predicate whose complement consists of NP and S', the active-passive pair is "cognitively non-synonymous" in sharp contrast with the pairs in (12) and (13). (See Chomsky (1965, 22) for a classical argument for assigning different structures to the complement of *expect* and *persuade*.)

Thus, it seems plausible to analyze a gerundive infinitival as a clausal complement of a predicate.

4.2.2.4. Against AGR as a SUBJECT

We now are ready to present the crucial data in (15) and (16) below, which will allow us to evaluate our prediction that AGR independent of [+Nom] **does not** create an opaque domain with respect to binding.

(15) Eles$_1$ sonharam [ɐ$_1$ con$s$igo$_1$ a roubarem
     they   dreamed   with=themselves at stealing=3=PL

     galinhas]
     chickens

     'They saw themselves stealing chickens
     in their dream.'

(16) Eles$_1$ deram [ɐ$_1$ con$s$igo$_1$ a beijarem
     they   found   with=themselves at kissing=3=PL

     as professoras]
     the teachers

     'They found themselves kissing the teachers.'

In these examples, a reflexive anaphor as the subject of a gerundive infinitival may be bound by the matrix subject despite the clear presence of agreement in the gerundive infinitival. Exactly the same binding property can be observed with an embedded reciprocal subject:

(17) Eles$_1$ sonharam [ɐ$_1$ *um com outro*$_1$ a roubarem
     they   dreamed   each other   at stealing=3=PL

     galinhas]
     chickens

     'They saw each other stealing chickens
     in their dreams.'

(18) Eles₁ deram [cɪ um com outro₁ a beijarem
      they found   each other   at kissing=3=PL

      as professoras]
      the teachers

      'They found each other kissing the teachers.'

Compare (15)-(18) above with (19a) and (19b) below, which involve complementation of a tensed clause and an inflected infinitival, respectively.

(19) a. *Eles sonharam [que { si
         they dreamed   that   themselves
                                 um ao outro
                                 each other   }

         tinham roubado galinhas]
         had   stolen chickens

     b. *Eles lamentam [{ si
         they regret   themselves
                            um ao outro
                            each other   }

         terem   gasto esse dinheiro]
         to=have=3=PL spent that money

In both (19a) and (19b), the anaphor in the embedded subject position cannot be bound by the matrix subject. These facts strongly suggest that it is not AGR that is responsible for the presence of opacity in (19a-b) and its absence in (15)-(18).

If we replace a lexical anaphor in the subject position of the gerundive infinitival with a pronoun, it is disjoint in reference from the matrix subject, as illustrated in (20) below:

(20) a. Eles$_1$ sonharam [ₑᵢ com eles$_{2/*1}$ a roubarem
       they dreamed   with them   at stealing=3=PL

       galinhas]
       chickens

       'They saw them stealing chickens in their dream.'

   b. Eles$_1$ deram [ₑᵢ com eles$_{2/*1}$ a beijarem
       they found   with them   at kissing=3=PL

       as professoras]
       the teachers

       'They found them kissing the teachers.'

This, in fact, is exactly what our hypothesis predicts, given the Binding Theory (B).[6]

Summarizing our analyses of Portuguese, we can come up with the following chart, which suggests the direct correlation between the referential opacity of an embedded clause and the Nominative Case assigning property of INFL rather than AGR:[7]

(21)

	Tns	AGR	NOM	Anaphoric Binding	Pronominal Binding
Finite Clause	+	+	+	−	+
Inflected Infinitival	−	+	+	−	+
Gerundive Infinitival	−	+	−	+	−

Thus, with respect to Portuguese, we reject the "SUBJECT" approach to the binding theory, which crucially assumes that AGR functions as a SUBJECT and creates opacity for binding.[8]

4.3. Case Marking and Binding

4.3.1. Case Island and the V^{max}--Internal Subject

The Portuguese facts we have examined in the previous section certainly provide us with a good motivation to re-examine the possibility of accounting for the contrast in (1) below in terms of the NIC:

(1) a. They$_1$ believe (that) [$_{IP}$ { *each other / they$_1$ } will win]

 b. They$_1$ [$_{VP}$ believe { each other$_1$ / *them$_1$ } to have won]

As has already been pointed out, however, if we adopt the NIC in its present form,[7] we will be forced to give up the unification of the two binding conditions. The contrast in (2) below will require us to retain the SSC, since Nominative Case marking has nothing to do with this contrast.

(2) a. They$_1$ expected [Mary to like { *each other / them$_1$ }]

 b. They$_1$ expected [PRO$_1$ to like { each other$_1$ / *them$_1$ }]

This dilemma can be solved, however, if we extend the NIC in the following way. First, we hypothesize that opacity in binding is created by **Case marking in general** rather than just Nominative Case marking. We thus extend the notion "Nominative island" into a more general notion "**Case island**". (A similar proposal has been made by Cole and Hermon (1980) and Rouveret and Vergnaud (1980).)

Second, we will define "binding category" as in (3) below, as our first approximation:

(3) *Binding Category* (First Approximation):

The binding category for ß is the maximal projection of ß's Case marker; where ß = an anaphor or a pronominal.

This definition plays a role in the familiar principles of the binding theory as in (4) below:

(4) *The Binding Theory*:

A: An anaphor is bound in its binding category.
B: A pronominal is free in its binding category.

Roughly speaking, then, (3) combined with (4) requires anaphors to be bound and pronominals to be free within the maximal projection, i.e., within the head-government domain, of their Case assigner.

The effect of this "Case Island" Approach to binding theory is straightforward in (1a) above --- the binding category for ß is the complement IP, since ß receives Nominative Case from the embedded INFL. Therefore, a

pronominal but not an anaphor may appear as ß, lacking any
legitimate binder within the binding category.

Given the traditional phrase structure analysis of
English, on the other hand, this theory immediately runs
into trouble. In (1b), for example, it seems plausible to
assume that ß receives Accusative Case from the matrix verb
believe. ß's binding category, therefore, is the maximal
projection of the matrix verb, according to the definition
in (3). It seems impossible, therefore, to subsume the SSC
under the NIC as long as we assume that subjects are
base-generated immediately under the IP node and stays
there throughout the derivation. Notice, however, that
this problem is immediately solved if we have a phrase
structure analysis of English that permits us to locate the
subject of a sentence under the V^{max} node. In other words,
the moment we combine the proposed binding theory with the
notion V^{max}-internal subject we have argued for in the
previous chapter, the problem will disappear. In this
analysis, the matrix V^{max} in (1b) contains a trace bound by
the subject *they*, as illustrated in (5) below. Let us
continue to label such a subject as "T-subject":

(5) They$_1$ [$_{Vmax}$ believe [{ *each other*$_1$ / *them$_1$ } to win] t_1]

The embedded subject position in (5) (= (1b)), therefore,
is accessible from the matrix subject, via its T-subject

trace within the matrix V^{max}, permitting an anaphor but not a pronominal.

With the notion T-subject, the Case Island Approach not only accounts for the contrast in (1) (= NIC effects) but also the contrast in (2) (= SSC effects).

In (6) below (=(2a) above with our analysis), ß receives Accusative Case from the complement verb *like*. The binding category, therefore, is the complement V^{max}. Although this V^{max} contains a T-subject trace (t_2), it is not a legitimate binder for either *them* or *each other*, being bound by a singular NP *Mary*. As a result, *them* but not *each other* becomes possible in the embedded object position:

(6) They$_1$ expected Mary$_2$ to [$_{Vmax}$ like { them$_1$ / *each other$_1$ } t_2]

If the T-subject trace in the complement V^{max} is bound by a plural antecedent as in (7) (=(2b)) or (8) below, on the other hand, the binding category for ß will contain a legitimate antecedent. The complementarity of an anaphor and a pronominal, therefore, will be reversed.

(7) They$_1$ expected PRO$_1$ to [$_{Vmax}$ like { each other$_1$ / *them$_2$ } t_1]

(8) John expected Mary and Susan$_1$ to
　　　[$_{Vmax}$ like { each other$_1$ / *them$_1$ } t_1]

Thus, the Case Island Approach to binding permits us to unify the NIC and SSC without recourse to the assumption that AGR functions as a SUBJECT --- an assumption whose validity has been questioned in the previous section. It seems to us that this is a significant improvement of the theory of binding, which can be brought about only when we incorporate the notion T-subject into the theory.

4.3.2. Problems in the Binding Theory of Japanese

In this section, we will introduce two well-known problems in the binding theory of Japanese. Both problems are concerned with the complementarity of anaphors and pronominals.

4.3.2.1. Reflexive Anaphors

Many interesting works on reflexivization have appeared in the generative literature of Japanese, based upon the behavior of *zibun* (self) --- Kuroda (1965a), Kuno (1973), Inoue (1976), N. McCawley (1976) to name only a few. One problem that *zibun* poses for the theory of binding is that, unlike English reflexive anaphors, it may be bound from outside a tensed clause, as illustrated in (9) below:

(9) Taroo$_1$ ga [Hanako$_2$ ga zibun$_{1/2}$ o seme-ru] to wa
    NOM   NOM   self   ACC blame-PRES COMP TOP
    omottemominakatta (koto)[10]
    never=thought   (fact)

    'Taro never thought that Hanako would blame herself/him.'

Note that all of the binding theories introduced above would incorrectly disallow such a long-distance binding as long as *zibun* is identified as an anaphor.

Recently, however, it was pointed out by Ueda (1984) and Fukui (1984) that *zibun*, in fact, may not be a pure anaphor but a type of pronoun. (See Appendix for details. See also Yang (1983) for a different view.) Moreover, Kurata (1986) has pointed out that *zibun-zisin* (self-self), another reflexive item in Japanese, behaves more like an anaphor, exhibiting the familiar locality condition peculiar to anaphoric binding, as in (10) below. Compare carefully (9) and (10):

(10) Taroo$_1$ ga [Hanako$_2$ ga *zibun-zisin*$_{2/*1}$ o   seme-ru]
     NOM   NOM   self   ACC blame-PRES
     to   wa omottemominakatta (koto)
     COMP TOP never=thought   (fact)

    'Taro never thought that Hanako would blame herself.'

Let us also point out here that still another reflexive item *mizukara* (self) is also a "well-behaved" anaphor, as illustrated in (11):

(11) Taroo₁ ga [Hanako₂ ga mizukara₂/*₁ o   seme-ru]
            NOM   NOM   self   ACC blame-PRES

to   wa omottemominakatta (koto)
COMP TOP never=thought   (fact)

'Taro never thought that Hanako would blame herself.'

Mizukara (self) is somewhat less colloquial than the other two forms, but it still is in the vocabulary of modern Japanese, and by no means archaic.

In short, there seems to be good reason to treat zibunzisin and mizukara rather than zibun as pure reflexive anaphors in Japanese.[11] In this thesis, therefore, we will pay our attention to zibunzisin and mizukara, rather than zibun, to investigate the properties of anaphoric binding in Japanese. Since the contrast between zibun and zibunzisin/mizukara becomes sharper when they are juxtaposed, I will constantly compare the binding properties of these items below even when the binding of zibun is irrelevant.[12]

4.3.2.2. A Subject-Object Assymetry

It has been observed by Huang (1982) that Chinese, unlike English, exhibits a subject-object asymmetry with respect to anaphoric binding into tensed clauses. In Japanese as well, we can observe this phenomenon. Put differently, Japanese anaphors observe the SSC but are immune to the NIC. Compare the Japanese examples in (12) and (13) below with their English translations:

(12) a. Taroo$_1$ wa [{ *zibunzisin*$_1$ / self / *mizukara*$_1$ / self } ga syoo o
        TOP   NOM award ACC

to-**ru**] to wa omottemominakatta
get-**pres** COMP TOP never=thought

'*Taro never thought that himself would win the award.'

b. Taroo$_1$ ga [Hanako$_2$ ga { *zibun*$_{1/2}$ / *zibunzisin*$_{2/*1}$ / *mizukara*$_{2/*1}$ / self } o
          NOM   NOM   ACC

seme-**ru**] to wa omottemominakatta (koto)
blame-**PRES** COMP TOP never=thought (fact)

'Taro never thought that Hanako would blame herself/*himself.'

(13) a. karera$_1$ wa [{ *otagai*$_1$ / each other / *sorezore*$_1$ / each / *onoono*$_1$ / each } ga yakusoku o
       they   TOP   NOM promise ACC

mamo-**ru**] to sinziteiru
keep-**PRES**] COMP believe

'*They$_1$ believe that *each other*$_1$ will keep a promise.'

b. karera₁ ga [hutari₂ ga { *otagai*₂/*₁ } o
   they   NOM   two   NOM   each other   ACC
                         *sorezore*₂/*₁
                         each
                         *onoono*₂/*₁
                         each

   seme-ru   to] wa omottemominakatta (koto)
   blame-PRES COMP TOP never=thought   (fact)

   'They never thought that the two would blame themselves.'

Under the "SUBJECT" approach, the well-formedness of (12a) and (13a) might naturally be ascribed to the lack of AGR in the INFL of Japanese, since Japanese lacks overt subject-verb agreement. In (12a), for example, the only SUBJECT that can enter into the binding of the anaphor *zibunzisin/mizukara* (self) is the matrix subject *Taroo*. Thus, the sentence is well-formed, the anaphor being bound in its governing category, the matrix sentence.

There is good reason to cast doubt on such an analysis, however. It makes an empirically incorrect prediction concerning pronominal binding in Japanese. If the governing category of the embedded subject in (14a-b) below were the higher sentence due to the lack of AGR in the embedded sentence, an embedded pronominal subject there should be disjoint in reference from the higher subject, given the binding theory in (4) above. This, however, is not the case, as is well-known (cf. Huang (1982)):[13]

(14) a. Taroo₁ ga [{ ?kare₁ / he / pro₁ } ga kanarazu
           NOM   NOM surely

katu to] omoikondeiru (koto)
win COMP be=convinced (fact)

'Taro₁ is convinced that he₁ will surely win.'

b. Taroo₁ ga [{ ?kare₁ / he / pro₁ } ga Hanako ni hurareta to]
           NOM   NOM   by jilted COMP

omoikondeiru koto to boku ga kanozyo ni kyuukon
be=convinced fact and I   NOM she   to propose

sita koto to wa mukankei da
did fact and TOP unrelated PRES

'That Taro₁ is convinced that he₁ was jilted by
Hanako and that I proposed to her are
unrelated.'

It should be clear that, if one considers that the Tensed S Condition blocks the application of the disjoint reference rule (cf. Oshima (1979)), it would be impossible to account for the successful binding of anaphors in (12) and (13).

The overt pronominals here are not perfect, possibly due to the Avoid Pronoun Strategy (Chomsky (1981)). There is a sharp contrast, however, between sentences like (14a-b) above and those like (15) below:

(15) *Taroo₁ ga *kare₁* o semeta (koto)
            NOM he   ACC blamed (fact)

'Taro blamed him.'

Furthermore, as is well-known, zero pronominals are perfectly acceptable in the same position (see (14a-b)), despite the fact that they are also subject to the Binding Theory (B), as illustrated by (16) below (cf. Kuno (1983)):[14]

(16) *Taroo to Ziroo$_1$ ga pro$_1$ semeta (koto)
'Taro and Jiro blamed them.'

We will regard (14a-b) as grammatical.

Thus, under the "SUBJECT" approach, there does not seem to be a natural way to account simultaneously for both (i) the subject-object asymmetry in the binding of anaphors, as illustrated by the contrast in (12) and (13), and (ii) the lack of complementarity between anaphors and pronominals, as illustrated by the contrast between (12)-(13) and (14).[15]

4.3.3. Lexical versus Non-lexical Case

On the other hand, our Case Island Approach in its present form fares no better. While it accounts for the lack of disjoint reference in (14), it does not predict the possibility of successful binding of anaphors in (12a) and (13a). This is because the anaphors in (12a) and (13a) are marked with a nominative Case marker ga within their clause. Ga-marking should make these anaphors inaccessible from the higher clause, according to this approach.

In this subsection and 4.3.4. below, we will solve these problems. We first adopt an analysis of Case proposed by Chomsky (1981) and extended by Saito (1982;1983;1985), and modify the Case Island Approach appropriately. We will then demonstrate that the facts in (12)-(14) above fall under the Case Island Approach.

Following Chomsky (1981), let us assume that genitive Case in English is **non-lexical Case** in the sense that it is not assigned by a nominal head but is assigned (or licensed) by a N^{max} node in the context $[_{Nmax} \ldots \ldots]$.[16] In contrast, Nominative Case in English is considered to be **lexical Case**, which is assigned (or licensed) by the INFL as the head of a sentence.

Considering the fact that genitive marking of a specifier NP is exceptionless irrespective of the choice of nominal head, this is not an unreasonable assumption. Compare, for exmaple, the genitive marking in (17) below with the Nominative marking by INFL in (18). In (17), no specifier NP fails to receive genitive marking whether the nominal head is concrete, abstract or deverbal. In (18), on the other hand, whether the complement subject is marked with Nominative Case or not depends on the choice of INFL being finite or infinitival.[17]

(17) a. John's brother

   b. John's sincerity

   c. the enemy's destruction of the city

(18) a. We believe (that) *he* is honest

   b. We believe him to be honest

   c. I tried PRO to be nice

Saito (1982;1983;1985) extends this Case theory to Japanese, and claims that certain subject-object asymmetries in Japanese are derivable from the lexical status of the object Case marking (*o-* (ACC)) as opposed to the non-lexical status of the subject Case marking (*ga-* (NOM)).

For example, it is well-known that a *ga*-marked NP may optionally be realized as a *no*-marked (i.e., genitive) NP within a complex NP (Harada (1971), Bedell (1972)), whereas such an option is not allowed for an *o*-marked NP, as illustrated by the contrast between (19b) and (19c) below: (From now on, lexical Case will be represented by upper-case letters (e.g., ACC), and non-lexical Case by lower-case letters (e.g., nom).)

(19) a. [NP [S Taroo ga okane o otosita] toori]
Taroo nom money ACC dropped street

'the street where Taro dropped money'

b. Taroo no okane o otosita toori
gen ACC

c. *Taroo ga/no okane no otosita toori
nom/gen gen

Put into popular terms, while we frequently find the phenomena of "ga/no conversion", "o/no conversion" does not exist (Saito (1983)).

Elaborating Bedell's (1972) analysis, Saito assumes that "ga/no conversion" is the result of a restructuring rule at PF, which places a ga-marked NP in the domain of a higher NP. The effects of this rule are illustrated in (20) below:

(20)
a. [NP [S Taroo ga okane o otosita] toori] ===>
b. [NP Taroo ga [NP [S okane o otosita] toori]]

Since NPs are generally assigned genitive Case under a projection of N, an option of the "ga/no conversion" may arise, as in (21) below:[18]

(21) [NP Taroo no [NP [S okane o otosita] toori]]

With this analysis, Saito claims that the subject-object asymmetry in Case conversion can be derived from the dichotomy between the lexical and non-lexical Case marking. According to Saito, lexical Case and non-lexical

Case are crucially distinguished in that the former, but not the latter, involves abstract Case marking by a lexical head. Thus, when NP-*ga* is restructured, nothing precludes the conversion of *ga* into *no*. When NP-*o* is restructured, on the other hand, there would arise a conflict between the abstract Accusative Case lexically assigned to the NP and the genitive Case marker *no* acquired through the Case conversion.[19]

As a simple but important piece of motivation for the non-lexical status of subject Case marking, Saito also mentions Kuno's (1973) observation that *ga*-marking in principle can appear on **indefinitely many** NPs. These NPs function as "major subjects" (Kuroda (1984)), as illustrated in (22) below:

(22) [s bunmeikoku   *ga* [s dansei *ga*
       civilized=nation nom   male   nom

      [s heikinzyumyoo   *ga* mizikai]]]
        average=life=span nom short

    'It is in civilized nations that men are such that
    their average life-span is short.'

    (Kuno (1973, 71))

This stacking can be explained if we assume that NP-*ga* involves non-lexical Case marking (or licensing) in the context [s __ S] (or [ɪ·ᴄ·ᵐᶦⁿᵃ __ Iᶜ·ᵐᵃˣ] in our terms). This property of *ga*-marking remains mysterious, however, under the assumption that it involves Case marking (or licensing) by a lexical head.

Thus, the dichotomy between lexical and non-lexical Case marking seems to have a solid empirical ground.[20] In the next subsection, we will modify our Case Island Approach to binding, making a crucial appeal to this dichotomy.

4.3.4. Lexical Case Island

Recall first the subject-object asymmetry in (23) and (24) below (= (12) and (13)) with respect to the binding of anaphors in the tensed clauses of Japanese. We have left unexplained this fact:

(23) a. Taroo$_1$ wa   [mizukara$_1$ ga   syoo o   to-ru]
              TOP   self   NOM award ACC get-PRES

     to   wa   omottemominakatta
     COMP TOP never=thought

    '*Taro never thought that himself would win the award.'

   b. Taroo$_1$ ga   [Hanako$_2$ ga   mizukara$_{2/*1}$ o   seme-ru]
             NOM   NOM self   ACC blame

     to   wa   omottemominakatta (koto)
     COMP TOP never=thought   (fact)

    'Taro never thought that Hanako would blame herself/*himself.'

(24) a. karera₁ wa [sore-zore₁ ga yakusoku o
        they   TOP each (other) NOM promise ACC

        mamo-ru] to   sinziteiru
        keep-PRES COMP believe

        '*They₁ believe that each (other)₁ will keep a
        promise.'

    b. karera₁ ga [hutari₂ ga sorezore₂/*₁ o
       they   NOM   two   NOM each   ACC

       seme-ru   to] wa omottemominakatta (koto)
       blame-PRES COMP TOP never=thought   (fact)

       'They never thought that the two would blame
       themselves.'

Although we have viewed this asymmetry only in terms of the distinction between "subject" and "object", we now have another means to capture it --- the dichotomy between lexical and non-lexical Case marking. Let us hypothesize here, in other words, that Saito's Case approach to various subject-object asymmetries in Japanese can be extended to the binding theory as well. We then can come up with the following descriptive generalization, based upon (23) and (24):

(25) (i) If an anaphor is **lexically** Case marked (with
          "Accusative") in the embedded clause, it must
          be bound by the embedded subject.

     (ii) If an anaphor is only **non-lexically** Case marked
          (with ga) in the embedded clause, there is no
          such restriction.

Additionally, there is a similar lexical versus non-lexical Case asymmetry in the disjoint reference of pronominals, as in (26) below:

(26)
a. Taroo$_1$ ga [?kare$_1$ ga   kanarazu kat-u]
             nom   he   nom   surely   win-PRES

   to   omoikondeiru (koto)
   COMP be=convinced (fact)

   'Taro$_1$ is convinced that he$_1$ will surely win.'

b. Taroo$_1$ ga [Ziroo$_2$ ga   kare$_{1/*2}$ o   seme-ru] to
             nom   nom   he   ACC blame   COMP

   wa   omottemominakatta (koto)
   TOP never=thought   (fact)

   'Taro$_1$ never thought that Jiro$_2$ would blame him$_{1/*2}$.'

Thus, we may also state:

(27) (i) If a pronominal is **lexically** Case marked (with "Accusative") in the embedded clause, it must be disjoint in reference with the embedded subject.

   (ii) If a pronominal is only **non-lexically** Case marked (with *ga*) in the embedded clause, there is no such restriction.

Roughly speaking, the complement clause will be a binding category for anaphors and pronominals if they are lexically Case marked there. On the other hand, anaphors and pronominals lack a binding category if they are only non-lexically Case marked. Based upon these observations, let us now modify our Case Island Approach into the **Lexical**

Case Island Approach with the definition of "binding category" as in (28) below:

(28) *Binding Category* (Revised):

The binding category for ß is the maximal projection of ß's **lexical** Case marker; where ß = an anaphor or a pronominal.

With this definition, let us now return to (23) and (26) above with their proper analyses in (29) and (30) below, respectively:

(29) a. Taroo$_1$ wa [$_{Vmax}$ *mizukara*$_1$ ga syoo o to]-ru
      Taroo TOP   self   NOM award ACC get-PRES

   to wa omottemominakatta
   COMP TOP never=thought

   '*Taro never thought that himself would win the award.'

b. Taroo$_1$ ga [$_{Vmax}$ Hanako$_2$ ga *mizukara*$_{2/*1}$ o seme]
   Taroo NOM   Hanako NOM self   ACC blame

   -ru to wa omottemominakatta (koto)
   -PRES COMP TOP never=thought   (fact)

   'Taro never thought that Hanako would blame herself/*himself.'

(30)
a. Taroo to Ziroo$_1$ ga [$_{Vmax}$?*karera*$_1$ ga kanarazu kat]-u
    and   nom   they   *nom* surely   win-PRES

   to omoikondeiru (koto)
   COMP be=convinced (fact)

   'Taro and Jiro$_1$ are convinced that *they*$_1$ will surely win.'

b. Taroo to Ziroo$_1$ ga [$_{V^{max}}$ Saburoo to Siroo$_2$ ga
       and   nom   and   nom

   karera$_{1/*2}$ o   seme]-ru to   wa omottemominakatta
   they   ACC blame-PRES COMP TOP never=thought

   (koto)
   (fact)

   'Taro and Jiro$_1$ never thought that Saburo and Shiro$_2$
   would blame them$_{1/*2}$.'

Since the anaphor in (29b) and the pronominal in (30b) are both **lexically** Case marked by the embedded verb, the embedded V^{max} there becomes a binding category for both of them. Therefore, the anaphor must be bound and the pronominal must be free within the embedded V^{max} in (29b) and (30b), respectively.

As for the ga-marked anaphor in (29a) and the ga-marked pronominal in (30a), they lack a binding category since they lack a **lexical** Case marker. As a result, they can be freely bound from outside the embedded V^{max}.[21] Our claim here, in other words, is that the Binding Theory as stated in (4) does not impose any restrictions on either anaphors or pronominals when they lack a lexical Case assigner.

Thus, we have solved the problem for the binding theory of Japanese posed above in 4.3.2.2., by modifying the notion "Case Island" into "Lexical Case Island". The subject-object asymmetry in the binding of anaphors (cf. (29a) vs. (29b)) as well as the lack of complementarity between anaphors and pronominals (cf. (29a) vs. (30a)) are both reduced to the asymmetry in Case marking, i.e., to the lack of lexical Case marking in the subject position in Japanese.

The Lexical Island Approach may be further motivated in the following way. Suppose that both Chomsky's and Saito's proposals concerning subject Case marking are correct --- Nominative Case in English is lexical, as opposed to *ga*-marking in Japanese, which is non-lexical. The Lexical Case Island Approach, then, will also predict the contrast between Japanese and English concerning the NIC effect on anaphors as illustrated in (31) below:

(31) a. *They believe that [*each other* are intelligent]

b. karera$_1$ wa [*otagai*$_1$ ga tensai da]
they top *each other* nom genius is

to omotteiru
COMO think

'*They think that each other are geniuses.'

The Lexical Case Island Approach also has some desirable theoretical consequences. The binding category is now definable in terms of the notion "government" in such a way that the head-government domain of an anaphor's or a pronominal's lexical Case marker corresponds to the domain of its binding category. In fact, we may also rephrase the Binding Theory (4) as a type of licensing condition under the notion head-government as follows:[22]

(32) *Anaphor Licensing Condition*:

An indexed anaphor is licensed by a like-indexed item within the head-government domain of its lexical Case marker.

(33) *Pronominal Licensing Condition*:

An indexed pronominal is licensed by a like-indexed item from outside the head-government domain of its lexical Case marker.

Although these licensing conditions need to be further worked out, it should be clear how the (Lexical) Case Island Approach allows us to assimilate binding phenomena to other phenomena accountable under the notion government.

So far, we have presupposed that an NP lexically Case marked by a verb is located within the maximal projection of that verb in Japanese. To be precise, however, this assumption is only partially true. In Chapters Two and Three, we have argued that Japanese predicates in general are generated in the lexicon as complex predicates, and the tense and other affixes are separated from the root by the application of Move-alpha at LF. If this analysis is basically correct, the NP lexically Case marked by a verb comes to be located in the V^{max} only after the affix raising takes place at

LF, as illustrated by the schematic example in (34) below:[23]

(34) a.   S-structure/Pre-LF: b.   LF:

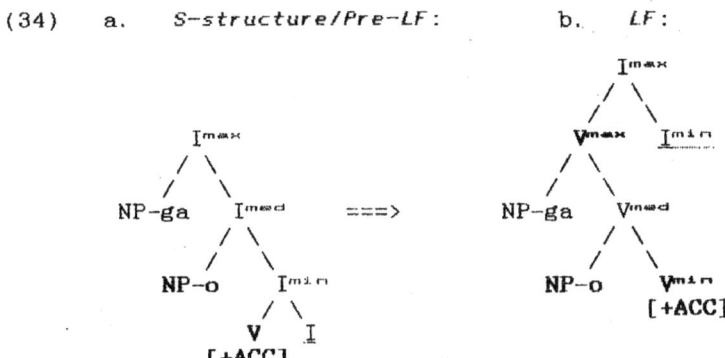

Notice, then, that the Lexical Case Island Approach to binding combined with the Affix Raising Analysis of Japanese predicates will lead us to hypothesize that Principles A and B of the Binding Theory hold at the level of Logical Form.

This hypothesis is also compatible with the following facts:

(35) a. Taroo$_1$ ga [$_{Vmax}$ otooto$_2$ ga { zibunzisin$_{2/*1}$ / kare$_{1/*2}$ } o
         Taroo nom   brother nom   self   he   ACC

         hidoku seme] ta
         badly blame PAST

         "It is Taro$_1$ whose younger brother$_2$ blamed him$_{1/*2}$/himself$_{2/*1}$ badly."

b. *konokotati*₁ ga [ᵥₘₐₓ ryoosin₂ ga { otagai₂/*₁ / karera₁/*₂ } o
   these=kids   nom   parents nom   each other / they   ACC

   hidoku nazit]-ta
   badly blame   PAST

   'These are the kids₁ whose parents₂ blamed
   each other₂/*₁/them₁/*₂ badly.'

First, object anaphors can (in fact must) be bound by a subject, but they cannot be bound by a major subject. Second, object pronominals must be disjoint in reference with a subject, but they may be bound by a major subject.

Again, only at LF do we find the representation that allows us to make a correct prediction. As illustrated in (36) below, the proper distinction between the major subject (NP_1) and the regular subject (NP_2) in terms of lexical Case island can be obtained only after affix raising takes place at LF:

(36) a. *S-structure/Pre-LF*:   b. *LF*:

[tree diagram a]: I^{max} dominating NP_1-ga and I^{med}; I^{med} dominating NP_2-ga and I^{med}; then β-o and I^{min}; I^{min} dominating V and I, with [+ACC]

===>

[tree diagram b]: I^{max} dominating NP_1-ga and I^{med}; I^{med} dominating V^{max} and I^{min}; V^{max} dominating NP_2-ga and V^{med}; V^{med} dominating β-o and V^{min} [+ACC]

Thus, we conclude that Principles A and B of the Binding Theory hold at LF in the grammar of Japanese.

4.3.5. Against the ECP Approach to the NIC

Before we further pursue the Lexical Case Island Approach to binding, let us compare our proposal to Chomsky's (1986a) suggestion that certain aspects of the NIC can be reduced to the Empty Category Principle (ECP).

Under this approach, both reciprocal and reflexive anaphors undergo LF-movement (adjunction) to the INFL position leaving a trace, as illustrated in the LF-representations in (37) and (38) below. (This analysis was first proposed in the literature by Lebeaux (1983)):

(37) a. They$_1$ love *each other*$_1$.
     b. LF: They$_1$ *each other*$_1$-INFL love t$_1$
(38) a. *They$_1$ think that *each other*$_1$ are intelligent.
     b. LF: They$_1$ *each other*$_1$-INFL think [$_{CP}$ that [$_{IP}$ t$_1$ are intelligent]]

Then, crucially in (38b) (though not in (37)), the trace left by this LF-movement violates the ECP, since it is neither lexically- nor antecedent-governed. Based upon this analysis, Chomsky claims that the NIC can be reduced to the ECP, at least with respect to the binding of anaphors.

Chomsky's approach constitutes an improvement of the binding theory over its predecessors in a number of areas, and has certain intuitive appeal. The LF-cliticization of anaphors parallels the syntactic cliticization of reflexives in many languages, e.g., the Romance. Nonetheless, there are several reasons to reject this approach.

First, this account forces us to predict that we can eliminate an ECP violation from (38a) by replacing the overt complementizer *that* with an empty complementizer. This prediction is incorrect. The ill-formedness of this sentence persists even in (39a) below:

(39) a. *They$_1$ think *each other*$_1$ are intelligent.
 b. LF: They each other$_1$-INFL think [$_{CP}$ e
 [$_{IP}$ t$_1$ are intelligent]]

Second, this account will incorrectly predict that (40) below would be as unacceptable as (38a) above:[24]

(40) ?They$_1$ would prefer for each other$_1$ to leave early.

If *each other* in (40) were LF-moved, as assumed in this approach, the trace left behind in the LF-representation (41) below would fail to be properly-governed, causing an ECP violation:

(41) LF: They$_1$ *each other*$_1$-would prefer [$_{CP}$ for [$_{IP}$ t$_1$ to leave early]]

That the complementizer *for* behaves on a par with *that* with respect to ECP can be demonstrated by the complete ill-formedness of both (42a-b) below, in which the extraction of a subject gives rise to an ECP violation:

(42) a. *who$_1$ would you prefer that t_1 leave early?
  b. *who$_1$ would you prefer for t_1 to leave early?

Even under the "Barriers" approach of Chomsky (1986b), there does not seem to be any natural way to account for the contrast between (38a) and (40). Suppose that the LF-cliticization of *each other* in (38a) and (40) is done in one step, without involving the specifier position of the COMP. The complement CP, then, will be a barrier for the trace left behind, since the complement IP is a blocking category, from which the CP can inherit barrierhood, according to Chomsky's definitions in (43)-(45) below:

(43) *Blocking Category (BC)*:

  A is a BC for B iff A is not L-marked and A dominates B.

(44) *Barrier*:

  A is a barrier for B iff (i) or (ii):

  (i) A immediately dominate C, C a BC for B.

  (ii) A is a BC for B, $A \neq$ IP.

(45) *L-marking*:

   A L-marks *B* iff *A* is a lexical category that
   θ-governs *B* (i.e., *A* (X^{min}) θ-marks *B* under
   head-government [Y.K.])

This account, thus, would incorrectly rule out not only (38a) but also (40). In short, the LF-cliticization of anaphors in a complement clause onto the matrix INFL must not be done in one step.

Suppose, then, that *each other* first moves to the specifier position of the COMP, and then adjoins the matrix INFL. This analysis, however, will also yield an incorrect result because of the "narrower" minimality condition in (46) below, which Chomsky claims reduces the *that*-trace effect to an ECP violation:

(46) *Narrower Minimality Condition*:

   A is a barrier for *B* if *A* is the immediate projection
   of *C*, a zero-level category distinct from *B*.

As illustrated in (47) below, the trace of *each other* (= *B* in (46)) is protected by the complementizers *that* and *for* (= *C* in (46)) from antecedent-government by *each other*, since *each other* is located outside the immediate projection of *that* and *for* (= *A* in (46)).

(47)
```
                    CP
                   /  \
        each other₁   C'
                     /  \
                    /    IP
                   C    /  \
                   ┆   t₁
                   ┆
                  that
                   for
```

Thus, (38a) and (40) again would incorrectly be ruled out in a uniform way.

One possible way to distinguish (40) from (38a) is to assume that *for* is as featureless as an empty complementizer. This way, the C' headed by *for* does not serve as a barrier to government, just as a C' headed by an empty category is claimed not to function as a barrier. This assumption, however, will lead us back to the first prediction mentioned above, which is incorrect (cf. (39)).

Still another counterargument comes from Japanese. As pointed out in 4.3.2. above, anaphors in Japanese may freely appear as the subject of an embedded tensed clause. Anaphors in Japanese, in other words, may freely violate the NIC, unlike those in English. (See (12a-b) above.) While we accounted for this distinction between English and Japanese in terms of the notion "lexical Case island", Chomsky (1986a) tries to ascribe the lack of an NIC violation in Japanese to the lack of an ECP violation with respect to the subject position in this language (cf. Huang

(1982), Aoun (1984) and Lasnik and Saito (1984)). Anaphors in the subject position are claimed to be possible, in other words, because this position in Japanese may be considered to be properly governed for an independent reason, for example, with respect to wh-movement at LF.

The ECP approach, then, makes a prediction that, even in Japanese, anaphors will still be disallowed when they appear in a position which is not properly governed. In Chapter Three, we have argued that "major subjects" in Japanese are not properly-governed, based on the contrast in (48) below, among others:

(48)
a. anata wa [$_{NP}$ [$_{Imax}$ Yamada-san ga [$_{Vmax}$ *nanbanme-no*
    you   top   nom   which=order-gen

   musukosan ga   e1 gookakusare]-ta] daigaku$_1$] o
   son   nom   pass   PAST college   ACC

   zyukennasaru otumori   desu ka
   apply=to   intention is   Q

   '*Which son of Yamada-san's do you intend to apply to the college which he succeeded to get in?'

b. *anata wa [$_{NP}$ [$_{Imax}$ *donata*   ga [$_{Vmax}$ *gotyoonan* ga
   you   top   which=person nom   eldest=don nom

   e1 gookakusare]-ta] daigaku$_1$] o
      pass   PAST college   ACC

   zyukennasaru otumori   desu ka
   apply=to   intention is   Q

   '*Whisch person is such that you intend to apply to the college which he has succeeded to get in?'

In the ECP approach to the NIC, therefore, it is predicted that anaphors may not appear as a major subject in Japanese. This, however, turns out to be an incorrect prediction, as illustrated by the well-formedness of (49)-(50) below:

(49) karera₁ wa [NP [IP (matigainaku) { otagai₁ / onoono₁ } ga
     they   top   (surely)   each other / each   nom

     [Vmax rieki ga agar] u] yoona   koohee de
           profit nom rise PRES such=that fair   and

     minoaru torihiki] o nozondeiru
     fruitful deal   ACC desire

     'They are desiring a fair and fruitful deal which brings profit to each of the party.'

(50) Taroo₁ wa [NP [NP [IP (ituka) { zibunzisin₁ / mizukara₁ } ga
         top   someday self   nom

     [Vmax hataraki-guti ga nakunat] ta] toki] no
           job   nom disappear PAST when   gen

     koto] o soozoositemita
     scene ACC tried=to=imagine

     'Taro tried to imagine the day when he will lose his job.'

In (49) and (50), an anaphor as a major subject appears in a complex NP without causing an ECP violation.

Thus, even in the "Barriers" approach, there does not seem to be any natural way to account for the well-formedness of (49) and (50) because the complex NP acts as a barrier for antecedent-government, inheriting barrierhood from the modifier IP it is immediately dominating.[25]

A similar discrepancy between wh-movement and LF-cliticization in English has been pointed out to me by David Pesetsky (personal communication). Observe the contrast between (51) and (52) below:

(51) *Who(m)$_1$ did John say that as for t$_1$ Mary appeared to be intelligent?

(52) a. John$_1$ said that as for himself$_1$, Mary appeared to be intelligent

  b. LF: John$_1$ himself$_1$-INFL that as for t$_1$ Mary appeared to be intelligent

Note that the ECP approach fails to distinguish the representations (52b) from (51), hence would incorrectly rule out (52a) in addition to (51).[26]

The fourth counterargument comes from some of the Romance languages like Italian and Spanish. As pointed out to me by David Pesetsky (personal communication), if the "inverted" subjects in these languages are properly-governed within the VP, as proposed by Rizzi (1982) (cf. 3.2.2.1), anaphors are predicted to freely violate the NIC when they appear in the inverted subject position. This prediction, however, is incorrect. Even the anaphors in the inverted subject position exhibit an NIC violation.

The above observations all cast serious doubt on Chomsky's suggestion that the NIC can be reduced to the ECP. We thus reject the ECP approach to the NIC.

4.3.6. Long-Distance Binding and BT-Compatibility

Consider now the so-called "long-distance" binding as in (53) below, in which a genitive-marked anaphor within the embedded subject NP is bound by the matrix subject:

(53) They$_1$ thought that [[each other$_1$'s pictures] were on sale

This example is known to pose at least two interesting problems in English (cf. Chomsky (1980;1981;1986a)).[27]

First, combined with (54) below, it shows a position in which the normal complementarity of anaphors and pronominals exceptionally breaks down:

(54) They$_1$ thought that [[their$_1$ pictures] were on sale]

Second, when (53) is paired with (55) below, we observe that the binding of anaphor is permitted in (53) but not in (55), despite the fact that the anaphor is located in a more deeply embedded position in the former:

(55) *They$_1$ think that [each other$_1$ are intelligent]

This fact is rather surprising when we consider that the binding of anaphors usually requires a certain locality.

In this subsection, we will first examine how several different alternatives fail to provide an account for these problems. We will then show how the Lexical Island Approach can handle them.

Let us start with the SUBJECT approach (Chomsky (1981)), in which "SUBJECT" (= subject and AGR) is regarded to be a potential binder and an opacity creater at the same time. As is well-known, this approach crucially relies on the idea that a potential violation of the i-within-i condition (cf footnote 28) permits the governing category for an anaphor or pronominal to be expanded from the lower S to the higher S, for example, as in (56) below (=(53)): (GC = governig category)

(56) [$_{S=GC}$ They$_1$ thought that [$_{S=GC}$ [$_{NP_1}$ each other$_1$'s pictures] AGR$_1$ are on sale]]

Here, the "agreement" coindexation between the subject NP and the AGR in the lower S causes a potential violation of the i-within-i condition, interacting with the coindexation involved in the binding of *each other* within that subject NP.[28]

This approach, however, would also prohibit, incorrectly, the binding of the pronominal in (57) below (=(54)) by the matrix subject:

(57) [$_S$ They$_1$ thought that [$_S$ [$_{NP_1}$ their$_1$ pictures] AGR$_1$ be on sale]]

Notice that the potential violation of the i-within-i condition in (57) would make the higher S rather than the lower S the governing category of *their*, imposing a disjoint reference with the matrix subject (cf. Huang (1983)).

If AGR as a SUBJECT acts both as a potential binder and a crucial element to create opacity, the SUBJECT approach would also yield an incorrect result in (58) below (=(55)):

(58) *They$_1$ think that [$_S$ *each other*$_1$ AGR$_1$ are intelligent]

Notice that the anaphor *each other* is bound by AGR as a binder within the governing category defined by the AGR as an opacity creater. It is probably true that this example can still be ruled out if we consider that AGR cannot behave as a "proper" antecedent, lacking referential content. It should be clear, however, that the idea that AGR acts as a potential binder, which plays a crucial role in the account of long-distance binding in (56) is troublesome given that AGR cannot act as a real binder.

In short, the SUBJECT approach as outlined in Chomsky (1981) does not seem to provide a satisfactory account for either of the two problems introduced above.[29]

Extending the work of Huang (1983), Chomsky (1986a) redefines the notion of governing category. This definition can be summarized as in (59) below:

(59) *Governing Category*:

A governing category for ß (ß = anaphor or pronominal) is the least Complete Functional Complex (CFC) containing a governer of ß in which some indexing is available such that this indexing is "BT-compatible" with ß and the CFC.

The CFC here refers to a category in which "all grammatical functions compatible with its head are realized" (p.169) The "BT-compatible indexing" here refers to the indexing that could satisfy the Binding Theory (A-B), within the CFC, i.e., legitimate coindexation for anaphors and lack of such coindexation for pronominals.

With the abandonment of the idea that AGR is a potential binder, this approach successfully accounts for the lack of anaphor-pronominal complementarity in (53) and (54) above. In both (53) and (54), the least CFC containing ß's governor (*pictures*) and ß is the lower S. In (53), no BT-compatible indexing is available within this CFC, since there is no legitimate binder available in it. The governing category for ß, therefore, is expanded to the higher S, the next CFC containing a legitimate binder (*they*).

In (54), on the other hand, the lack of a legitimate binder within the minimal CFC **does** in fact provide an indexing BT-compatible with ß and this CFC, namely, the lack of coindexation. Thus, the governing category for *their* will be the lower S, within which this pronominal is free.

When we turn to the example (60) below (=(55)), however, this approach will yield the wrong conclusion that *each other* as the embedded subject may be bound by the matrix subject.

(60)   *They$_1$ think that [$_{S=BC}$ *each other*$_1$ AGR are intelligent]

Here, the minimal CFC containing ß's governor (AGR) is again the lower S, within which no BT-compatible indexing is available for *each other*. The higher S, therefore, would incorrectly be regarded as the governing category for *each other*.

Chomsky attempts to rule out (60), making an appeal to the ECP violation caused by the LF-cliticization of anaphors. We have already argued against this idea, however, in 4.3.5. above. Thus, the BT-compatibility approach has problems with the contrast between (53) and (55) above, given the questionable status of the ECP approach to the NIC.

Finally, let us turn to the Lexical Case Island Approach we have proposed in 4.3.4. above, and demonstrate that it can handle both of the problems mentioned above (lack of anaphor-pronominal complementarity ((53)-(54)) and "inversed" locality of anaphor binding ((53) and (55)) in a straightforward way.

Recall that we have adopted Chomsky's proposal that Genitive Case in English is not lexically assigned by a nominal head. The moment we recognize the non-lexical status of genitive marking and the lexical status of Nominative marking in English, we obtain an account of the contrast between (53) and (55) as well as the lack of anaphor-pronominal complementarity between (53) and (54) repeated below.

(53) They$_1$ thought that [[each other$_1$'s pictures] were on sale

(54) They$_1$ thought that [[their$_1$ pictures] were on sale]

(55) *They$_1$ think that [$_{IP}$ each other$_1$ are intelligent]

In (55), for example, each other is lexically Case marked by the INFL of the complement clause. It therefore must be bound within the lexical Case island created by the

INFL, the lower IP. In (53), on the other hand, *each other* is **not** lexically Case marked by the nominal head. It therefore is free of a lexical Case island and is accessible from the matrix subject. Exactly the same story as that for (53) holds true of the pronominal in (54), hence the lack of the complementarity between anaphors and pronominals. Thus, although the account of the actual binding of the anaphor in (53) requires further complication (See 4.4.2. below), the Lexical Case Island Approach provides us with a simple account of the two problems stated at the outset of this subsection.

One advantage of taking this approach is that we can now assimilate the lack of anaphor-pronominal complementarity in (53) and (54) to that observed with respect to the subject position in Japanese, as in (62) below. The crucial similarities and distinctions in Case marking between Japanese and English (adopted from Chomsky (1981) and Saito (1985)) are summarized in (61):

(61)   Nominative   Accusative   Genitive
    English: lexical   lexical   non-lexical
    Japanese: non-lexical   lexical   non-lexical

(62) a. Taroo$_1$ wa [{ *zibunzisin$_1$* / *mizukara$_1$* / self } ga syoo o
top   nom award ACC

to-**ru**] to   wa omottemominakatta
get-**pres** COMP top never=thought

'*Taro never thought that himself would win the award.'

b. karera$_1$ wa [{ each other / *otagai$_1$* / *onoono$_1$* / each } ga yakusoku o
they TOP   nom promise ACC

mamo-ru]   to   sinziteiru
keep-PRES] COMP believe

'*They$_1$ believe that *each other$_1$* will keep a promise.'

c. Taroo to Ziroo$_1$ wa [{ they / *karera$_1$* / *pro$_1$* } ga kanarazu
      and   top   nom surely

katu to] omoikondeiru
win COMP be=convinced

'Taro and Jiro$_1$ are convinced that *they$_1$* will surely win.'

In short, the Lexical Case Island Approach makes it possible to account for the problems concerning the long-distance binding not only in English but also in Japanese. We thus have seen the advantages of adopting the Lexical Case Island Approach over the SUBJECT approach and the BT-compatibility approach.[30]

4.3.7. Binding in Exceptional Case Marking Constructions

Although it still is a matter of controversy whether the Accusative marked NP is located within the complement clause or not in a sentence involving exceptional Case marking (or raising-to-object), it seems reasonable to assume that the Accusative marking in question comes from the higher verb, in (63) below for example, from the matrix verb *expect*:

(63) We expect *him* to return by tomorrow morning

In the Lexical Case Island Approach to binding, therefore, the successful binding of the anaphor and the disjoint reference of the pronominal in (64) below are precisely as predicted: (Recall that we have a trace of the raised subject within the V^{max}.)

(64) They$_1$ [$_{Vmax}$ expected { *each other*$_1$ / *them*$_{*1}$ } to leave early t_1]

A more interesting interaction of exceptional Case marking (ECM) and binding can be observed in English gerunds, in which Accusative Case (= lexical Case) and genitive Case (= contextual Case) are known to alternate, as illustrated in (65) below:

(65) I would favor { *him* / *his* } leaving early.

The Lexical Case Island Approach to binding, then, predicts the following contrast between the pronominals and anaphors that appear in the position of *him/his* in (65):

(66) (i) Whether a **pronominal** is Accusative-marked or genitive-marked will result in the presence or absence, respectively, of disjoint reference with the matrix subject.

(ii) Whether an **anaphor** is Accusative-marked or genitive-marked, on the other hand, will uniformly yield the successful binding of the anaphor by the matrix subject.

(66i) follows, because the Accusative-marked pronominal will have the matrix V^{max} as a lexical Case island, whereas the genitive-marked pronominal lacks it. The former, therefore, must be free with respect to the matrix subject, while the latter need not be.

In the case of anaphors, on the other hand, nothing precludes either the Accusative- or genitive-marked anaphor to be bound by the matrix subject. The Accusative anaphor is succesfully bound within its lexical Case island (matrix V^{max}). The genitive anaphor lacks a lexical Case island in which it must be bound.

This prediction is borne out, as illustrated in (67a-b) below, supporting further the Lexical Case Island Approach:

(67) a. [$_{Vmax}$ They$_1$ would favor { $them_{*1}$ / $their_1$ } leaving early t_1]

b. [$_{VMAX}$ They$_1$ would favor { each other$_1$ / each other$_1$'s } leaving early t$_1$]

The binding facts in the infinitivals as in (68) below have been claimed to be a strong motivation for a raising-to-object analysis of this construction (Postal (1974)).

(68)
a. *[They$_1$ believe them$_1$ [e$_1$ to be intelligent]]
b. [They$_1$ believe each other$_1$ [e$_1$ to be intelligent]]

In the raising-to-object analysis, both the failure of pronominal binding in (68a) and the success of anaphor binding in (68b) are ascribed to the matrix status of them and each other, respectively.

This account could be extended to capture the contrast between the two types of pronominals in (67a), by assuming that Accusative marking, **but not genitive marking**, of the complement subject is the result of raising-to-object. Two distinct analyses as in (69) below are assigned, in other words, to (67a):

(69)
a. *[They$_1$ would favor them$_1$ [e$_1$ leaving early]]
b. [They$_1$ would favor [their$_1$ leaving early]]

Notice, however, that it would be left unexplained in this approach why even the genitive-marked anaphor in (67b) above can be bound by the matrix subject. This problem becomes clearer when two distinct analyses parallel to (69a-b) are assigned to (67b), as in (70a-b) below:

(70)
 a. [They$_1$ would favor *each other*$_1$ [*e*$_1$ leaving early]]
 b. [They$_1$ would favor [*each other*$_1$*'s* leaving early]]

This analysis incorrectly predicts that *each other* in (70b) cannot be bound by the matrix subject, located within the complement clause. A raising-to-object analysis, therefore, seems to be insufficient to account for the binding in English gerunds.

 Adopting the Lexical Case Island Approach to binding, on the other hand, we are able to offer an account of the pronominal-anaphor asymmetry not only in English gerunds in (67) above but also in Japanese finite complements as in (71) and (72) below (cf. Kuno (1976), Oshima (1979)). As illustrated in (71), whether a pronominal embedded subject is marked with *o* (ACC) or *ga* (nom) yields different results in binding --- only the *o*-marked pronominal is disjoint in reference with the matrix subject. As illustrated in (72) and (73), on the other hand, an anaphor in the same position may be bound by the matrix subject whether it is *o*-marked or *ga*-marked:

(71) [vmax sono syoonen₁ ga { kare*₁ o / kare₇₁ ga }
         that boy   nom   he ACC / kare nom

isan-no-soozokunin da to   sira] nai (koto)
heir   is COMP know   NEG (fact)

'That boy does not know that he is the heir.'

(72)
a. [vmax sono syoonen₁ ga { zibunzisin₁ o / zibunzisin₁ ga }
         that boy   nom self   ACC   nom

isan-no-soozokunin da to   sira] nai (koto)
heir   is COMP know   NEG (fact)

'*That boy does not know that himself is the heir.'

b. [vmax karera₁ ga { otagai₁ o / otagai₁ ga } zituno kyoodai da
         they   nom each other ACC   nom   real   brothers are

to   sira] nai (koto)
COMP know   NEG (fact)

'*They do not know that each other are real brothers.'

Again, the dichotomy between the lexical Case (Accusative) and the non-lexical Case (nominative) provides us with a correct account of all the binding facts in (71) and (72). (See the summary of Case marking in (61) above.)

Also, just as in the case of English gerunds in (67), the raising-to-object analysis as schematized in (73a-b) below is insufficient to deal with this paradigm, leaving the successful binding of the nominative-marked anaphors in

(72a-b) unexplained. In other words, the raising-to-object analysis cannot explain the paradigm in (72) without stipulating that the NIC does not hold in Japanese.

(73) a. [... NP_1-o [$_{CP}$ e_1 ...]]
     b. [... [$_{CP}$ NP-ga ...]]

For exactly the same reason, it will also be insufficient to merely assume that the Accusative NPs in (71) and (72a-b) are located in the matrix, and control an empty subject in the complement clause interpreted as an empty pronominal, as illustrated in (74) below:

(74) [sono syoonen$_1$ ga kare$_{*1}$ o [pro_1 isan-no-soozokunin
       that boy   nom he   ACC   heir

       da to] sira nai (koto)
       is COMP know NEG (fact)

'That boy does not know that he is the heir.'

Suppose, then, that the examples in (71) and (72a-b) involve exceptional Case marking. That is to say, the Accusative-marked NPs in (71) and (72a-b) are located within the complement clause, as schematized in (75) below, and receives Accusative Case from the matrix verb across the clausal boundary.

(75) [$_{Vmax}$ ... V [$_{CP}$ NP-o ...]]

If this indeed is the case, the binding facts in (71) and
(72) above will provide us with a further motivation to
assume that the locality condition in binding should be
stated in terms of **Case and government**, as we have argued,
rather than solely in terms of government, as Chomsky
(1981;1986a) has argued. That is, there seems to exist
little or no reason to assume that NP-*o* in (71), for
example, is governed but NP-*ga* is not, once the NP-*o* there
is assumed to be located within the complement clause. The
crucial assumption is that the *o*-marked subject and the
ga-marked subject are free variants in this example.
Notice that the complement clause must be analyzed as a CP
for both NP-*o* and NP-*ga* in (71), since an overt
complementizer *to* appears with either of them. It is
highly unlikely, therefore, that NP-*ga* is protected from
government, contained in a CP, while NP-*o* is not protected
from government, contained in only an IP.[31] The government
approach, then, would fail to account for the contrast
between *kare o* and *kare ga* in (71).

4.3.8. Scrambling and Binding

The application of scrambling appears to cause us a
problem. Observe the following paradigm, in which
scrambling changes the possibility of the binding of

o-marked anaphors by a matrix subject: (This contrast has also been observed, independently, by Kurata (1986).)

(76)
a. Taroo$_1$ wa [$_{V^{max}}$ Hanako ga { zibun$_1$ / zibunzisin$_{*1}$ / mizukara$_{*1}$ } o seme
       top   nom   self   ACC blame

-ru to wa omottemominakatta
-PRES COMP top never=thought

'*Taro never thought that Hanako would blame himself.'

b. Taroo$_1$ wa { zibunzisin$_1$ / mizukara$_1$ } o Hanako ga t_1 seme-ru

to wa omottemominakatta

(77) a. karera$_1$ ga [hutari$_2$ ga sorezore$_{2/*1}$ o
       they   nom   two   nom each   ACC

seme-ru   to] wa omottemominakatta (koto)
blame-PRES COMP top never=thought   (fact)

'They never thought that the two would blame themselves.'

b. karera$_1$ ga sorezore$_1$ o hutari ga seme-ru t_1 to wa omottemominakatta (koto)

The embedded V^{max} in (76a) and (77a), in other words, suddenly ceases to function as the binding category of an o-marked anaphor when this anaphor is scrambled, as in (76b) and (77b).

This effect of scrambling is in fact predicted by our binding theory, which incorporates the Case theory proposed by Saito (1985). Recall that this theory dissociates abstract Case from overt Case markers. Then, given the one-to-one relation between an instance of *o*-marking and Accusative Case marking (or licensing), and the principle (78) below suggested by Chomsky (1981), we may consider that the preposed anaphors in (76b) and (77b) above lack abstract Case, unlike their traces (= variables) left behind:[32]

(78) Variables must have abstract Case.

Once we assume that the scrambled anaphors in (76b) and (77b) lack their abstract Case, we predict that they may be bound from outside the V^{max}, since they now lack their binding categories.[33]

Another potential problem for our approach comes from the binding of anaphors in relative clauses (RC) as in (79) below: (The observation here is due to Kurata (1986).)

(79)
a. kare$_1$ wa [$_{RC}$ [$_{Vmax}$ e$_2$ *zibunzisin*$_1$ *o* kubinisita]
    he   top   self   ACC fired

    gakubutyoo$_2$] ni sae kitinto   nengazyoo   o
    dean   to even regularly new=year=card ACC

    okuri tuzuketa
    send continued

    '*He$_1$ continued to send a new year card even to
     the dean who fired himself$_1$.'

b. hutarino kyoozyu$_1$ wa [$_{RC}$ [$_{Vmax}$ e$_2$ otagai$_1$ o
    two   professors top   each other ACC

   hihansi] ta   gakuseitati$_2$] o   sikarituketa
   criticize PAST students   ACC scolded

   '*The two professors$_1$ scolded the students who
     criticized each other$_1$.'

Since the anaphors in (79) are marked with o, our binding theory predicts that they must be bound within the V^{max}. This prediction, however, is incorrect.

As pointed out by Kurata (Ibid.), however, nothing precludes us from assuming that the o-marked anaphors in (79) are actually located to the left of the empty category coindexed with the head noun due to the application of scrambling. (79a-b), in other words, are not the only possible (LF) representations for these sentences. They may as well be analyzed as in (80a) and (80b) below, respectively.

(80)
a. kare$_1$ wa [$_{RC}$ zibunzisin$_1$ o e$_2$ t$_1$ kubinisita gakubutyoo$_2$] ni sae kitinto nengazyoo o okuri tuzuketa

b. hutarino kyoozyu$_1$ wa [$_{RC}$ otagai$_1$ o e$_2$ t$_1$ hihansi ta gakuseitati$_2$] o sikarituketa

Note, then, the problem here can be completely assimilated to that involving "regular" scrambling as in (76b) and (77b) above. We thus account for the successful binding in (79a-b), again, in terms of the lack of lexical Case on the scrambled anaphors.[34]

4.3.9. Binding into Prepositional Phrases

Let us assume that the prepositional complementizer *for* in (81) below assigns an abstract Case to the complement subject, and turns the complement CP into a lexical Case island:[35]

(81) They$_1$ would [$_{Vmax}$ prefer [$_{CP}$ for { *each other*?$_1$ / *them*?*$_1$ } to win] t$_1$]

The judgments indicated here concerning the anaphor- and pronominal-binding, then, would provide us with a counterexample to our definition of "binding category" (82) below (= (28)):

(82) *Binding Category*:
   The binding category of ß is the maximal projection of ß's lexical Case marker: where ß = an anaphor or a pronominal.

Obviously, therefore, we must allow a lexical Case island to be extended from the maximal projection of ß's lexical Case marker to the next maximal projection up in some cases. In (81), for example, the lexical Case island is extended from the complement CP to the matrix V^{max}. (It clearly is not the case that the complement subject in (81) simply lacks the binding category, since the complement pronominal subject must be disjoint in reference with the matrix subject.)

Such an extension of lexical Case islands, in fact, seems to be nothing peculiar to the prepositional complementizer *for* but to be something general about prepositions, as illustrated by the similar binding facts in (83) and (84) below:[36]

(83) They$_1$ [$_{Vmax}$ told Mary [$_{PP}$ about { *each other*$_1$ / *them*$*_1$ }] t$_1$]

(84) [$_{NP}$ the students'$_1$ criticism [$_{PP}$ of { *each other*$_1$ / *them*$*_1$ }]]

Characterizing the same phenomenon in different terms, we may probably consider that a prepositional phrase in general lacks the capability of functioning as a G-root, being transparent to "upward node-counting". (Recall that G-root refers to the topmost node in the government domain.) Let us hypothesize, then, that when the maximal projection of ß's lexical Case assigner cannot function as a G-root, the next available maximal projection becomes the G-root, and eventually becomes ß's lexical Case island. We will modify (82), in other words, as in (85) below:

(85) *Binding Category* (final):

   The binding category of ß is the **G-root** of ß's lexical Case marker: where ß = an anaphor or a pronominal.

In (83), for example, the lexical Case-marker of *each other* and *them* is the preposition *about*. Since its maximal projection, PP, is transparent, the next available maximal node, V^{max}, becomes the G-root, hence the binding category. Since this binding category contains the T-subject trace bound by the I-subject *they*, the anaphor will be well-formed and the pronominal ill-formed with the indexing indicated there.

Such a marked property of prepositional phrases, in fact, can be independently demonstrated when we closely examine how they interact with Principle C of the Binding Theory (Binding Theory (C)).

Recall, first, the paradigm in (86) below (from Reinhart (1976)), which we used in Chapter Three to support our proposal that the base-generated "extraposed" clause is located within the V^{max}:

(86)
a. [$_{CP2}$ That *Rosa*$_1$ failed] (should have) [$_{Vmax}$ bothered her$_1$ t_2]

b. *It (should have) [$_{Vmax}$ bothered her$_1$ that *Rosa*$_1$ has failed]

The contrast between (86b) above and (87) below clearly shows that the Binding Theory (C) is responsible for the ungrammaticality of (86b).

(87) It (should have) [$_{Vmax}$ bothered her$_1$ that *she*$_1$ has failed]

Moreover, the contrast between (86a) and (86b), on the other hand, and that between (86b) above and (88) below, on the other hand, suggests that the Binding Theory (C) concerns whether or not the R-expression (*Rosa*) is max-governed by another NP (*her*):

(88) It (should have) [$_{Vmax}$ bothered [$_{NP}$ her$_1$ friends] that *Rosa*$_1$ has failed]

Observe now the following paradigm, part of which is from Chomsky (1986a, 183):

(89)
a. *It [$_{Vmax}$ seems [$_{PP}$ to him$_1$] that *John*$_1$ is a failure]
b. It [$_{Vmax}$ seems [$_{PP}$ to him$_1$] that *he*$_1$ is a failure]
c. It [$_{Vmax}$ seems [$_{PP}$ to [$_{NP}$ his$_1$ friends]] that *John*$_1$ is a failure]

From the contrast between (89a) and (89b), we can conclude that it is the Binding Theory (C) that rules out (89a). If we follow the same reasoning as above, then, the contrast between (89a) and (89c) will lead us to conclude that *him* in (89a) does max-govern *John* despite the presence of a PP node, while *his* in (89c) does not. The PP in (89a), in other words, does not count as the G-root. We

ni-marked NP *Ziroo*. With this analysis, we can assimilate the pronominal binding in (90) to that in "regular" complementation structures in (91) below:

(91)　　Taroo$_1$ ga [Ziroo$_2$ ga　*kare*$_{1/*2}$　o　　hihansuru]
　　　　　　　nom　　　　　nom　*he*　　　ACC criticize

　　　　to　wa　omottemominakatta (koto)
　　　　COMP TOP never=thought　　(fact)

　　　'Taro never thought that Jiro would criticize him.'

Quite unexpectedly in this analysis, however, the Accusative-marked anaphors may be bound by the "matrix" subject. Compare, for example, causative (92a) below with a sentence involving regular complementation in (92b):

(92) a.　Taroo$_1$ ga [Ziroo$_2$ ni　aete　　　　{ *zibun*$_{1/2}$
　　　　　　　　nom　　　　　　DAT purposefully　*zibunzisin*$_{1/2}$ }
　　　　　　　　　　　　　　　　　　　　　　　　　mizukara$_{1/2}$
　　　　　　　　　　　　　　　　　　　　　　　　　self

　　　　o　hihans] aseta　(koto)
　　　　ACC criticize caused (fact)

　　　'Taro purposefully made Jiro criticize himself."

　b.　Taroo$_1$ ga [Ziroo$_2$ ga { *zibun*$_{1/2}$
　　　　　　　nom　　　　　nom　 *zibunzisin*$_{2/*1}$ } o
　　　　　　　　　　　　　　　　　 mizukara$_{2/*1}$　　　ACC
　　　　　　　　　　　　　　　　　 self

　　　　hihansuru] to　wa　omottemominakatta (koto)
　　　　criticize　　COMP top never=thought　　(fact)

　　　'Taro never thought that Jiro would criticize himself.'

thus have independent motivation to assume that prepositional phrases lack the capability to function as a G-root for max-government.[37] The binding facts in (81), (83) and (84), therefore, can be accounted for in the Lexical Case Island Approach with a slight modification of the definition of "binding category" as in (82).[38]

4.3.10. Binding in the Causative Construction

Finally in this section, we will investigate anaphoric and pronominal binding in the causative construction in Japanese.

Let us first present Oshima's (1979) observation concerning pronominal binding in the causative construction in (90):

(90) Taroo$_1$ ga [Ziroo$_2$ ni aete   kare$_{1/*2}$ o
       nom   DAT purposefully he   ACC

       hihans] aseta (koto)
       criticize caused (fact)

       'Taro purposefully made Jiro criticize him.'

Two facts in (90) suggest that we should assume the presence of a complement as indicated there in this causative sentence at the level where the Binding Theory (B) holds. First, the o-marked pronominal *kare* (he) in (90) may be bound by the *ga*-marked NP *Taroo*. Second, the same pronoun must be disjoint in reference with the

(93) a. Taroo to Ziroo$_1$ ga [Saburoo to Siroo$_2$ ni
        and   nom   and   DAT

    otagai$_{1/2}$ o mihar] aseta
    each other ACC watch caused

    'Taro and Jiro made Saburo and Siro keep an eye on each (other).'

b. Taroo to Ziroo$_1$' ga [Saburoo to Siroo$_2$ ga
      and   nom   and   nom

    otagai$_{2/*1}$ o semeru] to wa
    each other ACC blame   COMP TOP

    omottemominakatta (koto)
    never=thought   (fact)

    'Taro and Jiro never thought that Saburo and Shiro would blame each (other).'

Here we have a paradox --- the complement clause (the complement V^{max} in our terms) in the causative functions as a binding category for pronominals but not for anaphors. Obviously, we will not achieve a satisfactory account of this paradox by merely assuming that causatives involve complementation.[39]

In what follows, we will demonstrate that these seemingly paradoxical facts concerning the binding in the causative construction will be straightforwardly explained when we combine the following hypotheses we have proposed and argued for above: (i) the causative morpheme sase is raised at LF, (ii) the Binding Theory (A-B) hold at LF, and (iii) "binding category" is defined in terms of the notion lexical Case island.

First, recall that we have argued, in the light of adverbial interpretation, that any *ni*-causative sentence will come to have at LF the two representations as schematized in (94a) and (94b) below, before and after the application of Move-alpha, which raises the causative suffix *sase* out of the morphologically complex predicate V-*sase*: (Notice that the diagram (94a) presupposes that the tense morpheme has already been raised out of the complex predicate.)

(94)

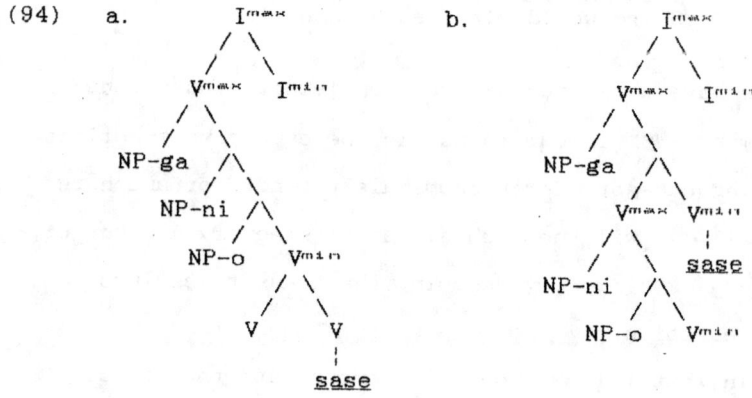

Then, the moment we adopt a (probably optimal) position that the Binding Theory (A-B) may hold anywhere in the LF component, i.e., the checking of anaphoric and pronominal binding does not have to be extrinsically ordered with respect to any operation at LF (e.g., application of Move-alpha), we can solve the above-mentioned paradox concerning binding.

The explication here requires clarification of the notion "well-formedness of derivation". Consider first the "standard" GB-approach to the raising construction, which assumes a D-structure as in (95) below:

(95) D-str: ___ seems [Mary to be sick]

We can come up with at least two possible derivations out of this D-structure representation. One derivation is well-formed, the Case Filter being satisfied as a result of applying Move-alpha, as in (96) below:

(96) S-structure: $Mary_1$ seems [t_1 to be sick]

Another derivation, which does not involve the application of Move-alpha, is ill-formed, causing the Case Filter violation, as in (97) below. (The ill-formed status of this derivation will remain the same with or without the insertion of a pleonastic element *it* in the matrix subject position.)

(97) S-structure: *(It) seems [Mary to be sick]

Notice that, while the D-structure representation (95) may result into an ill-formed representation as in (97), it may still surface as a well-formed sentence as in (96), since at least one well-formed derivation for this representation is permitted by the grammar.

A similar story can be told about the pre-LF representation in (94a) above. Suppose that the *o*-marked NP in (94a) is realized as an anaphor, as in (98) below:

(98) [$_{Vmax}$ NP-ga NP-ni mizukara o [$_V$ V-sase]]
                        self   ACC   CAUSE

(98) may serve as an underlying representation of two possible derivations. In one derivation, the Binding Theory checks the binding of the anaphor after Move-alpha has raised the causative affix *sase*, i.e., in the representation (99) below:

(99) [$_{Vmax}$ NP$_1$ ga [$_{Vmax}$ NP-ni mizukara$_1$ o V] sase]

If the intended binding is as indicated in (99), the Binding Theory rules out this representation since the accusative-marked anaphor *mizukara* is not bound within its lexical Case island, i.e., complement V^{max}. The underlying LF representation (98), however, may still be realized as a well-formed LF, since it may involve a well-formed derivation in which the Binding Theory checks the anaphor-binding before Move-alpha raises the causative affix *sase*, i.e., in the representation (98) above. In this representation, the binding of *mizukara* (self) by NP-*ga* is permitted since the binding category of this anaphor is the maximal projection of the complex predicate V-*sase*, which contains the NP-*ga* inside.

We can make an appeal to exactly the same reasoning to account for the pronominal binding in (90) above (repeated below):

(90) Taroo$_1$ ga [Ziroo$_2$ ni aete kare$_{1/*2}$ o
     nom   DAT purposefully he   ACC
     hihans] aseta (koto)
     criticize caused (fact)

'Taro purposefully made Jiro criticize him.'

(90) may be realized as a well-formed sentence because a well-formed derivation of this sentence is permitted by the grammar in which the Binding Theory checks the pronominal binding after the affix raising has taken place, i.e., in a representation like (100) below:

(100) [$_{Vmax}$ NP$_1$ ga [$_{Vmax}$ NP-ni kare$_1$ o V] sase]
                                         he   ACC   CAUSE

The Binding Theory permits the binding relation in (100) because the accusative-marked pronominal *kare* is free within its binding category, the complement V^{max}.

In short, not only the example (96) above (= raising construction) but also (90) (= pronominal binding), (92a) and (93a) (= anaphoric binding) have one well-formed derivation each, which permits them to surface as well-formed sentences. Thus, the seemingly contradictory facts concerning the binding in (90) and (92-3a) above follow straightforwardly from the affix raising analysis of Japanese causatives.

The contrast between the causatives and the "regular" complement construction as in (91) and (92-3b) above is also a natural consequence since the latter does not involve any affix raising (except for that of tense morphemes, which has no effect on binding).

We thus have seen that the Affix Raising Hypothesis for Japanese couched in the Lexical Case Island Approach to binding provides us with a straightforward account of otherwise puzzling properties of anaphoric and pronominal binding in the causative construction. We believe that this will provide further motivation for both these hypotheses.

4.4. Further Implications and Problems: An Initial Sketch

The purpose of this section is to point out further theoretical and empirical implications of the Lexical Case Island Hypothesis. We will provide some tentative analyses to cope with the predictions made in this hypothesis, although most of them will remain rather sketchy. We will also briefly discuss some of the apparent problems of this hypothesis.

4.4.1. PRO Theorem

Chomsky (1981, 191) derives (1) below as a theorem from Principles A and B of the Binding Theory. This proof depends on regarding PRO as a pronominal anaphor ([+anaphor, +pronominal]

(1) *PRO Theorem*:
PRO is ungoverned.

Since we have reformulated the Binding Theory (A-B) in terms of the notion "government by a lexical Case marker" rather than just "government", we necessarily modify the PRO Theorem as in (2) below:

(2) *Revised PRO Theorem*:
PRO is not governed **by a lexical Case marker**.

The Revised PRO Theorem (2) predicts that PRO may appear at LF in the positions listed in (3) below. (Recall that we have concluded that the Binding Theory (A-B) hold at LF):

(3) Non-Case Position
    a. English: I-subject of infinitivals (where there is no exceptional Case marking)

Non-lexical Case Position
    b. English: genitive position
    c. Japanese: nominative position
    d. Japanese: genitive position

A familiar control structure as in (4) below exemplifies (3a):

(4) He tried [$_{Imax}$ PRO to win]

With the example (5) below (among others), Chomsky (1986a) claims that PRO may appear in English in the genitive position ((3b)) as well:

(5) They$_1$ told [stories about them$_1$]

With the coreference relation indicated here, the sentence is ill-formed if the *stories* are *theirs*$_1$ but is well-formed if the *stories* are someone else's. Chomsky ascribes this contrast to the Binding Theory (B) on the following analysis, with PROs in the genitive positions:[40]

(6) a.   *They$_1$ told [*PRO*$_1$ stories about them$_1$]
     b.   They$_1$ told [*PRO*$_2$ stories about them$_1$]

Notice that the Revised PRO Theorem permits PRO to be governed by the nominal head.[41]

If PRO exists in Japanese, we predict that it may appear in the nominative position ((3c)), whether the sentence is tensed or not. In the literature, it has often been pointed out: (i) that, unlike in English, PRO in Japanese may appear as the subject of even a tensed clause

(Saito (1982), Hasegawa (to appear)), and (ii) that PRO may alternate with a lexical subject (Oshima (1979), Hasegawa (Ibid.)):

(7) a. kare₁ wa tuneni [{ PRO₁ / zibunzisin₁ ga } taiin-tati ni
       he   top always   self   nom   soldiers DAT

   mohan o   simesu yooni] tutome-te-iru
   model ACC exhibit COMP   trying

   'He always tries to present himself as a good model to the soldiers.'

   b. Taroo wa Hanako₁ ni [{ PRO₁ / kanozyo₁ ga } zibun de tegami
                  top   DAT   she   nom   self by letter

   o   kaku yooni] settokusi-ta
   ACC write COMP   persuaded

   'Taro persuaded Hanako to write a letter by herself.'

Both these observations are compatible with the revised PRO Theorem (2). The availability of non-lexical Case, in other words, allows PRO to occur in this position.[42]

It is possible that PRO appears in the genitive position in Japanese as well. It is, however, hard to detect:

(8) kare₁ ga [{ PRO₁ / zibun₁ no } sippai] o   kakusi-ta (koto)
    he   nom   self   gen   mistake ACC hide-PAST (fact)

   'He covered up his mistake.'

(9) [{ PRO$_{arb}$ } sippai] wa [{ PRO$_{arb}$ } seikoo]
      aru hito no failure top sono hito no success
      one person gen   that person gen

   no moto^{43}
   gen cause

   'Failure is the mother of success.'

Thus, an initial investigation suggests that the revised PRO Theorem (2) makes correct predictions concerning the distribution of PRO in English and Japanese.

4.4.2. Binding Domains

In 4.3.4. above, we have concluded that the Binding Theory as stated in (10) below does not impose any restrictions on either anaphors or pronominals when they lack a lexical Case assigner, in accordance with the definition of "binding category" in (11):

(10) *Binding Theory*:

    A: An anaphor is bound in its binding category.
    B: A pronominal is free in its binding category.

(11) *Binding Category*:

    The binding category for ß is the maximal projection (more precisely, G-root) of ß's **lexical** Case marker; where ß = an anaphor or a pronominal.

Observe, however, the contrast in the following pair of sentences:

(12) a. The students₁ believe that [the teachers₂ thought that [their₁/₂ pictures] were on sale]

b. We₁ believe that [ₛᴅ they₂ thought that [each other's₂/*₁ pictures] were on sale]

The pronominal binding in (12a) does not require any addition to the Lexical Case Island Hypothesis --- the Binding Theory (10) does not impose any restrictions on *their*, since it is not lexically Case marked.

That the genitive marked anaphor *each other* cannot be bound by *we* in (12b), on the other hand, suggests that the binding of an anaphor is not totally free even when the Binding Theory (10) does not impose any restrictions on it.

A similar locality condition on anaphors can be observed in the Japanese examples (13)-(17) below:

```
                              kare₁/₂
                              he
                              zibun₁/₂
(13) Taroo₁ ga [ₛᴅ titioya₂ ga [{ zibunzisin₂/*₁ } no
            nom      father   nom    mizukara₂/*₁        gen
                                     self

     sakuhin ] o   damatte  syuppinsi-te-ita ] to   wa
     art=work ACC silently  submited             COMP top

     siranakatta (koto)
     didn't=know (fact)
```

'Taro did not know that his father had submitted his work to an exhibition without telling it to him.'

(14) Taroo₁ ga [₍ᵦₚ₎ titioya₂ ga [{ kare₁/₂ / zibun₁/₂ / zibunzisin₂/*₁ / mizukara₂/*₁ } no
     nom   father   nom   he / self / self   gen

     sakuhin] ga nyuusensu-ru to   sinzitei-ru] to
     work   nom accepted   COMP believe-PRES COMP

     omot-te-iru (koto)
     think   (fact)

     'Taro thinks that his father believes that his work
     will be selected for the exhibition.'

(15) aru kasyu₁ ga [₍ᵦₚ₎ maneezyaa₂ ga
     one singer nom   manager   nom

     [{ kare₁/₂ / zibun₁/₂ / zibunzisin₂/*₁ / mizukara₂/*₁ }] no kai-ta kyoku] o
        he / self / self   gen wrote tune   ACC

     rekoodingusi-ta
     recorded

     'Some singer's manager recorded a song he wrote.'

(16) ano raibaru-kasyu-tati₁ ga [₍ᵦₚ₎ maneezyaa₂ ga
     those rival-singers   nom   managers   nom

     [otagai₂/*₁ no seikoo] o   netan]-de-iru
       each=other gen success   ACC envy

     'Those rival singers' managers are jealous of each
     other's success.'

(17) Taroo to Ziroo₁ ga [₍ᵦₚ₎ hahaoya₂ ga [sorezore₂/*₁ ga
     and   nom mother   nom each   nom

     ziman-banasi   o   si]-ta]
     boastful=account   ACC did

     'Taro and Jiro's mothers each gave a boastful
     account.'

In order to capture such an extra locality condition on anaphors, we introduce the notion "binding domain" defined in (18) below, and modify the Binding Theory (10) as in (19): (cf. Huang (1983))

(18) *Binding Domain*:

   A binding domain for ß is the minimal constituent containing ß and its potential binder; where ß = anaphor.

(19) Binding Theory *(Revised)*:

   A: An anaphor is bound in its binding category **and binding domain**.

   B: A pronominal is free in its binding category. (no change)

This way, the restriction on the binding of anaphors in (12)-(17) above can be ascribed to the presence of the binding domains (BD) indicated in each example.

Making an appeal to the revised Binding Theory (19), we can also capture the locality of Subject Raising in English illustrated by the contrast in (20) below:

(20) a. It seems that [$_{BD}$ John$_1$ has [$_{Vmax}$ left t$_1$]]

   b. *John$_1$ seems that [$_{BD}$ it has [$_{Vmax}$ left t$_1$]]

Since the T-subject traces in (20a-b) do not seem to be bound by any operator, let us assume that they are anaphors. The anaphors in both (20a) and (20b) lack a binding category, since they are not lexically Case marked. The revised Binding Theory (19), however, correctly distinguishes the two cases, since the anaphor is bound in its binding domain in (20a), but not in (20b). Even if this problem is overcome in (20b) with the coindexation of the trace with the pleonastic *it*, the resulting representation will be thematically anomalous, since the agent θ-role of the complement verb *leave* is not assigned to an argument. Thus, the locality of Subject Raising in English is at least partly derivable from the revised Binding Theory (19).

4.4.3. Control Theory

The revision of the Binding Theory as in (19) above can be independently motivated in the area of control theory, along the line of Manzini (1983).

Manzini comes up with the descriptive generalizations in (21) and (22) below based upon (23)-(25) and (26)-(28), respectively:[44]

(21) A PRO in an object sentence of a sentence S is bound in S.

(22) A PRO in a subject sentence (co)refers freely.

(23) a. John₁ asked Bill [*PRO*₁ to be allowed to shave himself]
b. John asked Bill₁ [*PRO*₁ to shave himself][48]
c. *John asked Bill [*PRO*ₐᵣᵦ to behave oneself]

(24) a. John₁ promised Bill [*PRO*₁ to shave himself]
b. John promised Bill₁ [*PRO*₁ to be allowed to shave himself]
c. *John promised Bill [*PRO*ₐᵣᵦ to behave oneself]

(25) a. *Mary₁ said [that John asked Bill [*PRO*₁ to behave herself]
b. *Mary₁ said [that John promised Bill [*PRO*₁ to behave herself]

(26) [*PRO*ₐᵣᵦ to behave oneself in public] would help Bill

(27)
a. [*PRO*₁ to behave himself in public] would help Bill
b. [*PRO*₁ to behave himself in public] would help [Bill₁'s development]

(28) Mary₁ knows that [*PRO*₁ to behave herself in public] would help Bill

Although we will not go into the details, Manzini proposes to capture the generalizations in (21) and (22) in terms of the notion "domain-governing category", which is conceptually similar to our "binding domain".

The revised Binding Theory (19) accounts for the control phenomena in (23)-(28) by imposing a variety of restrictions on anaphors, pronominals and pronominal anaphors (PRO), depending on the presence/absence of a binding category and a binding domain, as summarized in (29) below:

(29)

	restriction on anaphor	restriction on pronominal	restriction on **pronominal anaphor**
If BC:	bound in BC	free in BC	bound & free in BC
If BD only:	bound in BD	none	bound in BD
If neither:	none	none	none

(BC = binding category, BD = binding domain)

If PRO (= pronominal anaphor) has a binding category, the Binding Theory will require it to be both bound and free in that binding category, which can never be satisfied. This of course is the effect of the PRO Theorem discussed in 4.4.1. above.

Suppose now that PRO lacks a binding category, but has a binding domain. The PRO, then, must behave as an anaphor since the Binding Theory (19) requires it to be bound within the binding domain. This straightforwardly accounts for the various control phenomena in (23)-(25) and (28), including the lack of "arb(itrary)" reading in (23c) and (24c), and the locality of control detected by the contrast between (25a-b) and (28).

Finally, the Binding Theory (19) imposes no locality restrictions on PRO when it has neither a binding category nor a binding domain. This opens up the possibility for PRO (perhaps as a pronominal) to acquire an "arb" reading as in (26), and to be bound by a non-c-commanding antecedent as in (27a-b).[46]

In short, we can capture the generalizations in (21) and (22) in terms of the presence versus absence of the binding domain for PRO, given the revised Binding Theory (19).

4.4.4. Remaining Problems

Huang (1983, 560) argues against a PRO Theorem defined in terms of Case, pointing out that PRO is sometimes disallowed even in Case-less positions, as illustrated by (30a-b) below:

(30) a. *It seems PRO$_{arb}$ to love one's own children.
  b. *It is confused PRO$_{arb}$ by such a strange sign.

We can possibly account for the ill-formedness of (30a-b), assuming that the PROs in (30a-b) violate the Binding Theory (19) since they are not bound within their binding domains. This problem may be overcome by coindexing PRO with the pleonastic *it*, but this will yield a semantic anomaly (or inconclusiveness) when PRO is semantically interpreted.[47]

A problem here is that the pleonastic *it* does not seem to count as a potential binder in the cases like (31a-b) below:

(31) a. John and Mary$_1$ think [*it* is likely [that each other$_1$'s dog will win the prize]
   b. Bill$_1$ thinks [*it* is tough [PRO$_1$ to be rich]]

Note that *each other* in (31a) and PRO in (31b) can be bound by the matrix subject. One possible solution to this problem is to let the sentential T-subject intrapose and replace the pleonastic *it* at LF along the line of Chomsky (1986a), as illustrated in (32) below:

(32) a. LF: John and Mary$_1$ think [**that each other$_1$'s dog will win the prize**] is likely __
   b. LF: Bill$_1$ thinks [**PRO$_1$ to be rich**] will be **tough** __

We then must stipulate that *seem* does not permit this LF Subject Raising to account for the ill-formedness of (30a). The ill-formedness of (33) below, in fact, is compatible with this assumption:

(33) *Bill$_1$ thinks [*it* seems [PRO$_1$ to be happy]]

Edwin Williams (personal communication) has also brought the following counterexample into my attention:

(34) John$_1$ [$_{Vmax}$ seems [$_{PP}$ to himself$_1$] [$_{Imax}$ t'$_1$ to have [$_{Vmax}$ won t$_1$]]]

Even if the PP is assumed to be transparent (cf. 4.3.9.), the anaphor *himself* is not bound within its binding category, V^{max}. Notice that the traces of *John* are located within the embedded clause, hence unable to behave as a possible antecedent. Yet the sentence is well-formed. One possibility that comes to mind is that the raised subject adjoins to the V^{max} headed by *seem* before it reaches the I-subject position. I must, however, leave this problem unsolved.

One non-trivial question that comes to mind is why there is an asymmetry between anaphors and pronominals with respect to binding domains. Put differently, we wonder why the Binding Theory is not defined symmetrically as in (35) below:

(35) *Binding Theory*:

    A: An anaphor is bound in its binding category and binding domain.

    B: A pronominal is free in its binding category **and binding domain**.

One possible answer is that the Binding Theory as in (35) is in fact necessary for some languages. Turkish, for example, exhibits the following contrast between anaphors and pronominals: (The data are from Enç (1985).)

(36) Yazar-lar₁ [birbirleri₁-nin₁ aptal ol-dug-un]-u
     author-PL   each other-GEN stupid be-GER-3SG-ACC

     san-ɨyor-du
     think-PROG-PAST

     'The authors thought each other were stupid.'

(37) *Ali₁ [on-un₁ hasta ol-dug-un]-u san-ɨyor-du
            he-GEN sick be-GER-3sg-ACC think-PROG-PAST

     'Ali thought he was sick.'

This contrast follows if: (i) genitive marking in Turkish is non-lexical, and (ii) the matrix clause is the binding domain for both the anaphor and pronominal in the examples (36) and (37).

Harbert (1982) also reports a similar contrast between anaphors and pronominals in the genitive position in Gothic, Icelandic, Russian, and Hindi. David Pesetsky (personal communication) has also informed me that the situation is the same also in Polish. If both versions of the Binding Theory ((19) and (35)) turn out to be necessary, it may even be the case that (35) constitutes the unmarked case. We must leave the pursuit of this topic, however, for future research.

4.5. Concluding Remarks

To sum up the entire thesis, we have argued that a sentence both in Japanese and English contains a subject governed by a verbal head at the level of Logical Form. If our proposal has any plausibility, it will allow us to take a significant step toward the minimization of the language particular variations in some basic features of Logical Form representations.

In the course of discussion, we have reassigned many functions of D-structures in the previous analyses to the Logical Form as a level of representation, especially in the grammar of Japanese. Although the presence of an S-structure Move-alpha as in the case of Scrambling (cf. Saito and Hoji (1983), Saito (1985), Hoji (1985), etc.) still argues for the need of D-structure as an independent level of representation, it seems to be a worthwhile task to re-examine the roles of D-structure as a level of representation. We must leave the pursuit of this topic, however, for future research.

Footnotes to Chapter IV

1. The Opacity Condition (Chomsky (1980)), though discarded eventually, also represents such an effort towards the synthesis, with the idea that both "tense" and "subject" are opacity-creating operators. In 4.3.5. below, we will examine a more recent claim by Chomsky (1986), in which the NIC is derived from the ECP.

2. I am extremely grateful to João Peres and Francisco Fagundes for patiently acting as my informants. Thanks are also due to Eduardo Raposo for helpful comments on this section. It should be kept in mind that we are concerned here with the European rather than Brazilian dialect of Portuguese.

3. Throughout, we will disregard the second person (i.e., non-anaphoric) reading of *si*.

4. The original meaning of *-go* from Latin *-cum* 'with' has disappeared in the present day Portuguese.

5. According to João Peres, the contrast between 2 and *1 in (5b) becomes stronger when *próprio* is added to *consigo*. In this paper, we will leave out the use of *próprio*, which is usually analyzed as an emphatic adjective in traditional grammar (e.g., Willis (1965,230)).

6. While Zubizarreta (1982,93) states that (non-emphatic) pronouns in general cannot be coreferential with the matrix subject even in the subject position of a finite embedded clause as in (i) below, this seems to be an overstatement of the facts:

(i) Eles acreditam [que *eles* são inteligentes]
     they believe   that *they* are intelligent

As has been pointed out to us by Eduardo Raposo, disjoint reference is simply **preferred** in this construction, in sharp contrast with (20a-b), in which disjoint reference is **obligatory**.

7. Edwin Williams (personal communication) pointed out to me that the existence of opacity in the English subjunctives as illustrated by (i) below may constitute another piece of evidence for our claim, since the INFL of subjunctives seems to be characterized as [-Tense, -AGR, +Nom] (at least in English) (cf. Picallo (1984)).

(i) They₁ suggested [ₛ· that { *they*₁ / *each other } be allowed

   to go home]

   Eduardo Raposo, on the other hand, brought into my attention the following counterexample from Portuguese:

(ii) Eles₁ desejam [ₛ· que   *eles*₂/*₁ sejam
      they wish   that they-**NOM** be-SUBJUNCTIVE

      inteligentes]
      intelligent

   'They want them to be intelligent.'

In the subjunctive complement here, the subject pronoun receives Nominative Case but cannot be bound by the matrix subject. See Meireles and Raposo (1984) for discussions.

8. As for Turkish, Enç (1985) reaches a similar conclusion to ours, examining the following paradigm:

(i) <u>Gerund (Genitive Subject)</u>:

Yazar-lar₁ [ₛ· *birbirleri*-nin₁ aptal ol-dug-un]-u
author-PL   each other-GEN   stupid be-GER-3SG-ACC

san-ɨyor-du
think-PROG-PAST

'The authors thought each other stupid.'

(ii) <u>Nominal (Genitive Subject)</u>:

Adam-lar₁ [NP *birbirleri*-nin₁ ev-in]-i   begen-iyor
man-PL   each other-GEN   house-3SG-ACC   like-PROG

'The men like each other's houses.'

(iii) <u>Tensed S (**Nominative** Subject)</u>:

*Çocuk-lar [ₛ· *birbirleri*   git-ti] san-ɨyor
 child-PL   each other-**NOM** go-PAST think-PROG

'The children think each other left.'

(iv)   Tensed S w/ ECM (Accusative Subject):

Çocuk-lar₁ [ₛ· *birbirlerin-i*₁ git-ti] san-ıyor
child-PL   each other-ACC go-PAST think-PROG

'The children think each other left.'

Notice that the binding of the reciprocal subject by a
higher subject is prohibited when and only when the
complement involves Nominative Case marking of the subject,
as in (iii).

Enç ascribes the ill-formedness of George and
Kornfilt's (1981) examples like (v) below to incorrect
number agreement rather than opacity of the complement,
stating that "although the reciprocal agrees with its
antecedent in person, it behaves like a third person
singular for the purpose of case assignment and agreement
-- [emphasis by Y.K.] (p.17)":

(v)   *Yazar-lar₁ [ₛ· *birbirleri*-nin₁   viski-yi
       author-PL   each other-3SG=GEN whisky-ACC

       iç-tik-**lerin**]-i san-ıyor-lar
       drink-GER-3PL-ACC think-PROG-3PL

       'The authors thought each other drank the whisky.'

She presents a well-formed example (vi) below as evidence
for this claim:

(vi) Yazar-lar₁ [ₛ· *birbirleri*-**nin**₁   viski-yi
      author-PL   each other-3SG=GEN whisky-ACC

      iç-tig-in]-i   san-ıyor-lar
      drink-GER-3SG-ACC think-PROG-3PL

      'The authors thought each other drank the whisky.'

Notice that (vi) differs from (v) only with respect to the
number on the verb of the gerund.

Kornfilt (1984), on the other hand, further argues
for the SUBJECT approach, providing some new obserbvations.

We will deal with pronominal coreference in Turkish
in 4.4. below. See also Cole and Hermon (1979) for
an argument that opacity for binding is created by [+Nom]
also in Imbabura Quecha, Ancash Quechua and Modern Greek.

9. Chomsky (1980, 13) defines the NIC as follows:

(i) *Nominative Island Condition*:

A nominative anaphor in S cannot be free in S' containing S.

10. In the Japanese examples below, we will often embed a sentence into an NP headed by *koto* (fact), in order to make its nominative marked subject sound natural. Such a sentence will be translated, however, as if it were used independently.

11. Although it is much less colloquial, *onore* (self) also seems to behave as a pure anaphor.

12. As for the status of *zibun*, we will tentatively adopt the following position, which was suggested by Fukui (1984, Appendix p.7) as a possible alternative to his claim.

Zibun is specified with the features [pronominal] and [anaphor] **disjunctively** rather than conjunctively, i.e., as [+pronominal or +anaphor]. With this hypothesis, we predict, first, that *zibun* as a pronominal may be bound from outside the local domain (in the relevant sense), for example, by the matrix subject *Taroo* in (9) above. Moreover, we predict that *zibun* as an anaphor may also be bound within such a local domain without giving rise to disjoint reference, for example, by the embedded subject *Hanako* in (9).

Sportiche (1986) claims that the pronominal function of *zibun* must further be restricted to that of bound pronouns, since *zibun* must be eventually bound even when it is functioning as a pronominal. We will leave the further pursuit of this topic for future reserach.

13. Chomsky (1986a) introduces a notion "BT-compatibility" to account for the possibility of having a pronominal in the Nominative subject position, among others. We will examine this approach in 4.3.6. below.

14. Hasegawa (to appear), on the contrary, analyzes this empty element as a variable, following Huang (1984).

15. Yang (1983) tries to solve the dilemma by giving up the synthesis of the principles A and B of the Binding Theory. This assumption, however, forces us not only to call the near complementarity of anaphors and pronominals

accidental, but also to give up predicting the distribution of PRO without a stipulation (since we must give up the PRO Theorem). His Reciprocal-Binding Principle, moreover, is problematic, since it crucially depends upon the assumption that AGR functions as a SUBJECT.

16. This presumably is the source of the SVO (rather than VOS) order in derived nominals in English.

17. Chomsky (1986a) proposes a Case theory in which a nominal head assigns "inherent" Case (which is lexical in our sense) to its complement. Even in this theory, however, contextual Case marking seems to be necessary for the base-generated specifier NPs, which cannot receive lexical Case from the head if we take seriously his claim that inherent Case marking is "uniformly to the right" (p.193) in English.

18. *Ga* is assumed to delete when it is followed by *no*.

19. "*θ/no* conversion" is disallowed even when the object NP is scrambled, as illustrated in the derivation (i) below:

(i) a. [NP [S e₂ hon o kaita] hito₂] ===>
                     book ACC wrote   person

   'the person who wrote a book'

   b. [NP [S hon₁ o [S e₂ t₁ kaita]] hito₂] ===>
                     acc

   c. *[NP hon₁ *no* [NP [S e₂ t₁ kaita]] hito₂]
                     gen

This suggests that the prohibition against Case conflict must be imposed on a chain. In (i), the chain (*hon*, *t*) has Case conflict between the genitive *no* and the abstract Case "Accusative".

20. Saito (1985) claims that this dichotomy of Case also creates a subject-object asymmetry in Case marker drop and scrambling.

21. This is not, in fact, entirely true. We will deal with further restrictions imposed on anaphoric binding in 4.4. below.

22. It may also be possible to consider that the maximal projection of a lexical Case assigner becomes a barrier for

the assignee of such Case, with respect to binding.

23. We assume here that Case marking in Japanese utilizes Selkirk's Percolation Conventions. We must leave the pursuit of this topic, however, for future research.

24. There is a dialectal variation concerning this judgment. We will briefly deal with this variation in 4.3.9. below.

25. Recall, however, our discussion of inalienable possession in 3.1.

26. It is highly unlikely that (52a) is saved by LF-pied piping as in (i) below, since (ii) below is still ill-formed:

(i) LF: John$_1$ [$_2$ as for himself$_1$]-INFL say that t$_2$ Mary

 appeared to be intelligent

(ii) LF: *[$_1$ as for whom] did John say that t$_1$ Mary

 appeared to be intelligent

27. We will deal with another such case, as in (i) below, in 4.4.1. below:

(i) They$_1$ thought that [[pictures of *each other*$_1$] were on sale.

28. The following are the definitions of the relevant notions proposed by Chomsky (1981):

(i)   *Agreement*:

 AGR is coindexed with the NP it governs.

(ii)   *Governing Category*:

 A is a governing category for *B* if and only if *A* is the minimal category containing *B*, a governor of *B*, and a SUBJECT accessible to *B*.

(iii) *Accessibility*:

 A is accessible to *B* if and only if *B* is in the

c-command domain of *A* and assignment to *B* of the
index of *A* would not violate the the i-within-i
condition.

(iv)   *i-within-i Condition*:

        *[ᵦ ... *A* ...], where *A* and *B* bear the same index.

29. The account of long-distance binding in terms of
the i-within-i condition is also based upon the mixture
of referential coindexation (in binding) and
non-referential coindexation (in agreement). The validity
of such a mixture, however, is not at all clear. (This
potential problem is also pointed out by Nakajima (1986).)

    Note also that the coindexation in agreement takes
place between a maximal phrase (NP) and an item within the
lexical head (AGR), while coindexation in binding in
general takes place between two maximal phrases (NPs).
This is another difference between the two types of
coindexation.

30. The NIC as proposed in Chomsky (1980) also successfully
accounts for the contrast between (53) and (55), on the one
hand, and the lack of anaphor-pronominal complementarity in
(53) and (54), on the other. As has already been pointed
out above, however, the adoption of NIC without
modification would preclude us from obtaining a unified
theory of binding, in which SSC and NIC are reduced to a
single condition.

31. Chomsky (1986a,1986b), for example, assumes that the
verb *consider* in English has an option of taking an IP
complement, which is transparent to government. This
allows ECM, as illustrated in (i) below:

(i)   I consider [ᵢₚ *him* to be a genius]

32. We are assuming here that scrambling involves
operator-variable binding. See Saito and Hoji (1983), Hoji
(1985), and Saito (1985) for arguments for the variable
status of the traces left behind by scrambling.

33. See Saito (1985, Chapter Three) for the crucial use of
the principle (78) in the account of the subject-object
asymmetry in scrambling.

    One possible alternative is to modify the definition
of "binding category" (28) as in (i) below:

(i) The binding category of ß is the maximal projection of ß's lexical Case marker **containing ß**; where ß = an anaphor or a pronominal.

As illustrated below in the derivation of the embedded IP in (76b), the scrambled phrase will not be contained in the V^{max} at LF after affix raising has taken place. Thus, (i) will allow the anaphor to lack a binding category, as desired.

(ii) a. *D-structure*   b. *S-structure*

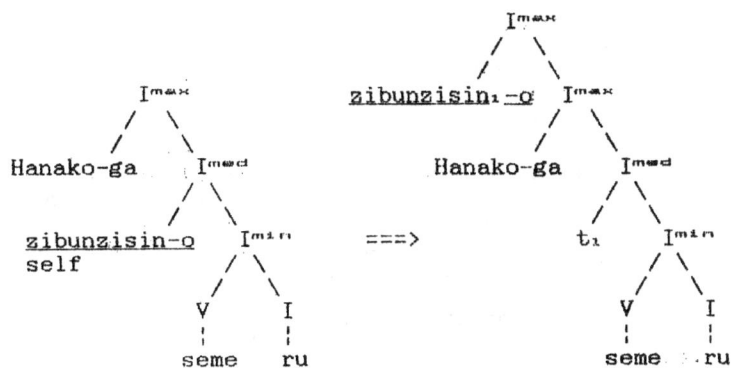

c.   *LF*

===>

34. An interesting fact pointed out to me also by Kiyoshi Kurata (personal communication) is that the anaphors in (76b) and (77b) above may be bound not only by the matrix subject but also by the embedded subject. (See Muraki (1974) for analogous facts concerning *zibun*.)

Let us also add our own observation here that, when Accusative pronominals are scrambled, they are not only bindable by the matrix subject (as predicted) but also obligatorily disjoint in reference with the embedded subject, as illustrated in (i) below:

(i) a. Taroo$_1$ wa *kare*$_{1/*2}$ o   Ziroo$_2$ ga t semeru to
       Taroo top him   ACC Ziroo nom   blame   COMP

   wa omottemominakatta
   top never=thought

   'Taro never thought that Jiro would blame him.'

b. Butyoo to Katyoo$_1$ wa *karera*$_{1/*2}$ o kitto
   dpt=head and sect=chief top they   ACC surely

   bukatati$_2$ ga t semeru daroo to   omotteita
   followers   nom   blame likely COMP think

   'The department head and the section chief thought that their men would probably blame them."

Although we will not go into the details here, this seems to be a case involving "reconstruction" discussed by Engdahl (1980), van Riemsdijk and Williams (1981), Barss (1984), Hoji (1985) and many others. I must leave the pursuit of this topic, however, to future research.

35. There is a well-known dialectal variation concerning the possibility of anaphoric and pronominal binding in (81). Many speakers find the anaphoric binding indicated there acceptable although it is less than perfect (e.g., Chomsky (1986)). Other speakers, on the other hand, find it unacceptable (e.g., Chomsky (1973), Postal (1974)). See Nakajima (1986) for an interesting discussion.

36. The situation seems to be the same with postpositions in Japanese:

(i) [$_{Vmax}$ Taroo to Hanako$_1$ ga [$_{PP}$ { otagai$_1$ / karera*$_1$ } kara]

```
    raburetaa    o    uketot ]-ta  (koto)
    love-letter  ACC  receive-PAST (fact)
```

'Taro and Hanako received a love letter from each other.'

37. Even if it turns out that the Binding Theory (C) must be stated in terms of c-command rather than max-government, a similar conclusion can be drawn concerning the transparency of PP nodes in the upward node-counting.

38. While we adopt the analysis sketched out above, there are at least two other possibilities that come into mind to deal with the same facts in the Lexical Case Island approach.

First, it might be possible to assume that the object of a preposition is "compositionally" Case-marked by the preposition and a higher predicate (V in (81) and (83), and N in (84)). This may possibly be done in a parallel way to the "compositional θ-role assignment" of prepositional objects suggested by Hagit Borer (as cited by Stowell (1981)).

Second, it might also be possible to assume that the Case in question actually comes from the higher predicates, and the prepositions are merely the "realizers" of Case, along the line of the Case theory proposed by Chomsky (1986a).

In either analysis, it follows that the Lexical Case Island is the V^{max} in (81) and (83), and the N^{max} in (84).

39. Saito (1985) points out a different type of paradox in causatives with respect to the Binding Theory (B) and the Double-*o* Constraint.

40. Williams (1985), on the other hand, argues against this proposal, providing the example (i) below, among others:

(i)   yesterday's attempt to leave

Notice that the genitive position in (i) is plugged up by *yesterday*. Nonetheless, (i) is interpreted as if PRO appeared in this position and controled another PRO, as in (ii) below:

(ii) PRO$_1$ attempt PRO$_1$ to leave

41. Alternatively to (6b), we may adopt (i) below, in which PRO does not appear:

(i) They$_1$ told [stories about them$_1$]

42. It has also been claimed by Saito (1982) and Kuroda (1983) that the nominative position in Japanese allows PRO$_{arb}$, unlike the Accusative position.

43. The two instances of PRO$_{arb}$ in (9) (if they exist) must be coreferential. A similar case is:

(i) PRO$_{arb}$ sakinzureba   PRO$_{arb}$ hito o   seisu
         forestall-COND   person ACC control

   'First come, first served.'

See Lebeaux (1984a) for a relevant discussion.

44. Hasegawa (to appear) points out that the generalizations in (21) and (22) hold also in Japanese.

45. Following Manzini (1983), we assume that the choice between subject and object control in (24) and (25) is determined outside the realm of binding.

46. One exception to this prediction is a PRO$_{arb}$ reading in indirect questions, as in (i) below:

(i) He always knows what PRO$_{arb}$ to do.

I must leave it for future reserach to figure our how exactly control into indirect questions is done.

47. On the same grounds, we can possibly eliminate (i) below, in which the Subject Raising has failed to apply to the PRO T-subject:

(i) *It may [$_{Vmax}$ love you PRO]

   (it = pleonastic)

Appendix

zibun

In 4.3.2.1., we have introduced Ueda's (1984) and Fukui's (1984) proposal that *zibun* (self) is a pronominal rather than an anaphor. Let us briefly introduce what we conceive as the strongest argument for the pronominal property of *zibun*, and later point out a problem in regarding *zibun* as a **pure** pronominal ([-anaphor, +pronominal]).

One strong basis for not regarding *zibun* as a pure anaphor is provided by the fact that, in some cases, it behaves more like a pronominal than an anaphor, taking split antecedents, as pointed out by Fukui (Ibid.,24):

(1) Gakutyoo$_1$ ga Gakubutyoo$_2$ ni [aru gakusei ga
    President nom Dean   DAT some student NOM

    kinoo   zibun-tati$_{1+2}$ o   kokusosita] to   tugeta
    yesterday self-PL   ACC sued   COMP told

    '*The president told the dean that some student sued themselves yesterday.'

One possible complication for this argument, which Fukui does not consider, comes from Lebeaux's (1984a) observation that even anaphors may take split antecedents when they are "non-locally" bound (= from outside the

minimal NP or S). Compare (2a) with (2b) below
(cf. Bouchard (1982)):

(2) a. *[John$_1$ told Mary$_2$ about themselves$_{1+2}$]

   b. John$_1$ told Mary$_2$ that [there were [pictures of themselves$_{1+2}$] inside]

Even if the proposed dichotomy between local- and non-local binding turns out to be correct, however, *zibun* must still be considered to have pronominal properties, since its plural form can take split antecedents even under the "local-binding" in Lebeaux's sense, as illustrated in (3) below:

(3) [Taroo$_1$ ga imooto$_2$ to issyoni
         nom younger=sister   and together

   zibuntati$_{1+2}$ o   urikonda]
   selves   ACC tried=to=sell

   'Together with his younger sister, Taro advertised themselves.'

Pursuing further the idea that *zibun* is a pure pronominal, Fukui and Ueda call the binding of *zibun* by the embedded subject in a sentence like (4) below "if not absolutely impossible, very weak (p. 23)" and "marked (p.38)", respectively, blaming it on the binding theory (B):

(4) Taroo₁ ga [Hanako₂ ga zibun₁/₂ o seme-ru] to   wa
             nom   nom self   ACC blame-PRES COMP top

    omottemominakatta (koto)
    never=thought   (fact)

    'Taro never thought that Hanako would blame
    herself/him.'

Since Fukui does not find the same restriction in simplex sentences, he further claims that a matrix subject position, unlike a complement subject position, does not enter into the binding of pronominals, being an A-bar position. This explanation, however, is incompatible with his claim that *zibun* must be A-bar-bound and function as a resumptive pronoun, since *zibun* in a nominal as in (5) below may be bound, even for Fukui, by the complement subject, which is in an A-position:

(5) Taroo₁ wa [Hanako₂ ga [zibun₁/₂ no okane] o
           top   nom self   gen money] ACC

    otosita] koto o siranai
    dropped   fact ACC don't=know

    'Taro does not know that Hanako dropped his/her
    money.'

Ueda (1984) also assumes that the Binding Theory (B) rules out the examples as in (6) below:

(6) a. ?Taroo₁ ga zibun₁ o   korosita (koto)
               nom self   ACC killed   (fact)

        'Taro killed himself.'

b. ?Taroo$_1$ ga zibun$_1$ o nagutta (koto)
       nom self   ACC hit   (fact)

   'Taro hit himself.'

c. ?Taroo$_1$ ga zibun$_1$ o ketta   (koto)
       nom self   ACC kicked (fact)

   'Taro kicked himself.'

Since similar examples in (7a-c) below are perfectly acceptable, Ueda claims that *zibun* (which is a pure pronominal also in his analysis) is exempt from the Binding Theory (B) just in case it is an object of a verb denoting an "abstract" rather than "physical" activity:

(7) a. Taroo$_1$ ga zibun$_1$ o semeta (koto)
          nom self   ACC blamed (fact)

   'Taro blamed himself.'

   b. Taroo$_1$ ga zibun$_1$ o ituwatta (koto)
         nom self   ACC deceived (fact)

   'Taro was dishonest to himself.'

   c. Taroo$_1$ ga zibun$_1$ o urikonda   (koto)
         nom self   ACC tried=to=sell (fact)

   'Taro advertised himself.'

This analysis is questionable, however, since the awkwardness of (6a-c) above is of much different nature from the ungrammaticality caused by the violation of the Binding Theory (B). This point can be clearly illustrated by comparing the somewhat awkward (6a-c) with the completely unacceptable (8a-c) below, each of which involves the disjoint reference of an overt pronominal *kare* (he) or a zero pronominal:

(8) a. **Taroo$_1$ ga { kare$_1$ / him / pro$_1$ } o korosita (koto)

    b. **Taroo$_1$ ga { kare$_1$ / him / pro$_1$ } o nagutta (koto)

    c. **Taroo$_1$ ga { kare$_1$ / him / pro$_1$ } o ketta (koto)

This conclusion can be confirmed by the fact that even *zibunzisin* (self) and *mizukara* (self) (which, as we have seen, behave as pure anaphors) sound awkward in this position:

(9)
  a. ?Taroo$_1$ ga *zibunzisin*$_1$/*mizukara*$_1$ o   korosita (koto)
          nom   self   ACC killed   (fact)

    'Taro killed himself.'

  b. ?Taroo$_1$ ga *zibunzisin*$_1$/*mizukara*$_1$ o nagutta (koto)
          nom   self   ACC punched (fact)

    'Taro hit himself.'

  c. ?Taroo$_1$ ga *zibunzisin*$_1$/*mizukara*$_1$ o ketta (koto)
          nom   self   ACC kicked (fact)

    'Taro kicked himself.'

While it seems to be true that *zibun* is more attuned to expressing an "abstract self", there are cases in which it is used to express a "physical self" but may be bound by a clause-mate subject, as in (10a-c) below:

(10)
  a. Taroo$_1$ ga sono pisutoru de   zibun$_1$ o   utta (koto)
       nom that pistol with self   ACC shot (fact)

    'Taro shot himself with that pistol.'

  b. Taroo$_1$ ga sono naihu de   zibun$_1$ o   sasita (koto)
       nom that knife with self   ACC stabbed (fact)

    'Taro stabbed himself with that knife.'

  c. yumedemo miteiru   nodewanaikato Taroo$_1$ wa
     dream   watching maybe   Taroo   top

    tyotto   zibun$_1$ o   tunettemita
    a=little self   ACC tried=pinching

    'He tried pinching himself, wondering whether he was dreaming.'

Thus, it is probably wrong to ascribe the awkwardness of (6a-c) to a violation of the Binding Theory (B). Although the exact cause for this awkwardness still remains mysterious, it seems to be rather clearly related to the idiosyncratic lexical meanings of the verbs involved there.

BIBLIOGRAPHY

Abe, Y. (1982) "On the Representation of Argument Structure," in Pustejovsky, J. and P. Sells eds., *Proceedings of the Twelfth Annual Meeting of the North-Eastern Linguistic Society*, 1-15.

Abe, Y. (1985) *A Theory of Categorial Morphology and Agglutination in Japanese*, Doctoral dissertation, University of Massachusetts at Amherst.

Allen, M. (1978) *Morphological Investigations*, Doctoral dissertation, University of Connecticut, Storrs.

Aoun, J. (1984) "Generalized Binding in Chinese," *Proceedings of the Fourteenth Annual Meeting of the North-Eastern Linguistic Society*.

Aoun, J. and D. Sportiche (1983) "On the Formal Theory of Governmnet," *The Linguistic Review* 2.3., 211-236.

Archangeli, D. and D. Pulleyblank (1984) "Extratonality and Japanese Accent" ms., Massachusetts Institute of Technology.

Aronoff, M. (1976) *Word Formation in Generative Grammar*, MIT Press, Cambridge, Massachusetts.

Bach, E. (1968) "Nouns and Noun Phrases," in Bach, E. an R. Harms eds., *Universals in Linguistic Theory*, Holt, Rinehart and Winston, New York.

Bach, E. (1971a) "Questions," *Linguistic Inquiry* 2., 153-166.

Bach, E. (1971b) "Syntax since *Aspects*," in R. O'Brien ed., *22nd Annual Round Table*, Georgetown University.

Bach, E. (1983) "On the Relationship between Word-grammar and Phrase-grammar," *Natural Language and Linguistic Theory* 1.1., 65-89.

Baker, M. (1985) "The Mirror Principle and Morphosyntactic Explanation," *Linguistic Inquiry* 16.3., 373-415.

Baltin, M. (1978) *Toward a Theory of Movement Rules*, Doctoral dissertation, Massachusetts Institute of Technology.

Baltin, M. (1982) "A Landing Site Theory of Movement Rules," *Linguistic Inquiry* 13.1, pp. 1-38.

Barss, A. (1984) "Chain Binding," ms., Massachusetts Institute of Technology.

Bedell, G. (1972) "On no," in Bedell, G. ed., *UCLA Papers in Syntax 3: Studies in East Asian Syntax*.

Bloomfield, L. (1933) *Language*, George Allen and Unwin, London.

Borer, H. (1986) "I-subjects," *Linguistic Inquiry* 17.3., 375-416.

Bresnan, J. (1978) "A Realistic Transformational Grammar," in M. Halle et al. eds., *Linguistic Theory and Psychological Reality*, MIT Press, Cambridge, Massachusetts.

Bresnan, J. (1982) "Control and Complementation," *Linguistic Inquiry* 13.3., 343-434.

Burzio, L. (1981) *Intransitive Verbs and Italian Auxiliaries*, Doctoral dissertation, Massachesetts Institute of Technology.

Burzio, L. (1986) *Italian Syntax: A Government and Binding Approach*, Reidel, Dordrecht.

Carlson, G. (1985) "Same and Different: Some Consequences for Syntax and Semantics," ms., University of Iowa.

Chew, J. (1961) *Transformational Analysis of Modern Colloquial Japanese*, Doctoral dissertation, Yale University.

Chomsky, N. (1965) *Aspects of The Theory of Syntax*, MIT Press, Cambridge, Massachusetts.

Chomsky, N. (1970) "Remarks on Nominalization," in R. Jacobs and P. Rosenbaum eds., *Readings in Transformational Grammar*, Blaisdell, Waltham, Massachesetts.

Chomsky, N. (1973) "Conditions on Transformations," in S. Anderson and P. Kiparsky eds., *A Festschrift for Morris Halle*, Holt, Rinehart and Winston, New York.

Chomsky, N. (1976) "Conditions on Rules of Grammar," *Linguistic Analysis* 2, 303-351.

Chomsky, N. (1980) "On Binding," *Linguistic Inquiry* 11.1., 1-46.

Chomsky, N. (1981) *Lectures on Government and Binding*, Foris, Dordrecht.

Chomsky, N. (1982) *Some Concepts and Consequences of the Theory of Government and Binding*, MIT Press, Cambridge, Massachusetts.

Chomsky, N. (1986a) *Knowledge of Language -- Its Nature, Origin, and Use*, Praeger, New York.

Chomsky, N. (1986b) *Barriers*, MIT Press, Cambridge, Massachusett.

Chomsky, N. and M. Halle (1968) *The Sound Pattern of English*, Harper and Row, New York.

Clark, M. (1983) "Japanese as a Tone Language," ms., University of New Hampshire, Durham.

Cole, P. and G. Hermon (1981) "Subjecthood and Islandhood: Evidence from Quechua," *Linguistic Inquiry* 12.1., 1-30.

Cole, P. and G. Harmon (1979) "Complement Structure and Islandhood in EST: A Crosslinguistic Study," in Clyne et al., eds., *Papers from the Fifteenth Regional Meeting of the Chicago Linguistic Society*, University of Chicago.

Contreras, H. (to appear) "Small Clauses in Spanish," in A. Hurtado ed., *Linguistic Theory and Spanish Syntax*, Reidel.

Davidson, D. (1976=1967) "The Logical Form of Action Sentences," in Davidson, D. and G. Harman eds., *The Logic of Grammar*, Dickenson, 235-245.

Emonds, J. (1970) *Root and Structure-Preserving Transformations*, Doctoral dissertation, Massachusetts Institute of Technology.

Emonds, J. (1976) *A Transformational Approach to English Syntax: Root, Structure-Preserving, and Local Transformations*, Academic Press, New York.

Enç, M. (1985) "Agreement and Governing Categories," ms., University of Southern California.

Engdahl, E. (1980) *The Syntax and Semantics of Questions in Swedish*, Doctoral dissertation, University of Massachusetts at Amherst.

Fabb, N. (1984) *Syntactic Affixation*, Doctoral dissertation, Massachesetts Institute of Technology.

Farmer, A. (1980) *On the Interaction of Morphology and Syntax*, Doctoral dissertation, Massachusetts Institute of Technology.

Fiengo, R. (1977) *On the Trace Theory*, Linguistic Inquiry 8, 35-61.

Fiengo, R. and J. Higginbotham (1980) "Opacity in NP," *Linguistic Analysis* 7, 395-421.

Fillmore, C. (1963) "The Position of Embedding Transformations in a Grammar," *Word* 19, 208-231.

Fillmore, C. (1968) "Case for Case," *Universals in Linguistic Theory*, Holt, Rinehart and Winston, New York.

Freidin, R. (1978) "Cyclicity and the Theory of Grammar," *Linguistic Inquiry*, 9.4., pp. 519-549.

Fukui, N. (1984) "Studies on Japanese Anaphora I: the Adjunct Subject Hypothesis and 'zibun'," ms., Massachusetts Institute of Technology.

George, L. and J. Kornfilt (1981) "Finiteness and Boundness in Turkish," in F. W. Heny ed., *Binding and Filtering*, MIT Press, Cambridge, Massachusetts.

Gruber, J. (1976) *Studies in Lexical Relations*, North-Holland, Amsterdam.

Haïk, I. (1985) *The Syntax of Operators*, Doctoral dissertation, Massachusetts Institute of Technology.

Hale, K. (1980) "Remarks on Japanese Phrase Structure: Comments on the Papers on Japanese Syntax," in Y. Otsu and A. Farmer eds., *MIT Working Papers in Linguistics: Theoretical Issues in Japanese Linguistics*, Massachusetts Institute of Technology.

Hale, K. (1983) "Warlpiri and the Grammar of
    Non-configurational Languages," *Natural Language and
    Linguistic Theory*, 1.1., 5-47.

Halle, M. (1973) "Prolegomena to a Theory of Word
    Formation," *Linguistic Inquiry* 4.1., 3-16.

Halle, M. and K. Mohanan (1985) "Segmental Phonolgy of
    Modern Engish," *Linguistic Inquiry* 16.1., 57-116.

Harada, S. I. (1971) "Ga-No Conversion and Idiolectal
    Variations in Japanese," *Gengo Kenkyu* 60.

Harada, S. I. (1976) "Honorifics," in Shibatani, M. ed.,
    Japanese Generative Grammar, Syntax and Semantics 5,
    Academic Press, New York.

Harada, S. I. (1977) "Nihongo ni Henkei wa Hituyoo da,"
    Gengo 6, 11-12.

Haraguchi, S. (1977) *The Tone Pattern of Japanese: An
    Autosegmental Theory of Tonology*, Kaitakusha, Tokyo.

Harbert, W., (1982) "Should Binding Refer to
    SUBJECT?" *Proceedings of the Twelfth Annual Meeting
    of the North-Eastern Linguistic Society.*

Harman, G. (1975) "Logical Form," in Davidson, D. and
    G. Harman eds., *The Logic of Grammar*, Dickenson
    Publishing, 289-307.

Hasegawa, N. (1980) "The VP Constituent in Japanese,"
    Linguistic Analysis 6.2., 115-130.

Hasegawa, N. (1981) *A Lexical Interpretive Theory with
    Emphasis on the Role of Subject*, Doctoral
    dissertation, University of Washington.

Hasegawa, N. (to appear) "On the so-called 'zero pronouns'
    in Japanese," *The Linguistic Review.*

Hayata, T. (1971) "Nihongo Onkeiron," in S. Higa ed.,
    Onsei-zyoohoo-syori, University of Tokyo Press.

Hayes, B. (1981) *A Metrical Theory of Stress Rules*, Indiana
    University Linguistics Club.

Higginbotham, J. (1983) "Logical Form, Binding, and
    Nominals," *Linguistic Inquiry* 14.3., 395-420.

Higgins, F. R. (1973) "On J. Emonds's Analysis of Extraposition," in J. Kimball ed., *Syntax and Semantics* 2, Academic Press, New York.

Hinds, J. (1973) "Some Remarks on soo su- *Papers in Japanese Linguistics* 2, 18-30.

Hoji, H. (1985) *Logical Form Constraints and Configurational Structures in Japanese*, Doctoral dissertation, University of Washington.

Horvath, J. (1981) *Aspects of Hungarian Syntax and the Theory of Grammar*, Doctoral dissertation, University of California, Los Angeles.

Howard, I. and A. Niyekawa-Howard (1976) "Passivization," in Shibatani, M. ed., *Japanese Generative Grammar, Syntax and Semantics* 5, Academic Press, New York.

Huang, C.-T. J. (1982) *Logical Relations in Chinese and the Theory of Grammar*, Doctoral dissertation, Massachusetts Institute of Technology.

Huang, C.-T. J. (1983) "A Note on the Binding Theory," *Linguistic Inquiry* 14.3.

Huang, C.-T. J. (1984) "On the Distribution and Reference of Empty Pronouns," *Linguistic Inquiry* 15.4.

Inoue, K. (1976a) *Henkei-bunpoo to Nihon-go*, Taisyukan, Tokyo.

Inoue, K. (1976b) "Reflexivization: An Interpretive Approach," in Shibatani, M. ed., *Japanese Generative Grammar, Syntax and Semantics* 5, Academic Press, New York.

Ito, J. and A. Mester (1986) "The Phonology of Voicing in Japanese: Theoretical Consequences for Morphological Accessibility", *Linguistic Inquiry* 17.1., 49-73.

Jackendoff, R., (1972) *Semantic Interpretation in Generative Grammar*, MIT Press, Cambridge, Massachusetts.

Jackendoff, R. (1975) "Morphological and Semantic Regularities in the Lexicon," *Language* 51, 639-671.

Jackendoff, R. (1977) *X-bar Syntax: A Study of Phrase Structure*, MIT Press, Cambridge, Massachusetts.

Karttunen, L. (1976) "Discourse Referents," in McCawley J. ed., *Notes from the Linguistic Underground, Syntax and Semantics* 7, Academic Press, New York.

Kawakami, S. (1973) "Doosi karano Tensei-meisi no Akusento," *Imaizumi Hakase Koki Kinen Kokugogaku Ronsoo*, 55-70.

Kayne, R. (1981) "Unambiguous Paths," in May, R. and J. Koster eds., *Levels of Syntactic Representation*, Foris, Dordrecht.

Kiparsky, P. (1982) "Lexical Morphology and Phonology," in The Linguistic Society of Korea eds., *Linguistics in the Morning Calm*, Hanshin, Seoul.

Kiparsky, P. and C. Kiparsky (1971) "Facts," in D. Steinberg and L. Jakobovits eds., *Semantics: An Interdisciplinary Reader in Philosophy, Linguistics and Psychology*, Cambridge University Press.

Kitagawa, C. (1974) "Case Marking and Causativization," *Papers in Japanese Linguistics* 3, 43-56.

Kitagawa, C. (1981) "Anaphora in Japanese: kare and zibun," in Farmer, A. and C. Kitagawa eds., *Coyote Papers* 2, 61-75.

Kitagawa, C. (1982) "Topic Constructions in Japanese," *Lingua* 57.1.

Kitagawa, Y. (1979) "Notes on Semantics of Japanese Causativization," *Attempts in Linguistics and Literature* 7, 17-30.

Kitagawa, Y. (1984) "SUBJECT, Subject and the Extended Projection Principle," ms., University of Massachusetts, Amherst.

Kitagawa, Y. (1986a) "More on Bracketing Paradoxes," *Linguistic Inquiry*, 17.1., 177-183.

Kitagawa, Y. (1986b) "Barriers to Government," *Proceedings of the Sixteenth Annual Meeting of the North-Eastern Linguistic Society*, 249-273.

Klima, E. (1964) "Negation in English," in J. Fodor and J. Katz eds., *The Structure of Language*, Prentice-Hall, Englewood Cliffs.

Koopman, H. (1984) "On Deriving Deep and Surface Order," *Proceedings of the Fourteenth Annual Meeting of the North-Eastern Linguistic Society*, 220-235.

Koopman H. and D. Sportiche (1982) "Variables and the Bijection Principle," *The Linguistic Review* 2.2., 139-160.

Kornfilt, J. (1984) *Case Marking, Agreement, and Empty Categories in Turkish*, Doctoral dissertation, Harvard University.

Koster, J. (1978) "Why Subject Sentences Don't Exist," in S. J. Keyser ed., *Recent Transformational Studies in European Languages*, MIT Press, Cambridge, Massachusetts.

Kratzer, A. (1984) "On Deriving Syntactic Differences between German and English," ms., Technische Universitaet Berlin.

Kuno, S. (1973) *The Structure of the Japanese Language*, MIT Press, Cambridge, Massachusetts.

Kuno, S. (1976) "Subject Raising," in Shibatani, M. ed., *Japanese Generative Grammar, Syntax and Semantics* 5, Academic Press, New York.

Kuno, S. (1980) "Comments on Lekach's Paper," in Y. Otsu and A. Farmer eds., *MIT Working Papers in Linguistics: Theoretical Issues in Japanese Linguistics*, Massachusetts Institute of Technology.

Kuno, S. (1983) *Sin Nihon Bunpoo Kenkyu*, Taishukan, Tokyo.

Kuno, S. (1986) "Blended Quasi-Direct Discourse in Japanese," ms., Harvard University.

Kurata, K. (1984) "Some Aspects of Japanese Phonology -- Autosegmental Approach," ms., University of Massachusetts at Amherst.

Kurata, K. (1986) "Asymmetries in Japanese," ms., University of Massachusetts at Amherst.

Kuroda, S.-Y. (1965a) *Generative Grammatical Studies in the Japanese Language*, Doctoral dissertation, Massachusetts Institute of Technology.

Kuroda, S.-Y. (1965b) "Causative Forms in Japanese," *Foundations of Language* 1, 31-50.

Kuroda, S.-Y. (1978) "Case Marking, Canonical Sentence Patterns, and Counter Equi in Japanese," in Hinds, J. and I. Howard eds., *Problems in Japanese Syntax and Semantics*, Kaitakusha, Tokyo.

Kuroda, S.-Y. (1981) "Some Recent Trends in Syntactic Theory and the Japanese Language," in Farmer, A. and C. Kitagawa eds., *Coyote Papers* 2, 103-121.

Kuroda, S.-Y. (1984) "Movement of Noun Phrases in Japanese," ms., University of California, San Diego.

Kuroda, S.-Y. (1985) "Whether You Agree or Not: Rough Ideas about the Comparative Grammar of English and Japanese", ms., University of California San Diego.

Ladusaw, W. (1979) *Polarity Sensitivity as Inherent Scope Relations*, Doctoral dissertation, University of Texas.

Lakoff, R. (1969) "A Syntactic Argument for Negative Transformation," in R. I. Binnick et al. eds., *Papers from the Fifth Regional Meeding of Chicago Linguistic Society*, University of Chicago.

Lapointe, S. (to appear) "An Autolexical Approach to Certain Syntax/Semantics Mismatches," in Huck, G. and A. Ojeda eds., *Syntax and Semantics* 20, Academic Press.

Lasnik, H. and J. Kupin (1977) "A Restrictive Theory of Transformational Grammar," *Theoretical Linguistics* 4, 173-196.

Lasnik, H. and M. Saito (1984) "On the Nature of Proper Government," *Linguistic Inquiry* 15.2., 235-289.

Lebeaux, D. (1983) "A Distributional Difference between Rciprocals and Reflexives," *Linguistic Inquiry* 15.2.

Lebeaux, D. (1984a) "Anaphoric Binding and the Definition of PRO," *Proceedings of the Fourteenth Annual Meeting of the North-Eastern Linguistic Society*, 253-274.

Lebeaux, D. (1984b) "Nominalizations, Argument Structure and the Organization of the Grammar," ms., University of Massachusetts at Amherst.

Leben, W. (1973) *Suprasegmental Phonolgy*, Indiana University Linguistics Club.

Lieber, R. (1981) *On the Organization of the Lexicon*, Indiana University Linguistics Club.

Linebarger, M. (1980) *The Grammar of Negative Polarity*, Doctoral dissertation, Massachusetts Institute of Technology.

Manzini, M. R. (1983) "On Control and Control Theory," *Linguistic Inquiry* 14.3, pp. 421-446.

Marantz, A. (1981) *On the Nature of Grammatical Relations*, Doctoral dissertation, Massachesetts Institute of Technology.

Martin, S. (1975) *A Reference Grammar of Japanese*, Yale University Press, New Haven.

May, R. (1977) *The Grammar of Quantification*, Doctoral dissertation, Massachusetts Institute of Technology.

May, R. (1985) *Logical Form: Its Structure and Derivation*, MIT Press.

McCawley, J. D. (1968) *The Phonological Component of a Grammar of Japanese*, Mouton.

McCawley, J. D. (1970a) "English as a VSO Language," *Language* 46, 286-299.

McCawley, J. D. (1970b) "Where do noun phrases come from?" in Jacobs, R. and P. Rosenbaum eds., *Readings in English Transformational Grammar*, Ginn, Boston.

McCawley, J. D. and K. Momoi (1986) "The Constituent Structure of -te Complements," in S.-Y. Kuroda ed., *Working Papers from the First SDF Workshop in Japanese Syntax*, University of California, San Diego.

McCawley, N. A. (1972a) *A Study of Japanese Reflexivization*, Doctoral dissertation, University of Chicago.

McCawley, N. A. (1972b) "On the Treatment of Japanese Pasives," in P. M. Peranteau, et al. eds., *Papers from the Eighth Regional Meeting of the Chicago Linguistic Society*, University of Chicago.

McCawley, N. A. (1976) "Reflexivization: A Transformational Approach," in Shibatani, M. ed., *Japanese Generative Grammar, Syntax and Semantics* 5, Academic Press, New York.

McGloin, N. H. (1972) *Some Aspects of Negation in Japanese*, Doctoral dissertation, University of Michigan.

McGloin, N. H. (1976) "Negation," in Shibatani, M. ed., *Japanese Generative Grammar, Syntax and Semantics* 5, Academic Press, New York.

Meireles, J. and E. Raposo (1984) "TENSE and Binding Theory in Portuguese," ms., Universidade de Lisboa and University of California, Santa Barbara.

Miyagawa, S. (1980) *Complex Verbs and the Lexicon*, Coyote Papers 1, University of Arizona, Tucson.

Miyara, S. (1981) *Complex Predicates, Case Marking, and Scrambling in Japanese*, Doctoral dissertation, University of Massachusetts at Amherst.

Mohanan, K. P. (1982) *Lexical Phonology*, Indiana University Linguistics Club.

Muraki, M. (1974) *Presupposition and Thematization*, Kaitakusya, Tokyo.

Muraki, M. (1978) "The sika nai Construction and Predicate Restructuring," in Hinds, J. and I. Howard eds., *Problems in Japanese Syntax and Semantics*, Kaitakusya, Tokyo.

Muysken, P. (1981) "Quecha Causatives and Logical Form: A Case Study in Markedness," in A. Belletti, et al. eds., *Theory of Markedness in Generative Grammar*, Scuola Normale Superiore Pisa.

Muysken, P. (1982) "Parametrizing the Notion 'Head'," *Journal of Linguistic Research* 2.3., 57-75.

Nakajima, H. (1984) "COMP as a SUBJECT," *The Linguistic Review* 4, 121-152.

Nebesky, L. (1979) "Graph Theory and Linguistics," in R. Wilson and L. Beineke eds., *Application of Graph Theory*, Academic Press, London.

Oshima, S. (1979) "Conditions on RUles: Anaphora in Japanese," in Bedell, et al. eds., *Explorations in Linguistics: Papers in Honor of Kazuko Inoue*, Kenkyusha, Tokyo.

Otsu, Y. (1980) "Some Aspects of rendaku in Japanese and Related Problems," in Y. Otsu and A. Farmer eds., *MIT Working Papers in Linguistics: Theoretical Issues in Japanese Linguistics*, Massachusetts Institute of Technology.

Oyakawa, T. (1975) "On the Japanese sika nai construction," *Gengokenkyuu* 67, 1-20.

Partee, B. (1975) "Montague Grammar and Transformational Grammar," *Linguistic Inquiry* 6.2, 203-300.

Pesetsky, D. (1979) "Russian Morphology and Lexical Theory," ms., Massachusetts Institute of Technology.

Pesetsky, D. (1982) *Paths and Categories*, Doctoral dissertation, Massachusetts Institute of Technology.

Pesetsky, D. (1985) "Morphology and Logical Form," *Linguistic Inquiry* 16.2., 193-246.

Picallo, M. C. (1984) "The Infl Node and the Null Subject Parameter," *Linguistic Inquiry* 15.1., 75-102.

Pierrehumbert, J. (1980) *The Phonolgy and Phonetics of English Intonation*, Doctoral dissertation, Massachusetts Institute of Technology.

Postal, P. (1971) *Cross-Over Phenomena*, Holt Rinehart and Winston.

Postal, P. (1974) *On Raising*, MIT Press, Cambridge, Massacuhusetts.

Prince, A. (1983) "Relating to the Grid," *Linguistic Inquiry* 14.1., pp. 19-100.

Pulleyblank, D. (1983) *Tone in Lexical Phonology*, Doctoral dissertation, Massachusetts Institute of Technology.

Quicoli, A. C. (1976) "On Portuguese Impersonal Verbs," in J. Schmidt-Radefeldt ed., *Readings in Portuguese Linguistics*, North-Holland.

Quine, W. (1950) *Word and Object*, MIT Press, Cambridge, Massachusetts.

Reinhart, T. (1976) The Syntactic Domain of Anaphora, Doctoral dissertation, Massachusetts Institute of Technology.

Rizzi, L. (1982) *Issues in Italian Syntax*, Foris, Dordrecht.

Rosenbaum, P. (1967) *The Grammar of English Predicate Complement Constructions*, MIT Press, Cambridge, Massachusetts.

Rothstein, S. (1983) *The Syntactic Form of Predication*, Doctoral dissertation, Massachesetts Institute of Technology.

Rouveret, A. (1980) "Sur la Notion de Proposition Finie," *Recherces Linguistiques* 9.

Rouveret, A. and J.-R. Vergnaud (1980) "Specifying Reference to the Subject: French Causatives and Conditions on Representations," *Linguistic Inquiry* 11.1., 97-202.

Sadock, J. (1985) "Autolexical Syntax: A Proposal for the Treatment of Noun Incorporation and Similar Phenomena," *Natural Language and Linguistic Theory* 3.4., 379-439.

Safir, K. (1982) *Syntactic Chains and the Deniniteness Effect*, Doctoral dissertation, Massachesetts Institute of Technology.

Safir, K. (1984) "Multiple Variable Binding," *Linguistic Inquiry* 15.4., 603-638.

Sag, I. (1976) *Deletion and Logical Form*, Doctoral dissertation, Massachesetts Institute of Technology.

Saito, M. (1982) "Case Marking in Japanese: A Priliminary Study," ms., Massachusetts Institute of Technology.

Saito, M. (1983a) "Case and Government in Japanese," in M. Barlow, et al. eds., *WCCFL* 2.

Saito, M. (1983b) "Comments on the Papers on Generative Syntax," Y. Otsu et al., eds., *Studies in Generative Grammar and Language Acquisition: A Report on Recent Trends in Linguistics*, International Christian University, Tokyo.

Saito, M. (1985) *Some Asymmetries in Japanese and Their Theoretical Implications*, Doctoral dissertation, Massachusetts Institute of Technology.

Saito, M. and H. Hoji (1983) "Weak Crossover and Move-alpha in Japanese," *Natural Language and Linguistic Theory* 1.2., 245-259.

Sapir, E. (1921) *Language*, Harcourt Brace and World, New York.

Selkirk, E. (1982) *The Syntax of Words*, MIT Press, Cambridge, Massachusetts.

Shibatani, M. (1973) "Semantics of Japanese Causativization," *Foundations of Language* 9, 327-373.

Shibatani, M. (1974) "Case Marking and Causativization: A Rejoinder," *Papers in Japanese Linguistics* 3, 233-240.

Shibatani, M. (1976) "Causativization," in Shibatani, M. ed., *Japanese Generative Grammar, Syntax and Semantics* 5, Academic Press, New York.

Siegel, D. (1974) *Topics in English Morphology*, Doctoral dissertation, Massachusetts Institute of Technology.

Spotiche, D. (1983) *Structural Invariance and Symmetry in Syntax*, Doctoral dissertation, Massachusetts Institute of Technology.

Sportiche, D. (1986) "ECP and Subjects," talk given at the Linguistics Colloquium, University of Massachusetts at Amherst.

Stockwell, R., P. Schachter and B. Partee (1973) *The Major Structures of English*, Holt, Rinehart and Winston, New York.

Stowell, T. (1978) "What was There Before There was There?" *Papers from the Fourteenth Regional Meeting of the Chicago Linguistic Society*, University of Chicago.

Stowell, T. (1981) *Origins of Phrase Structure*, Doctoral dissertation, Massachusetts Institute of Technology.

Stowell, T. (1983) "Subjects across Categories," *The Linguistic Review* 2, 285-312.

Sugioka, Y. (1984) *Interaction of Derivational Morphology and Syntax in Japanese and English*, Doctoral dissertation, University of Chicago.

Thomason, R. and R. Stalnaker (1973) "A Semantic Theory of Adverbs," *Linguistic Inquiry* 4.2, 195-220.

Tonoike, S. (1978) "On the Causative Constructions in Japanese," in Hinds, J. and I. Howard eds., *Problems in Japanese Syntax and Semantics*, Kaitakusya, Tokyo.

Travis, L. (1984) *Parameters and Effects of Word Order Variation*, Doctoral dissertation, Massachusetts Institute of Technology.

Ueda, M. (1984) "On a Japanese Reflexive zibun: A Non-parametrization Approach," ms., University of Massachusetts at Amherst.

van Riemsdijk, H. and E. Williams (1981) "NP Structure," *The Linguistic Review* 1.

Wasow, T. (1974) *Anaphora in Generative Grammar*, E. Story-Scientia, Ghent.

Westphal, G. (1985) "On the Expansion of S in Spanish," *Proceedings of the Eastern States Conference on Linguistics*, Ohio State University.

Whitman, J. (1982) "Configurationality Parameters," ms., Harvard University.

Williams, E. (1977) "Discourse and Logical Form," *Linguistic Inquiry* 8.1, 101-139.

Williams, E. (1980) "Predication," *Linguistic Inquiry* 11.1., 203-238.

Williams, E. (1981a) "On the Notions 'Lexically Related' and 'Head of a Word'," *Linguistic Inquiry* 12.2., pp. 245-274.

Williams, E. (1981b) "Argument Structure and Morphology," *The Linguistic Review* 1.1., pp. 81-114.

Williams, E. (1984a) "Bracketing Paradoxes," ms., University of Massachusetts at Amherst.

Williams, E. (1984b) "Coanalysis," ms., University of Massachusetts at Amherst.

Williams, E. (1985) "PRO and Subject of NP," *Natural Language and Linguistic Theory* 3.3., 297-315.

Willis, R. C. (1965) *An Essential Course in Modern Portuguese*, Harrap, London.

Yang. D.-W. (1983) "The Extended Binding Theory of Anaphors," ms., Seoul National University.

Zubizarreta, M. L. (1982) "Theoretical Implications of Subject Extraction in Portuguese," *The Linguistic Review* 2, 79-96.

Zubizarreta, M. L. (1985) "The Relation between Morphology and Morphosyntax: The Case of Romance Causatives," *Linguistic Inquiry*, 16.2., 247-289.

ADDITIONAL FOOTNOTES

1. The assumption here is that S-structure, the output of the overt syntactic component, is at the same time the initial LF representation (= pre-LF_1). All computations, in other words, are hypothesized to belong to components rather than to be intercomponential. The proposed analysis here is also accompanied by the hypothesis that rules and principles within a single component need not be extrinsically ordered, and hence LF licensing of various syntactic entities and syntactic encoding of such licensing may take place at any stage of derivation within this component (while there may exist certain conditions that must be satisfied on the final representation of the component).

2. Note that this hypothesis is in accordance with the Minimalist Approach.

3. The θ-marking properties of *ta* 'want' combined with that of *tabe* 'eat' correctly determine (23c) to be the resulting LF representation.

4. It must be kept in mind that the sentence-initial adverb *dammatte* in (44b) here is not followed by a pause. Otherwise, the sentence can be analyzed as involving scrambling, as in (i) below, which makes the lower scope interpretation of the adverb possible:

(i) **damatte**$_1$, Taroo ga Hanako o t_1 heya ni hair-ase-ta

5. The main point here, which should have been stated more clearly, is that the adverb has an opportunity to be licensed by both *sase* 'CAUSE,' as in (60b), and *hair* 'enter,' as in (61c), which explains why it may have ambiguous scope in the example (49a).

6. Similar ambiguity can be observed even when we reverse the linear (and therefore possibly hierarchical) order of the two types of quantified phrases, as in (i):

(i) Bill intends to visit [every museum in the city] [in some afternoon].   (INTEND > ∃ > ∀ / INTEND > ∀ > ∃)

7. The following example (i) with a desiderative construction perhaps involves ambiguity easier to detect as illustrated in (ii):

(i) Taroo wa ano ban   zyosidaisee-to-**sika**
     top that night with female college student-only

   odori-ta-gar-**ana**-katta
   dance-want-display-NEG-PAST

   'That night, Taro would dance only with female college
   students.'

(ii) a. ONLYx, x = with female college students [DISPLAY
        (John$_1$,WANT (e$_1$, DANCE (e$_1$, x)))]

        (That night, Taro proposed to dance only to female
        college students, though he usually would do that to any
        girl.)

     b. DISPLAY (John$_1$, WANT (e$_1$, ONLYx, x = with female college
        students [DANCE (e$_1$, x)]))

        (That night, Taro would dance only with female college
        students, while many other girls proposed to dance with
        him.)

8. It is claimed, in other words, that the so-called the
Lexical Integrity Hypothesis (Bresnan (1982), et al.), which
stipulates that any segment or structure internal to a word is
opaque to syntactic principles and operations, is too strong and
that it must be systematically weakened in the spirit of the
Atom Condition proposed by Williams (1981a: 253):

(i) The Atom Condition (AC):

   A restriction on the attachment of af$_x$ to Y can only refer
   to features realized on Y.

9. As pointed out to me by Joseph Aoun, the locality as well as
subject-orientation properties observed in all of reciprocalization, honorific politeness and humble politeness (see Additional
Footnote 10 below) reminds us of anaphor binding.

10. Note also the competition between the honorification in (i)
in the original Footnote 77 and that in (i) below:

(i) **watasi** ga Sensei ni   bansyaku-made
    I   nom Teacher DAT even daily drink

    o-yame-sase-**moosiage**-ta (koto)
    stop-CAUSE-HON-PAST   (fact)

    'I humbly made my teacher quit his daily drink at dinner.'

This example involves Harada's (Ibid.) "object honorification," which perhaps can be more correctly characterized in terms of Jorden and Noda's (1987, 165) notion "humble politeness." Humble politeness is licensed by the subject belonging to the speaker's "in-group," as opposed to "honorific politeness" (= Harada's subject honorification"), which is licensed by the subject belonging to the speaker's "out-group."

11. Kuno (1983, 65)) also provides similar examples. These examples, however, can be interpreted (somewhat marginally) only on a par with the "honorific passive" in the form of (i):

(i) X_1 ni okaremasite wa pro$_1$ o-V-ni-nar-are
     as for

They will, in fact, become unacceptable when a pure passive interpretation is forced, as in (ii) and (iii):

(ii) *watasi wa Sensei ni nanimokamo o-mitoosi-ni-nar-**are**-ta
      I   top Teacher dat everything see through-HON-PASS-PAST

     'I had everything in my mind told by our respectable teacher.'

(iii) *watakusidomo sonoyooni Sensei ni musuko o
       we   like that Teacher dat son   acc

      o-home-ni-nar-**are**-te wa kaette kyoosyuku-itasite-simaimasu
      praise-HON-PASS-if   rather be obliged

      'We feel uncomfortable if you praise our son like that.'

12. The underlying assumption here is that Italian permits a phonetically empty pleonastic subject (Rizzi (1982)), as illustrated in (i):

(i) [$_{CP}$ chi$_1$] credi che [$_{IP}$ [e] verrà-INFL t$_1$]

13. The examples in (i) and (iii) below illustrate the same point, as indicated by the informal interpretations in (ii) and (iv), respectively:

(i) Someone in our group must clean the room.

(ii) a. There is (at least) one person in our group who has been appointed as the cleaner of the room, whoever it may be. ($\exists$ > MUST)

     b. It is mandatory that we appoint (at least) one person in our group to clean the room.   (MUST > $\exists$)

(iii) Everyone must leave by 10.

(iv) a. Everyone has his or her own reason to have to leave by 10. ($\forall$ > MUST)

b. No one is allowed to stay here after 10 (eg., due to the building regulation). (MUST > $\forall$)

14. To be precise, the NIC as formulated by Chomsky (1980) does not say anything about pronominal binding. What I refer to here as the NIC, therefore, is in fact an extended version of the NIC, which covers pronominal binding as well. See the original Footnote 9 of this chapter.

15. Again, see what is stated in Additional Footnote 14.

16. Further investigation of various nominal proforms has now led me to conclude that pro rather than *kare* 'he' should be regarded as a pure pronomina in Japanese. Accordingly, each occurrence of *kare* in subsequent examples should be replaced by pro. See Kuroda (1965), Fiengo and Haruna (1987), and Hoji (1989), among others, for relevant discussion.

17. Some of Chomsky's (1986a, 171-172) original claims related to the BT-compatibility approach, in fact, need to be revised. First, Chomsky's original definition of governing category should be rewritten in such a way that the expression "there is an indexing j BT-compatible with" is replaced by "there **can be** an indexing j BT-compatible with". This revision is necessary to prohibit pronominal binding in sentences like (i a-b):

(i) a. *John$_1$ thinks [that **Bill**$_2$ hates **him**$_2$]
    b. *John$_1$ accepted [**Bill**$_2$'s criticism of **him**$_2$]

Note that the lower CFCs in (i a-b) actually do lack BT-compatible indexing.

Second, Chomsky assumes that AGR can be regarded as capable of making available BT-compatible indexing for anaphors (p. 172), perhaps in order to label the root sentences in (ii a-b) below as governing categories ("auxiliary hypothesis" on root sentences: Chomsky (1981, 219-220)):

(ii) a. *[Each other ate the apples].
     b. *[[For each other$_1$ to win] would be unfortunate (for them$_1$)].

Notice, however, that the lower S in our (53) cannot be regarded as the governing category despite the presence of AGR.

18. Note, for instance, that exceptional Case marking requires adjacency between the matrix verb (= Case assigner) and the complement subject (= assignee):

(i) a.   We **definitely** expect him to return by tomorrow.
     b.   *We expect **definitely** him to return by tomorrow.
(ii) a.   I **sincerely** believe him to be innocent.
     b.   *I believe **sincerely** him to be innocent.

19. We, in fact, cannot come up with relevant examples to test pronominal binding in (71) any longer if the newly adopted assumption in Additional Footnote 16 above is correct. The contrast in (71) between *kare o* 'he ACC' and *kare ga* 'he nom' also remains unaccounted for. See Hoji (To appear) for much relevant discussion.

20. Note that adverbial expressions can intervene between the matrix verb and the complementizer *for* as in (i) below, which suggests that reanalysis of the verb and prepositional complementizer is not what is responsible for the Case marking of the complement subject:

(i) They would prefer **very much** for John to win.

References in Additional Footnotes:

Bresnan, J. (1982) "Passive in Lexical Theory," in J. Bresnan ed., *The Mental Representation of Grammatical Relations*, 3-86, Cambridge, Massachusetts, MIT Press.

Di Sciullo, A.-M. and E. Williams (1987) *On the Definition of Word*, Cambridge, Massachusetts, MIT Press.

Fiengo, R. and M. Haruna (1987) "Parameters in Binding Theory — Some Suggestions Based on an Analysis of Japanese," in T. Imai and M. Saito eds., *Issues in Japanese Linguitics*, Foris Publication, Dordrecht.

Hoji, H. (To appear) *Theories of Anaphora and Aspects of Japanese Syntax*, MIT Press.

Jordan, E. H. and M. Noda (1987) *Japanese: The Spoken Language Part 1*, Yale University Press.

Kitagawa, Y. and S. -Y. Kuroda (1992) "Passive in Japanese," ms., University of Rochester and University of California at San Diego.

For Product Safety Concerns and Information please contact our EU representative GPSR@taylorandfrancis.com
Taylor & Francis Verlag GmbH, Kaufingerstraße 24, 80331 München, Germany

www.ingramcontent.com/pod-product-compliance
Lightning Source LLC
Chambersburg PA
CBHW071236300426
44116CB00008B/1054